To Sandy Christmas
merry Christmas
Love mom

How to Grow Wildflowers and Wild Shrubs and Trees in Your Own Garden

How to Grow Wildflowers and Wild Shrubs and Trees in Your Own Garden

by
Hal Bruce

Alfred A. Knopf
New York 1976

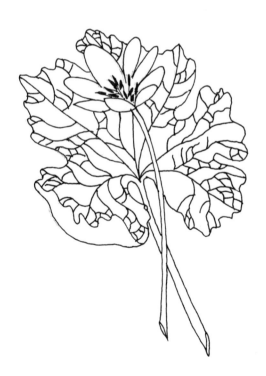

PHOTO CREDITS

Winterthur Museum: 1, 3, 4, 6, 7, 8, 10, 12, 13, 14, 15, 16,
  17, 18, 19, 26, 27, 28, 29, 31, 32, 33, 34.
Jane Garrett: 2.
Dick Ryan: 5, 9, 11, 20, 22, 23, 24, 25, 30.
author: 21.

THIS IS A BORZOI BOOK
PUBLISHED BY ALFRED A. KNOPF, INC.

Grateful acknowledgment is made to Oxford University Press for permission to reprint eight lines from the poem "God's Grandeur," from the book *Poems of Gerard Manley Hopkins*, edited by Robert Bridges (4th ed.).

Library of Congress Cataloging in Publication Data

Bruce, Hal.   How to grow wildflowers and wild shrubs
and trees in your own garden.

Includes index.
1. Wild flower gardening.   2. Trees.   3. Shrubs.
I. Title.
SB439.B75   1976   635.9'676   75-35974
ISBN 0-394-46577-6

Manufactured in the United States of America
First Edition

For Dick Ryan,
and all our forays into the fields

Generations have trod, have trod, have trod;
And all is seared with trade, bleared, smeared with toil;
And wears Man's smudge and shares Man's smell: the soil
Is bare now, nor can foot feel, being shod.

And for all this, nature is never spent;
There lives the dearest freshness deep down things;
And though the last lights off the black West went
Oh, morning, at the brown brink eastward, springs—

from "God's Grandeur"
by Gerard Manley Hopkins

*Color photographs of a variety
of wildflowers, shrubs, and trees
appear following pages 12, 76, and 236.*

Contents

Acknowledgments

A great many people have aided me in various ways during the preparation of this book. Some have given me plants, others advice and information, others help of various sorts, and still others the encouragement necessary to complete the task. To the following I express my gratitude: Mr. and Mrs. James Deeney, Dr. Charles Dunham, David Ewing, Theresa George, Mrs. Sidney Glass, John Kwasniewski, Dr. Richard Lighty, B. McLaughlin, Julie Morris, Mr. and Mrs. A. B. Root, Tom Scott, James Semenick, John and Irene Smith, Madeline Souder, Robert Stewart, Karin Suna, Edith (Jimmie) Ware, and Elizabeth Zimmerman.

For more specific though no less important help I offer thanks to Walter O. Petroll, head of the Gardens of Winterthur, and Charles van Ravenswaay, Director. Both men opened the magnificent gardens to me in the early stages of the book, and have allowed me to use appropriate photographs from the Garden collection. For shared experience in the plant world and for photographs as well, I am grateful to my fellow plantsman William H. Frederick, Jr. To Jackie (Mrs. A. B.) Root I am indebted for years of exchange of plants and plant lore, and for helping me with the manuscript when I most needed help. To June (Mrs. Walter) Jackle, my former teacher, I extend thanks for guidance and encouragement that go back many years. To my friend Tom Menendez I am grateful for help and encouragement more recent but no less important. The late Mabel Thatcher's garden appears again and again in this book, and her serenity has, I hope, influenced its style. My aunt, Frances Moore Ferguson, has offered me more love and help during the years of this book's inception and creation than I can ever hope to acknowledge. To her I am deeply grateful. Jane Garrett, my editor, has offered advice, encouragement, and patient understanding of a rare order during the same period. I feel privileged to work with her. My friend Dick Ryan not only accompanied me on many of the journeys described herein, but took the bulk of the photographs. This book is as much his as mine. And finally, the memory of my mother, Edna Crather Bruce, was much with me as I wrote. She was a true lover of nature, who taught me to name the wild things almost as soon as I could walk, and this book, whatever its worth, is a tribute to her teachings.

A Note on Terminology

All plants have a "scientific name" which in botanical parlance is called the binomial because it really consists of two names, that of the genus (the generic name) followed by that of the species (the specific epithet), which is usually an adjective modifying the generic name. Thus *Acer rubrum*, Red Maple, from Latin *Acer*, maple, and *rubrum*, red.

As part of the binomial, the generic name is always capitalized. Current practice is overwhelmingly in favor of writing the specific epithet in lower-case letters regardless of its origin or grammatical peculiarities.

It is perfectly acceptable to use the generic name as a common name, in which case it follows ordinary usage: *Trillium erectum*, but "trilliums, violets, and primulas"; *Rhododendron maximum*, but "pine, laurel, and rhododendron."

So-called common names really comprise names of varying origin and authenticity which have only one thing in common: none is sanctioned botanically. Some are ancient folk names (Mandrake, St.-John's-wort) whose application is now obscure. Others are manufactured or "book" names which are never used outside of botanical manuals. Others, though in general usage, are confusing because applied to different plants in different areas. "Blazing Star," for example, can be a *Liatris*, a *Chamaelirium*, or a *Mentzelia*, genera which belong to three different families. Similarly, "Bluebell" can be a squill, a bellflower, or a borage (*Mertensia*). I have heard hostas and forgetmenots called bluebells, and once was even asked by an acquaintance for cuttings of "bluebells" growing in my wild garden which turned out to be *Impatiens* with bright orange blossoms!

To compound confusion, there are plants which possess an over-abundance of common names. *Trillium erectum*, for example, is called Purple Wakerobin, Birthroot, Bethroot, Stinking Benjamin, Wet-dog Trillium, and Purple Trillium. I have used the last in this book, though I fear it is no more than a book name.

The point of all this is that common names are often undescriptive, misleading, or ambiguous. Throughout this book I have used scientific names in preference when such has been the case. To those who retreat in panic and bewilderment before an onslaught of Latin, I say only this: *Zinnia, Dahlia, Gardenia, Petunia, Camellia, Gladiolus, Anemone, Chrysanthemum, Azalea, Rhododendron, Amaryllis, Iris, Aster, Begonia, Asparagus*, and many other Latin (or Greek) generic names have become as familiar to most gardeners as any English names. Even the most formidable-looking epithet becomes familiar with use.

At present, the tendency among botanists and horticulturists alike is to minimize punctuation and capitalization. In my view, however, this often fosters ambiguity. I well remember a doctrinaire young editor who, by the excision of a few commas, hyphens, and capitals, turned a perfectly adequate comment of mine about blooming time and color of Plumleaf Azalea into a model of confusion: "the late blooming blood red plum leaf azalea." Accordingly, in this book common names are always capitalized when they refer specifically to a plant: Purple Trillium, Snow Trillium, the American Holly, etc. When the reference is to a group in general, the name is written in lower-case letters: trilliums, a trillium, any hollies, some hydrangeas, etc.

In keeping with a general trend among plantsmen, I have joined words into a single unit wherever this has seemed logically and aesthetically appropriate: Cardinalflower, Plumleaf, Longleaf, Beautyberry. In cases such as Yellow-wood a hyphen is necessary to eliminate a confusing and barbaric combination of w's which never occurs in natural English. When half of the name refers to the whole plant, rather than part (as leaf, berry, flower, etc.), I have let it stand free: Cucumber Tree, Sweet-pepper Bush. Finally, when a common name is falsely applied (i.e., "lily" to any plant outside the genus of true lilies, *Lilium*), the false application is shown through the use of a hyphen. *Lilium canadense* is Meadow Lily, for example, but *Hosta minor* is Dwarf Plantain-lily, and members of the genus *Erythronium* are trout-lilies or fawn-lilies. An exception is apparent in daylily (*Hemerocallis*), which is now a very popular garden plant and almost universally written as one word.

The following explanation of technical terms may be useful:

A SPECIES is an interbreeding population of living things, each member of which resembles externally, and is nearly identical to genetically, the other members of the population. In a VARIABLE SPECIES, individuals show some variation in external details such as height, hairiness, flower color, etc. These variable individuals are called VARIANTS, FORMS, VARIETIES, or sometimes SUBSPECIES. The TYPE is the usual, normal, nonvariant form of the species. Example: in New England Aster the type has purple flowers, but forms occur with flowers of pink or white.

A CLONE is a single individual propagated by cuttings or division (not seeds) in order to maintain its distinctive characteristics. A CULTIVAR (cultivated variety) is a clone of a species or hybrid which is perpetuated in cultivation because of certain ornamental characteristics.

A GENUS (plural GENERA) is a group of closely related species which are presumed to stem from a common ancestor. A FAMILY is a group of genera which are closely related and presumably of common descent.

A HYBRID is an individual created by crossing two different species. True species have evolved barriers against hybridization, so that hybrids occur infrequently in nature. Plant breeders, however, have bred them since the beginnings of gardens, so that the bulk of our garden plants are hybrids. A NATURAL HYBRID is one that does occur in nature.

The symbol *x* signifies hybridity. When it occurs in the binomial, between the generic and specific names, it denotes that the "species" is really a hybrid. Thus, *Magnolia x soulangeana* is really a cross, produced by a French nurseryman, of two true species. When the symbol *x* occurs between two specific names, it denotes "crossed by." We may grow an azalea that we call *arborescens x bakeri*, which tells us that this individual came from seed from a flower of *Rhododendron arborescens* pollinated by pollen of *R. bakeri*. Likewise, *Magnolia x soulangeana* may also be called *M. liliflora x denudata,* the names of its two parents.

STEMS or STALKS are plant parts which bear leaves or leaves and flowers together. What appears to be a leafless stem bearing only flowers (as in daffodils) is technically a SCAPE. Short, secondary stems bearing flowers are PEDUNCLES. The secondary stems which bear florets in compound flowerheads like those of onions are called PEDICELS. The short, secondary stems which terminate in leaves are called PETIOLES.

ROOTS are underground structures which draw water and dissolved nutrients from the soil into the plant. They may be confused with modified underground stems which may be more or less round in shape (BULBS, CORMS, TUBERS) or elongated (RHIZOMES). These function as storage organs during hard times. Very slender modified stems, either above ground or below, by which certain plants spread, are called STOLONS or RUNNERS.

LEAVES may be SIMPLE (e.g., elm) or COMPOUND (e.g., walnut, buckeye), and of many shapes, including OVAL or OVATE (egg-shaped, the narrower end outward), OBOVATE (the reverse of ovate), or LINEAR (very narrow, grasslike). In arrangement on the stem they may be OPPOSITE,

ALTERNATE, or WHORLED. In the first case, two leaves arise from each node on the stem, opposing each other on each side of the stem. In the second, one leaf arises from each node, alternating from left to right in the direction they point up and down the stem. In the third, three or more leaves arise from each node, forming a whorl or circle around the stem. Smooth leaves are GLABROUS; downy or hairy leaves are PUBESCENT.

A flower cluster is called an INFLORESCENCE, which may be elongated (a SPIKE, RACEME, THYRSE, PANICLE) or flattish and rounded (an UMBEL, CYME, CORYMB, HEAD) in shape. If borne at branch-tips, inflorescences are TERMINAL; if not, LATERAL. If they arise from the same point as a leaf, they are AXILLARY.

The parts of a flower are: CALYX, COROLLA, STAMENS, PISTILS. The calyx is composed of SEPALS, which are usually green and unshowy. The corolla is composed of PETALS, often colored and showy; these may be separate, or FREE (as in magnolia), or FUSED into a tube (azalea). The stamens and pistils are, respectively, the male (pollen-producing) and female (ovule-producing) reproductive organs.

Modified leaves which accompany flowers are BRACTS. They are often green, but may be some other color (as in poinsettia). When they occur at the base of the inflorescence, they are said to SUBTEND it.

Dry FRUITS are called CAPSULES, PODS, or a variety of more technical terms. BERRY has a specific and limited meaning in botany, but is used more loosely to signify any sort of fleshy fruit. DRUPE is the technical term for stone fruits like plum or cherry.

EXFOLIATING is the term applied to bark like that of the native sycamore, which flakes or falls away in large plates.

A GLANDULAR plant is one that bears quantities of minute growths which may exude a sticky or aromatic substance. These growths are called GLANDS, and may occur anywhere on the plant.

The PAPPUS is the tip of the calyx in plants of the Daisy Family. Usually minute, in some species (e.g., groundsel bush) it consists of long, white bristles.

BOREAL is applied to plants whose range is essentially northern. AUSTRAL is its opposite.

How to Grow Wildflowers and Wild Shrubs and Trees in Your Own Garden

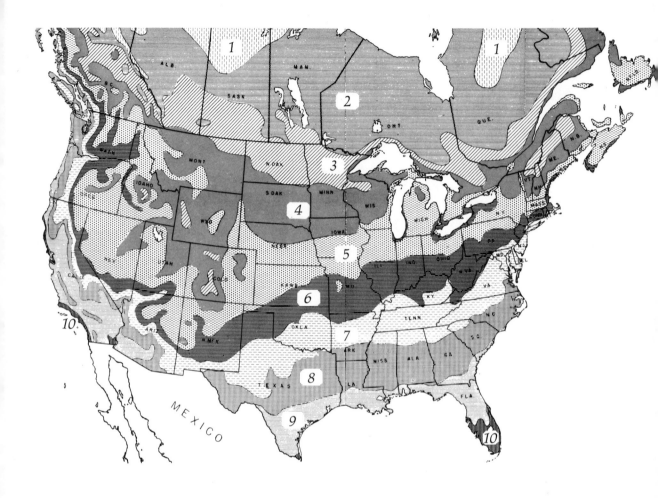

THE ZONES
OF PLANT HARDINESS

Approximate Range of
Average Annual Minimum
Temperatures for each Zone
in Degrees Fahrenheit

Zone 1	Below −50	
Zone 2	−50 to −40	
Zone 3	−40 to −30	
Zone 4	−30 to −20	
Zone 5	−20 to −10	
Zone 6	−10 to 0	
Zone 7	0 to 10	
Zone 8	10 to 20	
Zone 9	20 to 30	
Zone 10	30 to 40	

Labrador to Georgia . . .
Florida to New Jersey

The eastern half of North America is composed of a great plain sharply divided in two by a ridge of mountains running north and south from Quebec to Alabama. These have many names: in the North they are the Green Mountains, the Berkshires, the Catskills, the Poconos; in the South they are the Alleghenies, the Shenandoahs, the Smokies, the Blue Ridge. But they are all part of the Appalachian Chain, a mountain system which heaved itself out of the flatlands hundreds of millions of years ago, and which has profoundly affected the climate, the vegetation, and the animal life, including man himself, of North America.

The chain runs north and south, which means that it was no barrier to retreating plants and animals when the great glaciers four times marched out of the north between 1,000,000 and 15,000 years ago. Living things fled before the ice to the warmer south, there to dwell until the ice melted, and thereafter follow the withdrawing glaciers and recolonize themselves. In Europe, where the mountain chains run east and west, a different situation prevailed: the mountains effectively prevented the flight of many species which, trapped between them and advancing glaciers, became extinct. One result of this is that the plant life of eastern North America is much richer and more varied than that of Europe. As Nan Fairbrother points out in her brilliant ecological study of the modern world, *New Lives, New Landscapes,* there are more species of trees native in one small corner of North Carolina alone than in the whole of Europe.

On either side of the Appalachian Chain there stretches a plateau, an elevated but more or less level tableland, of varying width. On the west it becomes the prairie and plains through which great river systems such as the Missouri-Mississippi wind. On the east it falls away gradually, sometimes broken by low hills, to a completely level stretch of land only a few feet above sea level called the Coastal Plain. This plain was once ocean bottom; part of it is emersed land and part of it is sediment from the many rivers which drained the mountains and the tableland, the Piedmont Plateau, to the west. The width of Piedmont and Coastal Plain varies. At the extreme north, on the Gaspé Peninsula, the mountains come right down to the ocean; there is neither Piedmont nor Coastal Plain here. Along the coast of New England the Piedmont varies from a few to as many as fifty miles in width. There is no Coastal Plain in rocky New England. Not until we reach New Jersey do we find a true Coastal Plain. Much of New Jersey south and east of Trenton is Coastal Plain; almost the whole of Delaware, the eastern shore of Maryland, and "tidewater" Virginia are also. As we progress southward, both Piedmont and Coastal Plain become broader. In South Carolina, Charleston lies in the Coastal Plain, while Columbia, a hundred miles to the west, lies on the edge of the Piedmont. Here the mountains are some 250 miles from the coast.

So much, for the moment, for mountains. Off the coast of the United States there flows northward the current known as the Gulf Stream, passing close to Florida and sweeping gradually farther away from the coasts of Georgia and the Carolinas until it angles sharply eastward off Cape Hatteras. This current brings warm water from the tropics, greatly influencing the climate along the shore from New Jersey southward. In coastal North Carolina palmettoes and gardenias grow with abandon which a hundred miles due west would be cut to the ground by frosts.

Interacting with the warming effect of the Gulf Stream are very different factors produced by the Appalachian Chain. Mean temperatures fall as elevations rise; arctic conditions would prevail even on mountains at the equator if those mountains were high enough. Now, although none of the peaks in southern Appalachia is high enough to produce truly *arctic* conditions, many of them, such as 6,684-foot-high Mount Mitchell in western North Carolina, come very close to doing so. The flora and the fauna of the Appalachians, then, contain many boreal elements, just as the flora and fauna of the coast contain many austral, even subtropical, elements.

The phrase "Labrador to Georgia" occurs again and again in botanical manuals, almost invariably referring to those essentially northern plants like spruce, fir, hemlock, Small Cranberry (*Vaccinium oxycoccos*), Leatherleaf (*Chamaedaphne*), *Clintonia*, and Creeping Snowberry (*Chiogenes*), which are widespread in the upper part of their range but extend south only in the mountains. Conversely, the phrase "Florida to New Jersey (or Delaware, or Virginia)" occurs nearly as frequently, referring here usually to plants like Spanish-moss, Live Oak, Sorrel Tree, Yellow Jessamine, and Bald-cypress, which are abundant in the lowlands and hills of the Deep South but occupy only a narrow coastal strip at the northernmost limits of their range.

The point of all this is that in the East it is possible to travel from a typically southern to a typically northern climate by going not north but west. In the space of little more than two hundred miles one can journey the equivalent of, say, the 1,100 miles from Savannah to Montreal. This fact has enormous importance for the gardener. The Red Bay (*Persea borbonia*), for example, has an apparently wide range—southern Delaware to Florida and the Gulf States—but its range is somewhat diminished when we consider that only in the southern extremity does it leave the coast. Thus a Red Bay collected in Wilmington, North Carolina, would be far more likely to live if planted three hundred miles north in Pocomoke City, Maryland, than if planted three hundred miles west in Asheville, in the same state but among the mountains. The reverse applies to mountain plants, many of which languish along the coast because of hot summers and mild winters.

About midway between Maine and Florida on the East Coast of the United States lies a spit of land some two hundred miles long and, at its widest point, about seventy miles in breadth. Parts of three states are contained in it: almost the whole of Delaware, over a third of Maryland (the famous "Eastern Shore" of that state), and two counties of Virginia. It lies between the 37th and 40th parallels North and between 75 and 77 degrees of longitude West. The land area is a little over 6,000 square miles. To its inhabitants it is usually known by the coined term "Delmarva" (from the names of the three states composing it).

The Delmarva Peninsula is bounded on the north by the state of Pennsylvania; on its western edge its boundaries are the Chesapeake Bay with its countless inlets and tributaries; on the east its boundaries are the Delaware Bay and River, and the state of New Jersey. The southern half faces the open Atlantic. In topography the peninsula is almost entirely Coastal Plain. Only in the extreme north do we enter the Piedmont Province, the Fall Line (the point at which the Piedmont pitches steeply down to join the Coastal Plain) running in a southwesterly direction from the city of Wilmington in northern Delaware to the mouth of the Susquehanna River in northern Maryland. A low ridge, however, runs down the center of peninsula for about half its length, and along this ridge certain Piedmont plants extend southward, while along the flat coastal area typically southern species reach far northward.

Delmarva is a kind of microcosm, in terms of vegetation, of the whole East Coast. Even though its area is comparatively small, location and geography provide an enormous amount of variability in terms of climate, terrain, and types of plants. Two biological life-zones, the Upper Austral and the Austral, each with accompanying animals and plants, meet here. Outlying representatives of mountain flora occur in the foothills of the north (the Poconos begin only about seventy-five miles north of Wilmington, Delaware), and representatives of the subtropical flora which follows the Gulf Stream north occur in the cypress swamps and savannahs of the southern portion. Within fifty miles one may travel from a typical upland forest of beech, oak, and tulip-poplar to a typical southern lowland forest of pine, holly, and wax-myrtle, or from a landscape of hills and fast-running streams to the endless salt marshes and meadows of the Delaware and Chesapeake bays.

Within the limits of Delmarva such boreal species as Canadian Hemlock push down the central ridge as far as Caroline County in Maryland, over sixty miles south of the Mason-Dixon line, while twenty-five miles due east the southern Loblolly Pine marches north to form great, pure stands in the Ellendale Forest near Milford, Delaware. Other boreal plants which reach Delmarva are Gray Birch, Shinleaf, Teaberry, Nodding Trillium, and, along the sea coast, Sea-beach Sandwort (*Arenaria peploides*). The number of austral plants which reach the peninsula is even more surprising, considering that its latitude is roughly that of such midwestern cities as Indianapolis, Cincinnati, Topeka, and Kansas City. Loblolly Pine, Pond Pine, Black Jack Oak, Water Oak, Willow Oak, Persimmon, American Holly, Snowy Orchis, Ruellias, Saltmarsh Milkweed, Wax-myrtle, Bald-cypress are some that press into Delaware and along the coast a bit farther (a very few pushing sporadically as far as Long Island). Mistletoe comes into Delaware also, and the Sweetleaf (*Symplocos tinctoria*) and Red Bay (*Persea borbonia*) cross over into the extreme southern part of the state. Finally, in extreme southern Delmarva, one encounters truly southern plants: Cross Vine (*Bignonia capreolata*), Yellow Jessamine, Spanish-moss, and (dwarfed specimens) Live Oaks.

Thus many different habitats are compressed into the 6,000 square

miles that make up Delmarva: Piedmont hillside, with mixed deciduous hardwoods; coastal pine forests; tangles of Water Oak, cypress,
and Muscadine Grape; holly thickets; pine barrens; sand dunes; salt
marshes and meadows; seashore; freshwater swamps, bogs, and
marshes; shores of tidal rivers. One may feel justified in applying
observations made here to the rest of the East.

There is another justification for comparing Delmarva to the country
at large: the northern portion of the peninsula lies in the path of
Megalopolis, that dismal complex of neon, concrete, and asphalt
which is fast stretching from Boston to Richmond and leveling all
things in its path. New Castle County, the northernmost in Delaware,
is one of the most industrialized and heavily populated in the country.
In the past twenty years, as industry has boomed, literally thousands
of acres of woodland, field, and marsh have been leveled, graded,
and built up with refineries, factories, shopping centers, or housing
developments. As children my brothers and I often walked with our
mother to some nearby woods to pick blueberries or blackberries in
summer; today those woods, where thrushes caroled the summer
away while we gathered berries, are a complex of asphalt streets,
postage-stamp yards, and identical houses which stretch for miles
in all directions. The marsh where I once hunted ducks is an oil
refinery. The field where I first found Closed Gentians is a gaping
hole, the aftermath of a gravel pit.

There is little land left in New Castle County to exploit, yet
developers, real estate men, chiefs of industry continue to develop
it as though there were enough to last for years to come. This is
no new trend. R. R. Tatnall's *Flora of Delaware and the Eastern
Shore*, published in 1946, is full of references to habitat destruction.
One particularly interesting locality near the coast held at least three
of the rarest plants in the country: the southern False Asphodel,
Tofieldia racemosa, the Whorled Pogonia orchid, *Cleistes divaricata*,
and a hybrid Fringed Orchis, *Habenaria x canbyi*. Tatnall's manual
had this to say in 1946 about the location: "now destroyed." Mr.
Tatnall further said about *Arethusa bulbosa*, one of the loveliest of

the bog orchids, "The Hudson Pond station is perhaps the last stand of *Arethusa* on the Peninsula, and recent draining of the pond may have exterminated it." Hudson Pond is no more, and the last stand of *Arethusa* apparently perished with it. One wonders what Tatnall would say if he were alive today.

I could go on to talk about other vanishing plants. The point I want to make, though, is this: the wilderness has vanished today in tiny, urbanized Delaware; it can vanish tomorrow just as easily somewhere else. The size or remoteness of an area is no longer a guarantee against its development. Indeed, as land close to the industrial centers becomes used up (and it *is* being used up, every acre of it), industry and population, ever expanding, move deeper into undeveloped areas.

As I have noted, the trend is not new. It is accelerating, however, at an alarming rate. Since I began work on this book in 1968, I have watched the countryside closely, and I have seen more roadside acreage destroyed—that is, bulldozed and graded—in order to build shopping centers, housing developments, industrial complexes, than ever. In the autumn of 1969, I stopped my car by a field gorgeous with purple and gold flowers. Goldenrod covered the higher ground, joined by Bur-marigolds, Ironweed, and Joe-pye in the lower areas, and through the center, along a wash, ran a stand of Purple Gerardia like a river of purple through the gold. The following spring I drove past the field and was shocked to see the entire twenty-odd acres stripped, scraped of every blade of grass, every ounce of topsoil, and graded. There it lay, like an open sore, while a sign proudly read, "Another tract being developed by Blank Developers, Inc." In a few months, asphalt was spread on the raw earth, a complex of buildings was built in the center of the expanse, and white lines were painted on the rest of it. It is now an enormous parking lot surrounding a shopping mall. Thus twenty more acres was cleared of every living thing, and will not soon produce or support life again. Only twenty acres, you may say, but multiply that by thousands for the country as a whole and you have statistics on a lot of destruction.

It is not only happening near industrial centers, however. In

Delmarva the only recorded station for the One-sided Wintergreen (*Pyrola secunda*) is an oak-pine forest bordering an arm of the Indian River in the south of Delaware. In 1970 I went in search of this elusive northerner and found that the oak-pine wood is no more. It has been developed into a community of "waterfront estates," large summer houses surrounded by hedges and clipped lawns. Thus another species probably has vanished from the region.

Land near the ocean is presently changing at a rate equal to that near the big cities. This is even sadder to contemplate, since land near the cities is mainly "disturbed landscape" anyway, while ocean-side land, because it is useless for agriculture and produces no sizable timber, has remained closer to its original state than any comparable area, and supports a totally unique flora.

But between Population Boom and Affluent Society, the resort towns along the coast have become too small to accommodate the new group of pleasure-lovers. Their boundaries have been extended. Seashore motels and villages have sprung up on the dunes. Trailer parks are everywhere. Marinas to accommodate boat people have been built at every convenient spot. Sand dunes are trampled, "useless" salt marshes are ditched and drained, bays and inlets are filled in, the whole area is drenched with poisons all summer long in an attempt to kill the mosquitoes which annoy the newly arrived vacationers. And so it goes.

To date we have not handled the ecological crisis at all well. We talk about it in the newspapers, we hear it discussed on TV talk shows, college students protest against pollution and pick up a few beer cans, but little is done that is effective. Powerful forces are on the side of the destroyers and the polluters. Environmental control boards and their like are manned by people who are too often figure-heads, committed to the destroying agents—industry, businesses, transportation agencies, municipalities themselves—rather than to the environment. Their chiefs see their jobs as explaining to the public that everything is all right, when it is obvious that a great deal is wrong, and as defending local industries against "extremist" conservation groups.

The Pioneer Myth of this country is to blame for much of the public apathy, I think. Man is regarded as a lone figure pitted against that great enemy The Wilderness, replete with vicious animals, poisonous snakes, mammoth trees, and encroaching vines which must be destroyed before he can wrest a living from the land. Man the brave individual, the Daniel Boone or Davy Crockett, is of course a romantic figment. The real roots of contemporary America lie in the work of the Robber Barons of the nineteenth century. Davy Crockett and his ilk have provided bread and circuses for the public for a long time, but we can no longer afford to be entertained. We must understand that money, progress, affluence are the root reasons for the death of our environment. We have had our cake and eaten it too, but we cannot do it much longer. We cannot have the kind of economy we have and still have breathable air and clean water, let alone blue skies and pleasing landscapes—or wild orchids in the woods.

Many responsible experts feel that we cannot prevent the total destruction of our environment, that it is too late already. Many believe these predictions. Even the most optimistic pronouncements are grim. Whatever the outcome, it seems inevitable that some species of plants and animals will disappear from the face of the earth. We have already lost half a dozen birds, and others, like the ivory-billed woodpecker and the whooping crane, are all but extinct. The bluebird is declining rapidly in the populated regions of the East, and will very likely decline still more as English sparrows and starlings increase. Plant species, more adaptable than animals, do not show such alarming statistics—yet. But the more highly specialized, like the orchids, cannot endure the disturbances of civilization (those that can best do so are weedy, undesirable species like dandelion and pigweed, which have followed the march of progress), and it will be these most rare and beautiful species which will be lost. Perhaps the most compelling reason for using native American plants in our gardens is the chance that by so doing we might help save a species from oblivion. There will be some hope of survival for the next "last stand" if it is found in somebody's garden.

In 1967 I began teaching at a branch campus of the University of Delaware in Georgetown, a pretty colonial town in the heart of Delaware's southernmost county. The people of Georgetown were friendly, the job was enjoyable, my students were anxious to learn. The only hitch was that Georgetown is a long way from home for me: it is about ninety miles south of my home near Wilmington, or 125 miles south of Philadelphia—almost on the same latitude as Washington, D.C.

This meant that for a whole year I was forced to be one of those stereotypical Americans who commute vast distances each day, who spend as much time in transport as out. I borrowed a friend's summer cottage at a nearby resort on one of the salt-water bays that extend inland from the Atlantic. This, winterized, gave me a base of operations part of the time, but professional duties nevertheless required my frequent presence on the main campus, and personal affairs called me home oftener still. Not a week passed in which I did not travel at least five hundred miles by automobile. These trips, through autumn and the long grim winter, through a beautiful spring and into a marvelous summer, became the genesis of this book.

To my surprise the strain, fatigue, boredom of constantly driving the same route was mainly physical. For the first time in my life I found myself exposed repeatedly to a large segment of the American landscape. Monotony should have been what I found in this, and boredom the result. Instead, I found myself seeing more each time I looked, noticing more than I had ever had time or opportunity to notice.

After a time a strange visual effect began to take place. I became very familiar with certain landmarks—a particularly distinguished house, a well-planned garden, a picturesque patch of swamp or woodland, a pond or stream, even a well-shaped tree or a brightly blooming shrub. These I began to look for, anticipate half-consciously, as I sped down highways, noting, again only half-consciously, seasonal changes and seeing the landmarks each time in a different aspect or dimension. They became almost recurrent images imposed and

1. Black Oaks and
Tulip-poplars in snow.

2. Fruiting branches of Staghorn Sumac (*Rhus typhina*) during winter in Vermont.

3. *(left)* Swamp-pink, *Helonias bullata,* in early spring.

4. *(below)* Bloodroot *(Sanguinaria canadensis).* One of the earliest and most beautiful of woodland wildflowers.

5. *(left)* The author's garden in spring. Wild Columbine and Blue Phlox blooming with English Cowslips and the rare Japanese *Rhododendron yakusimanum.*

6. *(below) Viola striata,* the Cream Violet. One of the stemmed violet group and a most satisfactory species in the garden.

7. Purple or Wet-dog Trillium, *T. erectum*.

8. Marsh-marigold, *Caltha palustris*. A semi-aquatic relative of the Buttercup which is one of the first and brightest of spring flowers.

9. Birdsfoot Violet (*Viola pedata*) growing in dry soil beneath a Scrub Pine in the author's garden. Perhaps the finest of the violets, but requires dry, sterile soil and some sun.

10. The Double Trillium, a rare mutation of the Large-flowered Trillium, *T. grandiflorum.*

11. A good form of the Pinxterbloom Azalea *(Rhododendron nudiflorum)*, the earliest of the wild azaleas to bloom in the Northeast.

superimposed on my brain. The effect created was very much like that of time-lapse photography. My comprehension of the landscape grew with each passing week as I learned to see temporally as well as spatially, as I saw time and change as well as color and line in the countryside. I finally began to perceive the delicate balance between the permanent and the ephemeral from which much—perhaps all—of the beauty in art and nature arises.

My mind of course applied this somewhat rarefied philosophy long before it formulated it. For example, I swiftly became aware that color, in terms of visual effects in the landscape, is at once the most visually stimulating, the most appealing, and the most ephemeral attribute of plants. It is also the most wearying and cloying. Too often we choose garden plants for color only, and when their season of bloom is past, we have little remaining. Or we are seduced in early spring by bright pots of annuals at garden centers and overload our gardens with them. Form and mass and line are less obvious but paradoxically more important to the human sense of balance and design; they are also more permanent, more suitable as a framework in which to use color. A garden designed on the principles of form, line, and mass is much more satisfying than a garden crammed with eye-glutting geraniums or azaleas and little else. In Chekhov's *Three Sisters*, the vulgar Natasha, having succeeded in ousting the cultured Prozorov sisters from their family mansion, begins immediately making plans to destroy what must have been a fine old garden: "First of all I shall have this avenue of fir trees cut down," she says, "then that maple. . . . It's so unsightly in the evening. . . . And then I'll have flowers planted everywhere—flowers, flowers—and it will be fragrant. . . ." If a garden is not gaudy, it is in bad taste to Natasha. Chekhov, himself a gentleman farmer and an indefatigable planter of trees, works a great deal of irony into this scene as he has her planning the destruction of the very backbone of her garden while dreaming of its beauty.

I also learned much about succession of bloom on my trip. I saw for example that wave after wave of white sweeps through the woodlands of the East all through the spring, beginning with blossoms of Shad Bush in April and continuing at two-week intervals first with Flowering Dogwood, then with Chokeberry and Blackhaw Viburnum, and ending in June with Ironwood Viburnum and Elderberry. What I had recalled as one great, long burst of white flowers is really a series of overlapping shorter bursts, ebbing and flowing, varying greatly in species, in shade of white, even in details of individual blooms, but varying little in total effect. Several years ago, when I was a young horticulturist at Winterthur, the magnificent garden of the late H. F. du Pont, I learned that one of Mr. du Pont's major concerns was that his garden provide what he called "succession of bloom." I was not impressed by the idea then. I know now that Henry F. du Pont had been a close observer of nature during his eighty-odd years.

I saw also that in spite of what poets say about violets and rhodoras, spring can first be seen not in the flowers of the frozen ground, but in the trees which stand high in the warming sky, and in the birds which respond to lengthening days and warming sun. Weeks before the first Bloodroot shatters in the breeze or the first Marsh-marigold opens in cold woodland streams, even before the lurid hoods of Skunk-cabbage appear in swamps, the supple branches of willow glow green and gold in the thin sunshine of February, and the branches of Red Maples turn scarlet with swelling flower buds. In these, and in legions of returning blackbirds, is spring returned to us.

My journey began in late summer, a few weeks before the beginning of the school year, but I didn't begin really to *see* until there was little obvious to see—until winter had set in. When summer returned, I was a trained eye, and I saw more with each passing week than I'd ever seen before. For years I had, like everyone else, noticed the profusion of pink, white, mauve, purple, and yellow flowers which cover our fields and roadsides from August until almost frost (indeed, only a blind man could fail to notice them, so showy are they). I knew also that this profusion of blossoms was supplied by relatively few species: the Joe-pye Weeds (*Eupatorium purpureum, E. maculatum*), Boneset and Thoroughworts (*E. per-*

foliatum and others), Ironweed (*Vernonia*), Swamp Milkweed (*Asclepias incarnata* and its variety *pulchra*), and Flat-topped Goldenrod (*Solidago graminifolia*). It had never struck me that there existed between these species, many of them completely unrelated, a similarity so striking that one could call it mimicry. The Swamp Milkweed, for example, resembles the Joe-pye Weed with which it grows in color, form of inflorescence, even in superficial aspects of stem and leaf, far more than it does its bright orange relative Butterflyweed which blooms about the same time in uplands. Flat-top Goldenrod is yellow, like most *Solidago.* It is therefore different in color from its growing companions, but it closely resembles them in its broad, flat compound inflorescences, totally different from the upright spikes and tiered thyrses one usually associates with goldenrods.

Nor is this sort of mimicry limited to the plants of the summer swales and fields. When I finally found the delicate little Whorled Milkweed (*Asclepias verticillata*) of the Serpentine Barrens along the Mason-Dixon Line, I realized that I must have been looking at it for a long time without seeing it, so effectively did its narrow leaves and off-white flowers mimic the yarrow and mountain-mint with which it grows. Again, my plant-hunting friend Dick Ryan and I searched diligently for several seasons before we found a spike of the magnificent Purple Fringeless Orchis, and immediately after finding that one we found a full stand of it; once we had observed the plant, we began to detect other individuals among the similarly colored Joe-pye and Ironweed with which they grew.

Obviously these cases of mimicry are environmental adaptations. The survival value in the case of the orchid is apparent; the far more abundant and adaptable Joe-pye and Ironweed serve as a sort of floral smokescreen for it. Perhaps the same applies in the case of the milkweed. It also may be, though I have not proved this to my satisfaction, that the similarities in coloration and form may be adaptations to specific pollinators. In other words, the August and September bees and butterflies frequenting the orchid meadow may prefer colors in the mauve-magenta range to any others.

Such is certainly the explanation for mimicry in the summer swale

JOE-PYE WEED

association, though my job in Georgetown had been over for a full year before the reasons became clear to me.

Early one September afternoon I drove west on New Jersey Route 70 through the Pine Barrens on my way to spend a final weekend by the sea at Barnegat. It was the composite season: tall goldenrods with turreted, towered, steepled inflorescences bloomed everywhere upland, in dry fields, along sun-splashed roadsides, even in clearings among the pines. Here also were the first lavender flowers on the tiny *Aster concolor*, the long purple wands of *Liatris graminifolia*, the yellow bells of Fern-leaf False-foxglove (*Gerardia pedicularia*). In roadside swales the association of Swamp Milkweed, Joe-pye, Boneset, and Flat-top Goldenrod was at its height of bloom. The goldenrod was especially showy, with its great compound heads a foot across. Meadows, mounds, plains, plateaus of gold, rather than steeples, I thought to myself, as an immense butterfly, russet and black-spangled white, sailed majestically out of the sky to alight on one of the golden inflorescences.

This was it, of course! The answers to the most esoteric questions are often so obvious that they are ignored. My great, broad, mounded flowers were the landing fields of butterflies, their natural pollinators. Bees, flies, and such can move between the closely packed tiers of flowers in an inflorescence of ordinary goldenrod, can crawl up and down the fragile wands of liatris, can maneuver over and under the spherical heads of Common Milkweed; but three-inch monarch, viceroy, fritillary, or swallowtail butterflies need room to negotiate. Thus *Solidago graminifolia* and its smaller relative *S. tenuifolia* have adapted themselves to pollination by the big butterflies which appear late in the summer, as apparently have the Swamp Milkweeds, Joe-pye Weed, and others which share their habitat. This is not to say of course that *only* butterflies pollinate these plants; they are perhaps not so specialized as to be adapted to a single pollinator. But by making themselves easily accessible to large insects as well as small, they have vastly increased their chances of being cross-pollinated and setting seed.

I found in this more than mere natural history. It was one more natural application of the rules governing gardening. First, the color combination was varied but pleasing, both the contrasts between the whites, yellows, and purple shades, and the more subtle gradations from off-white to pink-mauve to purple. Second, there was an excellent balance between order and disorder, between uniformity and variation, in that the form of the flowers, their height, and general shape were nearly identical, while their colors varied enormously. The aim of the landscape gardener is to banish chaos and yet retain pleasing variation, to bring order to a landscape and yet avoid monotony. One way to do this is to bring a series of variations on a certain constant. In this case the constant was shape of inflorescence—flower form—while the variable was flower color.

Another realization came to me with great force as I traveled north and south. I saw many attractive gardens, many beautiful cultivated plants. In particular I remember a gorgeous Golden-chain Tree dominating a dooryard in one small town, every inch of the tree, from its glossy trunk to its finely divided leaves, its upright branches, its hanging clusters of yellow blossoms, proclaiming it an aristocrat. In another town I watched a Chinese Redbud so flagrantly magenta that it made my eyes ache, yet blooming so early that so much color seemed right. Farther south I recall a row, almost a hedge, of Crepe-myrtles, all of different colors and all large enough to be noteworthy in our fairly harsh climate. In midsummer they were truly spectacular.

But these sights were only a few among the many which delighted me. More often, the great effects which I saw were natural, not manmade; almost without exception, the beautiful individual plants I saw were wild plants. I realized that nature was still the greatest gardener of all, and I thought about writing a book like this, if only to tell of the sights I saw and record the thoughts which such sights brought to me. An example: in early April, when the cultivated landscape becomes blatant with forsythia, I watched closely a totally unique planting—a hillside so thickly grown with young maples that nothing save a few mountain-laurels grows beneath them. The absence of competing low growth, along with apparently abundant moisture and a northern exposure, has encouraged the growth of mosses on this hillside, so that the whole expanse is a carpet of green, yellow-green throughout the winter, gradually deepening with spring until it becomes that extremely vivid bronzy color known appropriately as "moss green." I remember watching that glowing hillside and thinking that, color for color, it was almost as bright as forsythia yellow, yet the latter color was gaudy in comparison. Because it was so over-used? Probably. At any rate, the effect of the ground itself glowing a vivid green was totally novel to me. I do not think that this moss garden was planned. It just happened. But apparently the people who own it have enough sense to leave it alone.

I took a side trip in late May through the Pine Barrens of New Jersey. Mile after mile of soft green Pitch, Scrub, Yellow Pines lined the narrow roads. Dozens of colorful herbaceous plants bloomed along the sandy roadsides. And back beneath the pines as far as the eye could see bloomed pink and white Mountain-laurel, a gorgeous, undulating pink carpet beneath the trees. I had never seen so much color concentrated in a single combination of plants before, yet the effect was far from overpowering, mainly because of the contrasts between the frilly flowers and the green needles and dark, rugged trunks and branches of the pines. Suddenly I came on a tiny bungalow sitting in the middle of a perfect rectangle of pale green grass. It stopped my car. Not a single pine remained in that rectangle chopped out of the wilderness. And not a single Mountain-laurel. All that relieved the stark house and starker yard were two Norway Maples and two pink weigelas. Weigelas! They were in bloom, and so resembled the laurels on first sight that I had to look a second time to ascertain that the house owner had not spared two laurels for his dooryard. But they were weigelas from far China, similar in flower, perhaps, to the native Mountain-laurel, but inferior in habit, foliage, winter interest, in every other way.

I wondered what the man who built the place thought of as he cleared his land. He perhaps felt like Daniel Boone putting his mark, imposing his personality on the wilderness, and that's a good, traditional, time-honored American feeling. The problem is that it is as out of date as Daniel Boone's muzzle-loader. I also thought of the many discerning gardeners in this country and abroad who would have given eyeteeth to have in their gardens a stand of mature Mountain-laurel like that obviously cleared from this land. One thing was certain, the anonymous owner of that property was incomparably poorer for his attitude toward his environment. All around him the forest blossomed, while his house sat in an angular desert of his own making.

Such sights were common on my travels. The pattern was everywhere the same: perfect squares or rectangles hacked out of the forest; a few trees perhaps left for shade, but more often than not the whole yard stripped clean; then exotic vegetation brought in: Scotch Pines, Norway Maples, Japanese Azaleas, Mock-orange, Forsythias, Lilacs. Everywhere total replacement—not even a compromise between exotic and native vegetation. Americans simply do not utilize their wildflower resources. Yet there is still time to begin. . . .

I

Beginnings

Six thirty A.M. of a frozen winter day, still dark and grimly cold outside, the air shrieking into the lungs with each breath and parching the nostrils, so cold it is. In the wan night light at my back door I see the rhododendrons standing with black leaves rolled thin as pencils hanging down against their stems. A border of Sweetwilliam which has (foolishly, to my human calculation) sent forth lush green winter rosettes is drooping and bruised-looking. The skeletal branches of deciduous shrubs rattle in the cutting winds that gust around the house, and on the frozen, opaque surface of my little backyard pond a sycamore leaf, moored to the ice by its petiole, husks a dry, dead ghost of a sound.

Pre-dawn, the coldest time of the day, so the meteorologists tell us, the dreariest hour of the dreariest season of the year, when one's garden and indeed the whole face of nature lies sealed and remote, still as death, against the harshness of the elements. Yet, not long after I start the reluctant motor of my car, ease it out my driveway too soon, while it is still cold and resistant, and turn with numb hands on the numbing wheel down the long road south, the earth begins to awaken. A hint of lilac tints the gray east. Roadside trees become darker presences before a paling horizon. The dark silhouette of a bird whirs across the beams of my headlights.

Slowly the east wakes. Long before the sun actually appears, its presence is felt. Once I had to drive my car for a few miserable days while the heater was "inoperative." Only then did I begin to comprehend the real power of the sun, for even before it appeared on the horizon, a warmth, a presence entered the chilled confines of the car. And when the disk finally appeared, red and glorious, low in the east, the vehicle was lit by a warmth that was only partly heat from the trapped rays; much of it came from within me, a kind of primitive joy in living, which must surely have been the feeling that inspired the first monotheist, Ikhnaton, to call the sun God and so praise it.

We are so far removed from that which is real in life, walled off by landscaped lawns surrounding trim houses, by jobs which carry us deep into the masses of metal, concrete, and glass which rise out of our hostile cities, by a technology more complex than any the world has yet known, which turns ultimately upon the most unreal notion of all: that some of earth's elements are more important than others, and that possession of them or their paper symbols gives us true power, true freedom, true peace. We litter our lives with molecular perversions like plastic and cellophane, true symbols of our culture—weightless, textureless, unnatural, dead. The irony is that, however like their symbols human hearts and minds become, man can never truly separate himself from nature so long as he lives and his life processes depend on the basic elements of oxygen, hydrogen, nitrogen, and carbon. He must have reasonably clean air to breathe, reasonably pure water to drink, and nourishment which comes, directly or indirectly, from the plant life of the earth.

———————————

As I speed southward, the new sun on my left, flooding my tiny auto, my microcosm, with light and heat, the world outside seems frozen tightly, yet even now there is life and movement beneath the rays of the sun. Few spectacles are more amazing than that of a winter flock of starlings wheeling and turning and settling against the leaden skies and dun fields. Thousands of black bodies move as one bird, fanning out in a great crescent against the landscape, veering suddenly skyward with ten thousand silvery underwings aflash against opaque, dark breasts, then suddenly dropping darkly earthward, in a tight black funnel, to fan out across the fields again. Later in the winter, when redwings and grackles return, we will see flocks more spectacular because of sheer numbers, but the native blackbirds have not the great ease and agility on the wing as the introduced starling.

To my winter-starved emotions, the starlings are intensely alive, therefore intensely pleasing in the dead winter landscape. The earth lies locked in a shell of cold; it is one of those periods dominated by Canadian air masses when the thermometer dips to near zero by night and, regardless of clear or cloudy skies, hardly climbs into the twenties by day. Herbaceous plants have long disappeared from sight. Deciduous trees and shrubs are mere skeletons. Even evergreens are hardly green. Pines and spruces are dull and blackish. Azaleas and andromedas are a bruised bronze-purple. The green of evergreens is now hardly the color of life.

But the illusion of death is only, after all, illusion, and is as temporary as this cold snap. Next week may come a thaw which will cause the green of conifers and broadleaved evergreens to soften almost immediately, freshen, revive. In spite of the winter's prevailing mood of death, there is always something to see during the season. What is unique about it is that there is no surfeit of visual delights; they are parceled out slowly, so that we have time to reflect on them.

If I were to stop my car for a walk in the woods I pass, I would notice, for example, the marvelously striped trunks of the shad bushes, the sinewy blue trunks of hornbeams, the snowy trunks and branches of river-bottom sycamores. In sheltered pockets I would easily find evergreen woodferns and Christmas fern. Perhaps I would see the club mosses called Ground-pine and Running-cedar, rising from the leafmold like miniature conifers, or would find a mat of Partridgeberry green of leaves and scarlet of berries. I might see a stand of Teaberry, its coral-pink, wintergreen-flavored berries nodding beneath polished leaves, or discover a clump of Spotted Wintergreen, its pointed, variegated leaves as garish as any popular houseplant, nestling among the fallen pine needles.

But all these are small treasures. I can't see Spotted Wintergreen from my window as I pass by at sixty mph. I can hardly make out the white trunks of sycamores along distant streams. The general picture *is* lifeless, so much so that even the female house sparrows, colorless puffs of dust by the roadside, are welcome sights. And the starling, his black glossed with purple and green and spangled with white, seems almost as bright as a tropical bird.

The plant world all but fails us in winter, for most of my impressions of those cold days of my journey linger on animals. Starlings, sparrows hopping with cold feet on the highway shoulder. A mockingbird, which sailed into a roadside hawthorn with great tail and white-spotted wings so floppy and askew that one wondered how such a disorganized and uncoordinated-looking creature could avoid impaling itself, let alone become as successful a species as it is. Or a mallard drake, which one morning scaled on set wings across the highway, almost touching the roof of my car, to pitch in a tidal stream nearby. For a second my brain was entirely dazzled by the speed, the grace, the bright colors, the *attitude* of that supple and efficient body flashing by my windshield.

Such a transitional region is Delmarva, however, that not many miles are covered before I begin to notice subtle changes outside, due as much to geography as to the height of the sun in the sky. Resident cardinals are far more common along the roads, as I move southward, as are flocks of wintering birds. Evergreens, both conifer and broadleaf, begin to predominate. The deciduous forest of the Piedmont gives way to Coastal Plain pines. The Carolinian elements of both flora and fauna begin to be much more in evidence.

Prehistoric America east of the Rockies was characterized (ignoring specialized areas like deserts, mountain peaks, bogs) by three basic types of environment. The Middle and Northern States from the Atlantic into the Mississippi Valley were covered by a "Climax Forest" of deciduous hardwoods: beech, maple, oak, tulip-poplar, chestnut, ash, hickory. Beyond the Mississippi–Missouri system began the prairies and the plains, with trees of any sort decreasing in both size and numbers westward as annual rainfall decreases. The Far North and the Southeast were both covered by evergreen forest, predominately pine in the South, mixed pine, fir, and spruce in the North.

To a native of the Middle States like me, pine forests mean the South—red sand roads, shrilling cicadas, clouds of biting flies, and the pungency of sun-baked pine needles (or pine "shats" as they are called in lower Delmarva), one of the most wonderful smells in nature. Even in winter they radiate a warmth that the chill woods of the Piedmont cannot.

NATIVE PINES

The transition from deciduous upland forest to coastal pine wood never seems so sudden and astonishing as during the bitter days of midwinter. Then, after miles upon miles of undulating brown fields and gray ghostlike woods, the soft green of pine forests with holly and wax-myrtle undergrowth is most fresh and most bright.

On such days I traveled the narrow back roads, where the pines are allowed to grow almost to the shoulder. The straight road stretched away from me for miles across the absolutely flat terrain. Huge trunks of pines, straight and tall, with bark of large broken plates stood, deep brown with pink, mauve, purple lights, supporting the great canopy of needles that only partially obstructed the pale winter sun. Between the trunks stood young pines: Loblolly, clothed from crown to root in long, abundant needles as bright as new grass; Pitch, shorter needled and less abundantly clothed, its trunk already beginning to curve in the manner so diagnostic of this species at maturity; Scrub, with short almost sprucelike needles, bushy, dense, deep bright green. Among these grew the hollies, seedling trees a few inches tall or gray-barked old giants forty or fifty feet tall, the vast majority ten or twenty feet in height, their normally deep green leaves turned somewhat bronzy by the cold winds of winter. Female hollies, especially those close to the brightly sunlit roadside, were heavy with red berries, in brilliant contrast to the green of their own foliage and that of pines and other evergreens—Mountain-laurel (here far from the mountains but growing magnificently) and Wax-myrtle, the evergreen bayberry.

As if to complete the seasonal contrast of red and green, cardinals were everywhere, fluttering from holly thicket to greenbrier tangle, darting across the road in front of the car, flying, with their typically undulating flight, along the shoulder ahead of the car for some distance before darting back into the pines. Other birds were present: mockingbirds quite common, the dazzling white flash of their wings signaling their presence, and wintering flocks of robins and hermit thrushes, persuaded to remain and brave the cold by the abundant crop of food in the form of holly berries.

But to get back to the three species of pine in these forests, the tall and abundant Loblolly, the usually low and bushy Scrub, and the gnarled and picturesque Pitch, I often wondered why they were not more often seen as lawn trees, either here where they were common or farther north. The houses on my trip were furnished with pines in abundance, but these were almost all foreign species— Japanese, Black, Scotch, Austrian, Mugho, or, the only native to be used in any numbers, White Pine. What is it about the natives that prevented people from using them? In the South, it is simply that they are too common in the wild. In the North it seems that everyone buys his pines from the local nurseryman, who often does not carry native pines. Nevertheless native pines have many uses. I do not for a moment suggest that they replace the foreign ornamental species; they are too different for that. Both types merit a place in any evergreen planting.

How are they different from the foreign pines? It is dangerous to generalize, but the foreign pines are nearly all fairly slow-growing, dense, almost shrubby trees with foliage of a gray- or nearly black-green. The native pines of the East are more open-growing, trees

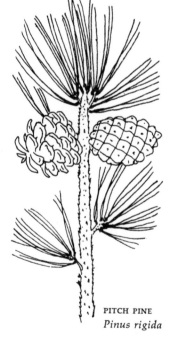

PITCH PINE
Pinus rigida

rather than shrubs, of often faster growth, and (with the exception of the White Pine, which ornamentally as well as botanically is in a class by itself) with bright grass-green needles. These are quite long in the Loblolly Pine, and enormously long in its close relative, the Longleaf Pine of farther south—so long in the latter species that one common name, "Broom Pine," alludes to the practice of making brooms from bundles of the dried needles. In the Pitch Pine they are also rather long. The Scrub Pine is an exception to just about everything I have said in this paragraph. I have seen large trees of this species, but more often it appears as a stunted and bushy plant with very short needles. A variant of the colloquial name, "Shrub Pine," alludes to this habit of growth.

It happens that all three of the common Coastal Plain species are growing in my garden, and I value each one highly. There are five Pitch Pines, dug several years ago along U.S. Route 40 in the red hills of eastern Maryland by the previous owner of the property. They are now about forty feet in height, with straight (but not ramrod straight) trunks and horizontal, twisted, and gnarled branches. The lower branches have long been cut away—to a height of ten feet or so—but I suspect that they would have died out anyway as the trees gained height. One tree is growing in good light in the center of the lawn, and is much the most attractive specimen, a moderately dense-headed tree becoming more open below. The others have had some competition from large deciduous trees and are less dense—one in fact, in the smothering embrace of a Black Locust, being very thin. The persistent cones of these trees are ornamental features also. One winter day I watched from my kitchen door three red crossbills, a dun female and two shining carmine males, feed on the seeds held in these cones.

Scrub Pine for impoverished soil.

There are six Scrub Pines obtained from the same place (the date is unknown to me, but it is certainly less than thirty years ago, since this house was built during the Second World War). These are in the neighborhood of thirty feet tall, but are much more rounded and broad in habit, and very much denser. They grow on a part of the property which is apparently composed of a completely sterile clay subsoil fill, and here they thrive. Beneath them I have planted many native heaths and other acid-loving plants, and (with summer watering) these grow very nicely, the short needles of the Scrub Pine forming an excellent mulch for them. Scrub Pine is perfect for impoverished soil, but it is also an excellent ornamental for other places.

Loblolly Pine is not common, if indeed it is found natively at all, in the northern part of the state, but is very common farther south. A vigorous young specimen of this species is among the most handsome of evergreens, with its dense bright green needles. It grows very rapidly, with tall straight trunks (it is a very valuable timber tree, one of the "yellow pines" of the lumber trade). Vigorous trees will reach sixty or seventy feet in twenty-five or thirty years. Its cones are not persistent like those of the Pitch Pines. One of its drawbacks is relative lack of hardiness. It is really a plant of the Austral Zone, reaching its northernmost limit in Delaware and southern New Jersey, but like most plants will survive well north of its natural range—to eastern Pennsylvania, Long Island, and Cape Cod (Zone 7). Near Wilmington I have several young specimens collected in southern Delaware, and they seem to do well with me, either summer or winter, with absolutely no pampering. At this latitude, however, I have noticed some winter browning of needles in exposed situations, a factor which counts against this otherwise highly ornamental species. The term "loblolly," incidentally, is a folk expression synonymous with "mudhole" or "swamp." It appears also in the common name of a beautiful southern relative of the camellias, *Gordonia lasianthus*, the Loblolly Bay. The Loblolly Pine is, however, found in drier woodlands as well as swamps.

Loblolly Pine for rapid growth.

All three of these local pines have different growth habits. Loblolly is a robust, upright optimist of a tree, always straight, fresh, and bright-looking. Even very old trees, like those, massive and spreading, in the forest of the Chincoteague wildlife refuge, have a youthfully vigorous look to them. Specimens often reach heights of a hundred feet. Pitch Pine is usually far lower in stature, a crabbed, bent, gnarled but fascinating-looking cynic who seems to bow beneath the force of the elements. Scrub Pine is somewhat similar when young but usually becomes bushy and round-headed in age. Occasionally it becomes a tall forest tree of a hundred feet. None of these cares for the shade of other trees. This applies to most conifers. Pitch Pine especially is intolerant of shade, dying rapidly in insufficient light. As to hardiness, Loblolly is hardy in Zone 7 and the others in Zone 5.

There are several native pines which do not grow naturally in this area. Some are seen rather often in gardens—the White Pine (*P. strobus*), the Red Pine (*P. resinosa*), which is also erroneously known as Norway Pine, and the Western Yellow Pine, *P. ponderosa*, are three of these. Those that are extensively grown do not need any futher discussion, I think. But I would like to say a few words about one of the most widely grown and one of the most attractive of American conifers, the White Pine. Originally native to the whole northeastern quarter of the continent, as far north as Newfoundland and Manitoba, and straggling in the mountains south to Georgia, the species has been transplanted all over the United States, and abroad as well.

It is unique among eastern pines in belonging to the so-called Soft Pine group (subgenus *Haploxylon*), a bit of botanical trivia which assumes more importance when we see that most members of this subgenus have definite characteristics which affect their ornamental qualities—in this case long, soft, somewhat drooping needles in clusters or "bundles" of five (rather than two or three), which are glaucous to really bluish green in color, and long, pendulous, soft cones, very different from the hard, spiny ovals of the other species. When young, it is a fairly dense evergreen, extremely attractive by reason of its feathery, light needles. A mature White Pine is a magnificent tree, all straight, thick, dark trunk and sparse but stout horizontal branches. As the trees mature they in effect prune themselves: great branches shear off near the trunk during ice and wind storms, so that by the time the tree reaches an advanced age, it is very open and sparsely branched but exceedingly picturesque. Therefore, do not grieve if your maturing White Pine loses a big branch now and again. This is the natural course of things. On the

White Pine for sheer attractiveness.

other hand, do not plant a White Pine too close to buildings and other breakable objects. A wet or ice-laden pine branch, plummeting earthward with jagged end down, is no mean projectile. *P. strobus* is hardy, as one may imagine, throughout Zone 5. It has two rather similar western relatives which should certainly be tried: *P. monticola*, Western White Pine, like its eastern counterpart a valuable timber tree and a giant which occasionally reaches 150 feet in height, and *P. lambertiana*, Sugar Pine, even more of a giant, sometimes reaching two hundred feet and also distinct for its enormous drooping cones, nearly two feet long. *P. monticola* will stand in Zone 6 in the East; *P. lambertiana* is just a shade more tender.

I want to discuss one more native pine in this chapter, one which unfortunately not everyone can grow because of its tenderness. This is the Longleaf Pine, *Pinus palustris* (*P. australis*), mentioned earlier in the discussion of its near relative, *P. taeda*. Native from Virginia to Florida and Mississippi on the Coastal Plain, the Longleaf is a strikingly characteristic plant, like Live Oak and Saw Palmetto, of its region. A mature hundred-foot tree is a splendid sight, but even more striking, to my mind, is a young plant. Several of these grow on a lawn in a town of southern Delaware, and no more exotic and striking an evergreen could be imagined as lawn plants.* Their thick, abundant needles, which reach incredible lengths of over a foot and a half, wave in bright green cascading plumes the year round. Noteworthy also, on older plants, are the big cones, widely sold as Christmas decorations far beyond the species' native range. These are handsome, a heavy, rich brown in color, and reach ten inches in length.

* I have seen young specimens growing in Newark, Delaware, also, and more recently observed one in the garden of Mr. Lee Raden near Kimberton, west of Philadelphia, on the southern edge of Zone 6.

II

Winter Flowers and Berries

Winter—officially December 22 to March 22. A longer period in the North, from the first really heavy frosts in November until the middle of April. And all this time the native plant life lies dormant. I am reluctant to admit it, but exotics give us most of our winter color—crocuses and snowdrops from the Mediterranean, rhododendrons, camellias, and witch-hazels from Japan and China, Christmas-roses from southern Europe. The climate of the American East is not kind to flowers which appear in winter, and plants which have evolved here do not show until winter is well past. The exotics, in other words, are plants from climates of less severe winters, and we are in effect placing them in abnormal situations by planting them in harsher climates. There is nothing therefore really "cheery" about a sasanqua camellia opening a gorgeous flower among the frost-blackened remains of others, on a mild day in December. The plant is flowering because it has been inalterably programmed to do so, and as long as the temperature remains high enough for physiological processes to function, it will continue to flower, until there are no more buds to open. The cheer is in the mind of the beholder; one might as legitimately feel gloom that the flower will not be able to pursue its normal course to fruition, but will be frozen in all its pristine delicacy that evening, and a blackened mass on the following day.

So I call the native plants (anthropomorphically, I admit) sensible in waiting until it is safe for them to flower. In light of this, we might as well, you say, forget about gardening with native plants until spring and summer arrive? No, because first, there are other sources of color and visual interest in winter, and secondly, not quite all of the native plant material is "sensible." There are a few very interesting plants which, for some obscure, renegade reason, bloom either very late in fall or early in spring, almost as early as the snowdrops and crocuses.

The ice seems hardly to have thawed from woodland ponds and bogs before the Marsh-marigold lifts its gleaming gold cups to the thin spring sun, and I have seen snows fall on the first Bloodroot and Hepatica. Still, none of these bloom until spring is obviously well along, in spite of what seem like resurgences of winter during their blooming period. The great bulk of color in native shrubs during the winter comes not from flowers but from fruits—those of Winter-berry Holly, Dogwood, Chokeberry, and the like—invaluable because one berried shrub on a frozen day can equal a whole grove of flowering shrubs in mid-spring, for nothing in the grim landscape competes with it.

There are, however, two native shrubs which together very nearly span the winter months with flowers. These are the native Witch-hazels, *Hamamelis*. The Vernal Witch-hazel, *H. vernalis*, native to the southern part of the Mississippi Valley, begins blooming during the first thaws of winter—in January and February in Delaware. Its naked branches are heavily studded with three-quarter-inch flowers of pale yellow, each with very narrow petals, spidery in effect

WITCH-HAZEL

but showy in mass. In cultivation also is another form, var. *carnea*, which has flowers the color and brightness of newly polished copper. It can be a real show on a cold day. Attractive as this witch-hazel is, it must compete with the two Asiatic species, the Japanese (*H. japonica*), and the Chinese (*H. mollis*), since it blooms at the same time. For me it holds its own with the Japanese species (it also usually blooms earlier), but not with the Chinese, which has larger and showier flowers—which is indeed one of the choicest of all flowering shrubs. The variety *carnea* is distinct enough to warrant planting anywhere, however.

The second species, the Common Witch-hazel (*H. virginiana*) of the East Coast from Quebec to Georgia and extending west to Minnesota and Missouri, is totally unique in blooming, incredibly enough, in November, just when its leaves begin to fall. Its flowers are in fact obscured by yellow leaves when they first open, and as the leaves fall, one looks at the shrub as though more were to fall, even when there are no more. Somehow, the idea of simultaneous flowers and falling leaves is especially poignant to me. It is also, I have found, amazing to those unfamiliar with the plant.

I first happened on it in the middle of an early November woods, on one of those dark, cold days so common to late autumn, the ground underfoot already noisy with beech leaves, yet the greater part of the trees—hickory, tulip, oak especially—still thick with saffron, gold, orange, and brown foliage overhead. I walked under a small, spreading tree (I took it to be a hornbeam from its general shape and appearance) which grew beneath the high canopy of oak and beech, and looking up, I saw to my surprise that the pale yellow festooning the dark branches was flowers, not dying leaves. The actual color was not too different from that of some of the leaves hanging from the different trees; hence my stumbling beneath the tree before noticing it in bloom. But the quality of the blossoms themselves was different—they possessed a living brightness, a translucence which somehow concentrated the pale autumn sunshine passing through them, which the dying leaves could never rival. Much later I came across Whittier's line: "The hazel's yellow blossoms shine" and knew precisely why he chose that verb "shine."

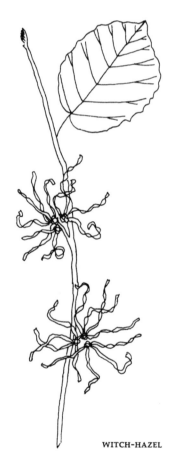

WITCH-HAZEL

That flowers of any sort, not to mention flowers of such translucent beauty, should open in this dark wood and dying year amazed me. What strange autumn-flying insect pollinated them, I wondered? Are they adapted to a specific creature, or do they simply open their miniature yellow starbursts to catch the last of the honeybees, as their cultivated Oriental relatives which bloom in January and February attract the bees that fly during early thaws. Whatever their genesis, these delicate flowers provoked a powerful emotion in me, and still do. This is strongest when I come on a wild plant blooming half-eclipsed in the golden autumn forest, but it also stirs when I see the plant in more contrived cultivated settings.

Common Witch-hazel for autumn bloom.

Common Witch-hazel makes some stunning effects in contrast with other colors—various berries, for example. Henry F. du Pont used it at Winterthur with Beautyberries (*Callicarpa*) and Japanese Winterberry (*Ilex serrata*)—a beautiful combination (even more so because it was one of the last of the year) of palest yellow, intense lilac, and glistening red. It also makes an excellent companion for the native Winterberry, *I. verticillata* (which keeps its fruit longer than *I. serrata*). Combine the two against a bank of evergreens and you have an even more effective show of color during the dark months of autumn and early winter.

Combine Witch-hazel with: Beautyberries, Winterberries, late flowering exotics, White Birches.

It might also be interesting to combine with some of the later-flowering exotics—like *Elaeagnus pungens,* the Evergreen "Russian Olive," or Holly-olive, *Osmanthus ilicifolius,* or the various clones and hybrids of *Camellia sasanqua* where these are hardy. In a wild garden it would be spectacular underplanted with the electric blue of the similarly late-flowering Closed Gentian (or, if one had the almost incredibly good fortune to be able to grow it, the Fringed Gentian). I like it alone as much as any place, or planted in a grove of White Birches, where it seems an echo of the gleaming yellow of their leaves after they have fallen. It is quite hardy, extending as it does into Canada (where it is called *Café du Diable,* Devil's Coffee, for some obscure reason). It will stand quite well throughout Zone 5. *H. vernalis* is somewhat tenderer, being best limited to Zone 6. *H. virginiana* has also a reddish form (*H. v. rubescens*), which I haven't seen, although I grow and highly appreciate the red form of *H. vernalis.*

Perhaps the greatest single difference in appearance between the Piedmont and the Coastal Plain, what really makes the former seem northern and the latter southern, is the increasing predominance of evergreen trees as one journeys southward. Winter landscapes in the Piedmont are gray, sere and brown, black with the naked branches of oaks and tulip-poplars. Those on the Coastal Plain, as in the true South, are eternally green with bright-needled pine and burnished holly. Even the deepest, darkest, coldest swamps on the Coastal Plain seem living, not dormant and waiting in the winter, with half-evergreen Sweet-bay, dense Wax-myrtle, clambering, evergreen *Smilax laurifolia,* and, showiest of all, bright-berried Holly.

HOLLY

In Delmarva the American Holly grows sporadically right up to the Fall Line, but is found in abundance closest to the sea. It is one of the most ornamentally valuable trees in the plant kingdom. No other can quite give the stunning effect of a mature female holly, with its pale bark and deep green leaves punctuated by masses of scarlet berries. Old specimens make dense, upright trees to fifty feet in height and a foot and a half in trunk diameter. Such are naturally worth their weight in gold. The species flowers and fruits when quite young, however, and is pleasing as a small tree or shrub. Hollies have sexes on different plants, so that to get berries one must have a female plant and a male plant within pollinating distance— that is, within the range of the flight of a bee. In areas where the species grows wild, one doesn't have to worry about male plants, since bees range widely. In other areas it is well to purchase a male plant, or to bring in a bucket of the branches of male flowers in late May, when the species blooms.

American Holly for long-lasting berries.

Few berry-bearing plants, native or exotic, can compete with *Ilex opaca* for brilliance of effect combined with longevity of berries. When fruits of pyracantha and crab-apple have been decimated by the birds or browned by winter winds, those of American Holly remain plump and red and dense in their clusters. Spring comes, and the berries are still red and firm. The clusters have been somewhat thinned by wintering birds, but enough remain to give a good effect. Only after the new crop of berries begins to turn from green to greenish orange in summer do last year's fruits fall. The plant is literally in fruit for most of the year.

Why do the fruits of some plants disappear quickly while others remain for months? The reason obviously has to do with palatability. Fruits of hollies (and, incidentally, all berried plants discussed in this chapter) are sufficiently astringent to be ignored by birds until nothing else is available. Perhaps also the long period of ripening and freezing enhances the taste of the berries. In any case, the berries of hollies and hawthorns serve as emergency rations for wildlife, and for that reason alone they deserve to be planted widely.

In the wild, American Holly is usually found with dogwoods as an understory in pine forests or with gum, maple, and magnolia in swamps. As might be expected, it prefers acid soil, but actually is rather adaptable, thriving in conditions very different from those it is accustomed to in nature. Under cultivation it usually makes a small tree, conical in outline, and clothed to the ground with densely foliaged branches. One of the prettiest combinations of native plants that I have ever encountered comes naturally in many gardens— *Combine: Holly and* native holly and Flowering Dogwood. Not only are the flowers of *Dogwood.* the latter greatly enhanced by a backdrop of foliage, so are its wine-red leaves in autumn and, later, its scarlet berries. A private home near the University of Delaware each winter provides the eye with a wonderful spectacle—a large dogwood, its horizontal branches hanging with berries, backed by an enormous holly, itself liberally studded with red fruits. A Christmas decoration closer to perfection could hardly be imagined.

American Holly is very variable; some individuals are exceptionally deep green and glossy of leaf, profuse of berry, or otherwise distinguished, but the vast majority of specimens are, when compared with English or Chinese hollies, a rather dull green ("Opaque" is the species' scientific name, after all). Many also tend to turn yellowish when exposed to winter winds. Any gardener who plans to use American Holly is therefore wise either to select wild plants carefully or to purchase named clones from nurseries.

There is an abundance of these. Some of the older cultivars include: 'Judge Brown,' a select female cultivar (in spite of its name) with good berries and glossy leaves; 'Old Heavy Berry,' whose name speaks for itself; 'Arden,' the original plant of which was found in northern Delaware by my friend Jimmy Ware, and 'Xanthocarpa,' a form with yellow, not red, berries. The latter, unfortunately, has rather poor foliage.

Some twenty additional newer clones are listed by holly specialists, all distinguished by good habit, dark foliage, and large berries. As might be expected, most named clones are female plants.

In the South are several species of holly with narrow, often glossy leaves, which are sometimes used in gardens. None is hardy north, but recently some hybrids with the northern holly have appeared on the market. I have tried a few of these ('Fosteri,' a cross of *cassine* and *opaca*), which are narrow-leafed and rather un-hollylike to me. They do have rich leaf gloss and bright red berries. They also tend to wind-burn during winter. The USDA has recently distributed some hybrids of *opaca* and the tiny-leaved *I. myrtifolia*, under bird names. Two of these, 'Oriole' and 'Tanager,' are interesting evergreens with small leaves, though young plants are very ungainly in habit.

For hardy American Holly: 'Cape Cod.'

The Ohio Agricultural Research and Development Center, at Wooster, has begun a holly test garden which may be of interest to enthusiasts who live in cold climates. According to their newsletter, the clone of American Holly which has proved hardiest thus far is 'Cape Cod.'* Since the original plant of the clone was discovered at the northern limit of *I. opaca*'s range, it might be expected to be inordinately hardy. 'Cape Cod Dwarf' is apparently another name for the clone; it is not dwarf, however. Other cultivars proving exceptionally good in Ohio are 'Arlene,' 'Ed Thomas,' 'Merry Christmas,' and 'Wyetta.' These apparently are all pure *opaca*.

A very different holly grows in coastal swamps, dune hollows, and borders of salt marshes—*Ilex glabra*, the Inkberry. In its small,

* Secrest Arboretum *Notes.* Autumn, 1972.

oblong or ovalish leaves without teeth and black berries it shows close relationship to the Japanese *I. crenata* now so commonly used in our parks and gardens. As it grows wild, it is often a very undistinguished plant, a straggly, suckering mass growing among Bayberry, Wax-myrtle, huckleberries, Sheep-laurel, and Groundsel Bush as underbrush in swamps, barrens, and marsh-edges. In such situations it is featureless, totally lacks individuality, shows little promise as an ornamental, but cultivated and tended for a year or so, it becomes a shapely, small-leaved evergreen bush, much like *I. crenata* but somewhat larger in all its parts and more willowy and open in habit. Very old specimens reach ten feet or so, but these are few in cultivation. It is found as far north as coastal Nova Scotia, so should prove to be hardy in many gardens where broadleaved evergreens are difficult to grow. Most manuals list it as the hardiest of evergreen native hollies—to Zone 4 (as opposed to *I. opaca's* Zone 6). Since the similar *I. crenata* is hardy only to about Zone 6, this species might well replace it in the North. Inkberry is also of much value as a shore plant, since it is extremely resistant to salt and winds. With exposure and cold temperatures, its leaves turn bronzy-purple, but do not become unattractive.

Inkberry if other broad-leaved evergreens are not hardy.

Suckers with as much root as possible may be detached from a clump and planted. Cut the plant back severely, else it will not survive such treatment. All hollies transplant poorly and should have tops trimmed in proportion to root loss. In larger wild specimens this may mean cutting back nearly to the ground.

Of the many natural garden spots I learned to look for on my triweekly journey, one of the most perpetually pleasing was a section of swamp south of Dover. Here Cardinalflowers glowed against the green of Sweet-pepper Bush and Sweet-bay, and pale Meadowbeauties starred the roadside. Here in earliest spring bloomed a small specimen of Red Maple with the deepest red flowers of any I'd ever seen, whose leaves in fall were correspondingly bright. Here also was a great Winterberry (*Ilex verticillata*) straggling above mud, alders, and marsh grasses, and brightening the landscape with its waxen scarlet berries through much of the winter. The spot remains—

Winterberry for a showy, long-season shrub.

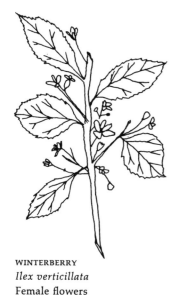

WINTERBERRY
Ilex verticillata
Female flowers

WINTERBERRY
Male flowers

though, being a "useless" wet area, it is in grave danger of "development," especially since it is close to a major road. I have not seen the berries of the Winterberry for the last year or two, however. Perhaps berry collectors have finished it.

Many delightful—almost magical—moments of my life are associated with Winterberry. I first encountered it on the edge of a place called "Thompson's Swamp" near Wilmington (I-95 now passes through the heart of this place). I was about ten years old, yet I can still feel the pure wonder that I felt on looking above me in the foot-soaking, toe-numbing, gray and dank woodland and seeing all the red in the world concentrated into pea-sized berries strung on narrow, straight dark stems, wands of scarlet against a leaden winter sky. The feeling is rekindled each time I encounter the plant, for it always makes an arresting contrast to its surroundings.

The wise gardener selects shrubs with more than one season of interest: flowering evergreens like rhododendrons and mountain-laurel, for example, or Flowering Dogwood, with bright autumn foliage and red berries as well as flowers in spring. *Ilex verticillata* has neither bright summer flowers nor evergreen foliage, nor is it particularly remarkable in leaf. So outstandingly showy are its berries, however, and so long do they last, that it easily classifies as a long-season shrub, one that every gardener should grow.

In the East this deciduous holly decorates swamps, bogs, wet woods, where it usually grows as a straggling tall shrub or small tree. In cultivation it grows well on drier soils, becoming a robust, bushy plant some eight or ten feet tall. The undistinguished foliage is bright green with no particular autumn color. The insignificant flowers are greenish also (insignificant to us, that is—bees love the flowers of all hollies). The bark is almost black, and pleasing in winter. The plant's glory is its fruit—spheres of scarlet aggregated in clusters along each twig. These do not drop until very late in the winter—plants usually remain colorful from November until well into February—nor are they readily eaten by birds. Since they are intact in late December, they are prized as Christmas decorations.

When at its best it is fully as showy as, say, forsythia is at its season, and its show is staged at a time when it has competition from very few other plants. Its comparative lack of distinction during the warmer months may be mitigated by placement **behind** or among other deciduous plants (those with showy flowers might be chosen, for example) which will deemphasize it until it comes into its own in autumn. A well-fruited plant is absolutely spectacular against a backdrop of evergreens, incidentally. Another virtue: it will grow in poorly drained soil. Along Interstate 295 in southern New Jersey is a drowned woodland created by banking of the highway. Most of the trees and shrubs therein have died, because the area is now under water for much of the year. Among the stumps and skeletons of trees grow several thriving plants of Winterberry, gorgeous above the dark water or pale ice when in fruit.

Poorly drained soil? Try Winterberry.

Winterberry's natural beauty has moved commercial people to stock it. Even big mail-order nurseries often offer it. Many, however, offer instead its Japanese counterpart, *I. serrata,* a somewhat more delicate plant with smaller berries. *I. verticillata* is native from Canada to Florida and west to the Mississippi Basin–Great Lakes region. It is hardy in Zone 4. Several variants occur, the most striking being a form with yellow fruits. There are several related (and usually much rarer) species of deciduous holly native in the East. *Ilex verticillata* is probably the most ornamental of them all, however. A final word: like all hollies the species has sexes on different plants. You need a female plant for berries, and a male plant somewhere in the area. In most places, there are sufficient wild plants to ensure a good fruit set on cultivated plants. If your female plant does not berry, get a male from a nursery or the wild.

There are perhaps half a dozen other deciduous hollies distributed across the eastern half of this country which, I must confess, I am not very familiar with. Of these *I. laevigata, I. dubia, I. longipes, I. montana,* and *I. decidua* are in cultivation. All are deciduous, red-fruited shrubs or low trees similar to *I. verticillata.* One interesting variation of the Possum-haw, *I. decidua,* is worth noting: the Spring 1970 volume of *The American Horticultural Magazine* carries a photograph and description of a yellow-fruited clone, described as "very

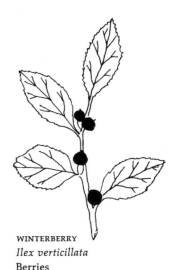

WINTERBERRY
Ilex verticillata
Berries

beautiful" by a research botanist of the U.S. National Arboretum. It has been registered under the name 'Byer's Golden.'

HAWTHORN

It sometimes happens that one notices, after years of seeing but not really remarking, a specific group of trees during a season. It is like suddenly truly hearing a piece of music, familiar but hitherto ignored, or finding beautiful for the first time a familiar face. The fall and winter of 1972 was for me the season of the hawthorns. All my life I had known them, from boyhood years in the fields of Delaware, and through many college semesters of English authors celebrating the "Mayhaw." One year I had even made jelly from the fruits (strongly adulterated with apple, I will admit) of wild trees. But until late in the year of 1972 they were simply a group of mildly interesting but rather undistinguished trees. That autumn I saw their real beauty for the first time. It seemed as though hawthorns everywhere put on a special show for me. Young trees along U.S. 40 near Elkton, Maryland, glowed like coral-red sentinels during the dark, wet (and it *was* a dark, wet season) days of November and December. The several species at Winterthur drooped beneath their abundance of berries. Specimens in the various local parks shone against trimmed, still-green lawn. A magnificent spreading hawthorn planted as a specimen in front of a tiny house in the city of Wilmington literally stopped traffic at Christmastime. Walking through the wintry fields in December I came across a most memorable sight —a small copse of hawthorns clustered in a tiny swale, surrounded by dead, brown grasses and backed by dark, somber woodlands. It was the most cheering sight of that winter.

Hawthorn for year-round interest and food for wildlife.

So much for winter cheer—which is reason enough to plant hawthorns. More reason is that they are really plants of year-round interest. Though nearly all are deciduous, they show great character in their "skeletons" after the birds have eaten their berries, for all are small, shapely trees with angular, often zigzag branches and long thorns, the latter frequently a polished purplish brown or deep maroon. In spring also they are extremely pretty, bearing large corymbs of white blossoms reminiscent of those of their close relatives apple and pear. Hawthorns are in addition very valuable to wildlife, their long-lasting fruits providing food late in the winter when food is scarce, and their spiny branches providing relatively predator-free havens for many birds and small mammals. Birds certainly seem to be cognizant of the safety of hawthorns, judging by the frequency with which the shedding of leaves in autumn reveals the current year's nests among their branches. Catbirds, mockers, and thrashers seem to be especially prone to nesting in them in my part of the country. The old nest remains rather a pretty sight in the bare tree throughout the winter.

Hawthorns are members of the apple subfamily (like apples, they bear "pome" fruits) of the rose family, *Rosaceae*. Their near relatives, besides apple and pear, are mountain-ash, shad bush, cotoneaster, firethorn, and chokeberry, most of which, it will be noticed, are valued for their brightly colored, long-lasting autumn fruits. The genus is enormous. Sargent lists 153 species in his *Manual of the Trees of North America*, and Rehder in addition gives about ninety species native to the Old World. To compound matters, many species intergrade, producing individuals which "splitters" describe as distinct species (those already described number well over a thousand!). Only a specialist can really hope to know the hawthorns intimately. For the practical gardener, though, this fact is of little significance, for he will choose his material living in field or nursery, and not be concerned with the abstractions of taxonomy.

The commonest species in my part of the country is probably Cockspur Thorn, *Crataegus crus-galli*, a small tree with prodigious thorns, glossy, small, teardrop-shaped leaves, and half-inch red *Try Cockspur Thorn or* berries. This has produced hybrids with various other species, two *Washington Thorn.* of which are sometimes encountered in the trade as *C. x lavallei* or *C. x carrierei*, and *C. x persistens*. According to the books, Cockspur Thorn reaches an ultimate of about forty feet in height, but like most hawthorns is usually seen as a much lower tree. Its crown is dense and its branches distinctly horizontal.

There are many other species available in the wild (though few, unfortunately, in nurseries), most of which differ from the foregoing mainly in size of fruit and in size and lobing of the leaves. One of the best is *P. phaenopyrum*, Washington Thorn. Originally native to a small area of the Southeast, west of the Appalachians, it has been cultivated more than probably any other native species and has become naturalized far beyond its original range. It is a more slender tree than the foregoing, with lobed leaves like those of a maple, and bright red berries half the size of the Cockspur Thorn's. It is often sold as *"Crataegus cordata."*

Combine: American and European Hawthorns.

There are many other thorns, most of which are extremely desirable. Sixteen of these are found in Delmarva alone. Those found in nurseries are often variants of the European species *C. oxycantha* (the "May" of English literature) or *C. monogyna*. There is no denying that these two are showy trees. The European species, having of course been in cultivation for much longer than their American counterparts, offer a wide array of mutations—cultivars with yellow fruit, yellow leaves, double flowers, or flowers of pink or red, for example. One of the most striking is known as 'Paul's Double Scarlet' in the trade, and a showy little tree it is when it blooms in late spring. Such mutations cannot be duplicated by the American species and should be grown right along with them. Here is another case where American plants complement rather than replace exotics.

Nursery-grown hawthorns offer little difficulty in transplanting. Wild material tends, if my limited experience is diagnostic, to be more difficult because the plants are often tap-rooted and lacking in fibrous roots which will hold a ball of soil. Small plants have a better chance of surviving the shock of transplanting than those of larger size, and since all hawthorns, because of their lethally armed branches, are extremely touchy subjects to haul about, it is no doubt best to select as small a plant as practical when collecting.

Cover and lace thorns for transplanting.

It is best to approach the transplanting of any size of thorn with an ample supply of light rope or heavy cord and lots of burlap. Tie one end of the cord around the trunk at the level of the lowest branches and gradually wind it around the plant, lacing the branches upward against the trunk as tightly as possible. After this is done, the now columnar plant should be covered with sheets of burlap and this laced also (needless to say, it is wise to wear gloves during the whole operation). Laced up and covered like this the plant may then be dug, transported, and set in its new position with relative ease.

Crataegus (rhymes with "fatigue us") derives from a Greek word meaning "strong" and alludes, so the books tell us, to the strength of the wood. I do not know of any commercial use of our native species, but Sargent mentions that it is used for the handles of tools, mallets, and other small items. The word "haw" (Old English *haga*) is the ancient word for the fruit of a European species. Apparently "Blackhaw" Viburnum was named by early settlers because of its external resemblance to thorns and its blue-black fruits. I have many times eaten a clear, rosy jelly made from the haws of our native thorns, with or without a generous admixture of apples, and found it very good.

III

Winter Trees

February, a month of changes, one day mild and the next freezing; today dry and tomorrow dripping with rain. One begins to look on sunny slopes and lawn borders for snowdrops or crocuses, but the first signs of spring are found in the air, not on the ground—in flocks of returning blackbirds and in the gradual coloring of branches and buds of trees. The delight of the blackbirds, for me, lies in their movement. They move, they are alive; I am suddenly aware of how *still* a season winter is. It is not only that landscapes are colorless and that nights are freezing cold in winter. The feeling of death is as much due to lack of movement as to either of these.

It is still cold and gray when the blackbirds make their spring invasion —still winter to the undiscerning eye. But in early February a change becomes noticeable in the landscape. Maples (at least the Red and the Silver species) and willows begin concentrating color in their twigs—red in the former and greenish gold in the latter. As the days slowly lengthen, as the temperature imperceptibly rises, the color deepens, until willows, especially forms of *Salix alba* (White Willow), radiate a golden glow and Red Maples show a true deep red against February skies.

It always seems a sudden thing to me. I seldom pay attention to either tree during the winter, and then one day in early February come upon a willow resplendent in gold, from the ends of its main branches to the tips of its supple twigs. Almost immediately afterward I notice the Red Maples turning red. And thus the spring begins. Soon elm buds swell into beads strung on slender, drooping branches. Then in early March the flowers of Silver Maple fuzz its branches—mainly a dull écru shade, but occasionally a good red. In wet woods and swamps the full brown catkins of alders dangle in the wind, while hooded Skunk-cabbage pushes through the black muck below. Finally, after the Silver Maple flowers are fading in mid-to-late March, the scarlet blossoms of Red Maple festoon the trees. Most of these early tree- and shrub-blossoms depend on wind for pollination (in the language of botany, they are "anemophilous"—lovers of the wind), rather than bees; thus they may open buds during windy March and not need to depend on early bees for a crop of seeds.

Willows for early spring color.

To return briefly to willow—it is perhaps not accurate to imply that all willows are brightly colored in spring, though most of them do have bark of chartreuse, yellow, or even light orange. The brightest of all are varieties of the White Willow, *Salix alba,* a large tree-willow which, though originally native to Europe, is widely naturalized in America. Its variety *vitellina,* the "Golden Willow" of horticulture, becomes brilliant yellow in February; a vigorously growing specimen can be almost as bright as forsythia, and even more welcome since it shows color when the winter landscape is at its most drab. More desirable, perhaps, is variety *tristis,* the "Golden Weeping Willow," which is just that. Its long, pendulous branches are golden for their entire length, and the unfolding leaves are golden too. The tree will light up the whole garden through March and April, and every garden of any size should have one. Even small gardens can accommodate a single small tree, which could be cut down and started anew whenever it might grow too large. This is not as heartless as it sounds: willows are trees which grow very fast but do not live long. They may be propagated simply by sticking a section of branch into the ground for about half its length; and as far as the Golden Willow is concerned, younger trees give a more concentrated brilliance, since they have proportionately larger expanses of young bark, where the greatest intensity of color occurs.

The common Weeping Willow, *Salix babylonica*, also a naturalized European, has greenish branches and new leaves, and, since all willows leaf out very early in the spring, makes a pretty sight in March. It is not nearly so bright, however, as the Golden Willow. One of the most pleasing spring sights of my trip was a planting of both kinds on a farm in middle Delaware, the green and gold combining spectacularly with the abundant Red Maples growing near them. This was color that was by no means overpowering, yet color on a grand scale. I am fairly sure that it was unpremeditated, but in its effect it rivaled anything to be found in many greater gardens.

RED (SWAMP) MAPLE

Acer rubrum is one of the commonest yet most useful and beautiful of native American trees. Flowering trees are not easy to come by, and really big flowering trees are even rarer. The Red Maple might be grown simply because of its bright spring flowers; but its virtues do not cease with blooming. It is hardy, long-lived (much longer-lived than its close relative *Acer saccharinum*, the Silver Maple), has pleasing habit and foliage, and what is more, is one of the most brilliant in coloration of all autumn trees.

Red Maple for spring and fall color.

It has perhaps the longest period of bright color of any tree of comparable size. In mid-February its twigs and branch-tips begin turning red; in mid-March its scarlet flowers, borne in tight fuzzy little clusters all along the branchlets, open, and, once fertilized, begin growing slowly into red fruit. Its name in the Onondaga Indian language was, according to one source, "red flower." The paired "keys" so typical of maples, bright red while young, become green before they fall in May or June. It has a similar, though not so prolonged, period of bright color in the fall.

Each spring I am newly amazed at the showiness of this common tree when it is in bloom, and my brain races with ideas for landscape designs utilizing it. It may be used in a particularly effective combination with two exotic Cornelian-cherries (really species of dogwood), *Cornus officinalis* and *C. mas.* These have an abundance of very small flowers arranged in rounded clusters like powder puffs along the twigs. In color they are a rather intense greenish yellow. The plants themselves become small trees, twenty or so feet in height. They bloom in March, at the same time as Red Maple. At Winterthur two medium-sized specimens of the maple grow along a small run which drains the area known as the Primula Quarry. Around them have been planted several very large specimens of the two *Cornus*, the whole combination being backed by a massive stone bridge across the low end of the Quarry. In the middle of March the yellow/red combination is really lovely. From a distance the trees seem stippled with color, as though painted by a *pointillist* painter.

Like many widespread species (it is native from Newfoundland to Florida and west to the prairies), it is variable. I have seen trees that were really flamboyant in spring, so intense was the pigmentation of twig, flower, and fruit, and these usually had bright red autumn coloration also. Other individuals have much less intensely pigmented flowers and fruits, some almost yellow, and these usually have yellow leaves in the fall. A collected tree should be observed carefully for color before it is dug, and a bought tree should be of a highly colored strain. Red Maple is fortunately rather common in the trade. Most roadside nurseries offer it, and several large mail order houses do also. There are many variants of the species listed, most of which vary in lobing of the leaves and habit.

A further use for this tree might be suggested: one of its common names, Swamp Maple, alludes to its frequent habitat in the wild. It is one of those trees which will grow in wet soil, and might be tried by gardeners who have poor drainage or similar problems in their gardens. The species is especially common in the wetter areas

Poor drainage? Try Red Maple.

of the Coastal Plain, where in swamps, sloughs, and along stream banks it grows abundantly with Water Oak (or Pin Oak in the North), Black Gum, and White-cedar. Here it is the commonest host of the mistletoe, and in some swamps nearly every maple will be festooned in winter with the green masses of this beautiful parasite.

Red Maple has the one great fault of all maples: its shallow feeder roots run close to the surface of the soil, greedily sucking moisture and nutrients up and away from any weaker plant nearby. It does not, however, seem so bad in this respect as either Silver or Norway Maple, and it has much more to recommend it. For sheer ornament, it is one of the best in its genus, and indeed one of the best of flowering trees.

During the summer, *Acer rubrum* is handsome with its abundance of bright green leaves, each silvery on the underside. During the winter, also, its light gray bark is distinctive and attractive. In cultivation it usually forms a tree with a rounded, somewhat irregular head and dense foliage, of medium height. It grows rapidly enough when young, but like all trees slows as it reaches maturity. The giants which occupy the austral forests of the southern part of Delaware must be ancient.

GUMS AND OTHER NATIVES

With Red Maple there are two other large trees which contribute much of the autumn color in my area. These are the two "gums," Sweet (*Liquidambar styraciflua*) and Black (*Nyssa sylvatica*). In spite of their common names, they are not related to each other, Sweet Gum belonging to the witch-hazel family, and Black Gum distantly related to dogwoods. Neither do they really resemble each other. Sweet Gum is a tall, upright tree, straight and usually single-trunked, with star-shaped leaves (it is very often misidentified as a maple), and conspicuous dry, spherical fruits which hang on the tree after the leaves fall. Its glossy deep leaves usually turn a rich claret or burgundy in color, though here there is considerable difference as to depth and clarity of color and time of turning. The Black Gum is often straight and single-trunked when young, but becomes gnarled and twisted, often in a most picturesque manner, and a spreading round-headed tree when old. Its rather small leaves are unlobed and untoothed, and turn a glorious crimson at the first hint of frost. Its fruits are small, blue, like miniature plums, and edible but not especially palatable due to their extreme tartness.

Sweet Gum transplants with relative ease. Black Gum is very deep-rooted and difficult to move, in large sizes at least. It is certainly a plant to cherish if one finds it growing on his property, for there is none with better fall color. Being deep-rooted, it is also good as shade for woodland plants such as rhododendrons. Both gums are worth growing for autumn color alone.

Many are the native trees which contribute to the show of color in the autumn woods. The oaks, always abundant, do not as a rule show much color, inclining toward browns and bronzes. The native Scarlet Oak (*Quercus coccinea*) does show a good clear red color, and is worth obtaining for this reason alone. In leaf form and habit the species is much like the better known and usually more abundant Red and Black Oaks. The various hickories (Carya) and ashes (Fraxinus) turn bright gold with frost, and both genera are quite showy. The two groups are superficially similar, but many ashes seem to me rather undistinguished trees, with often an abundance of dead twigs and little else to recommend them. Hickories, in contrast, are almost without exception handsome and distinguished. That they are not so widely grown as shade trees must surely be due to the fact that their deep taproots make them difficult to move except when small.

Less difficult to transplant (easy, in fact) is another native that is not so widely grown as it should be: the American Fringe Tree, *Chionanthus virginica*. This is among those trees valued for flowers as well as for other assets. The Fringe Tree is a superlative plant in almost every way, a fact which Europeans have long known, since they rate the tree as among the best of American imports (along with mountain-laurel, *Magnolia grandiflora*, American azaleas). The white flowers of Fringe Tree are very showy. It is a small, round-headed tree with blocky, thick branchlets, very late to leaf out in the spring. Its large, ovate leaves are attractive. Its fruits (on pistillate

The American Fringe Tree: A superlative plant—and it will grow in wet soil.

trees only), like bloomy blue grapes in hanging clusters, and the clear yellow color of its autumn foliage are both outstanding. It is valuable as a tree of moderate size (to forty feet). One of its many assets is that it will grow in wet soil.

The average gardener approaches trees in a very cavalier manner. He is often too ready to chop down those existing—not realizing that most trees require nearly a human lifetime of growth before they are truly impressive. And when he decides to plant one, he relies usually on the information given him at his local department store "garden mart." The true value of such information may be estimated when one realizes that the help at these places often don't know plants. I have had them attempt to sell me crab-apple as flowering plum and leucothoe as euonymus.

So the homeowner buys a Norway Maple from such a place, plants it in his well-drained, beautifully cared-for lawn and in a few years ruins the lawn completely. The density of the maple's shade kills grass beneath it, and its voracious roots, spreading out just beneath the surface of the ground, rob the surface soil of moisture and nutrients. In desperation, then, the owner thins out the maple a bit, attempting to let some light filter through its densely foliaged branches. The usual result?—sun-scald on the heretofore-shaded trunk and limbs, and shortly a dead tree, a ruined lawn, and several wasted years.

Perhaps the four commonest trees pushed by garden centers are Norway Maple, Silver Maple, Chinese Elm and Sycamore ("London Planes," the hybrid, actually). All four of these have the advantage of being easy and quick to grow. The Norway Maple makes an especially effective shade tree, in addition, and the London Plane is especially resistant to air pollution (at least according to authorities). But all four of these trees have grave faults. Those of the Norway Maple have already been outlined. It is a robber tree. The Silver Maple has pretty foliage and grows very quickly, but it is short-lived, soft-wooded and brittle, very prone to storm destruction. The Chinese Elm is less brittle but is also rather short-lived and is in addition not a particularly attractive tree—not a fraction as pretty as its relative the American Elm, for example. The London Plane, one of the commonest trees in America, is also one of the least interesting. A hybrid of the native Sycamore (*Platanus occidentalis*) and the Oriental Plane (*P. orientalis*), it lacks the personality of either. The native Sycamore's inner bark is snowy white—there are few more attractive sights in winter or summer than that of a stand of native Sycamores growing tall in the rich bottomland along some river, their massive trunks and branches gleaming white, patched with dun and russet. But the inner bark of the London Plane is a dingy yellowish olive-gray. In addition, like all *Platanus*, it is constantly shedding bark and seed-heads (which makes it a "dirty" tree), and like its relatives it exudes a curious odor which some—I among them—find rank and faintly obnoxious. In addition, all four of these trees mentioned are surface-rooted and, unless provided with a tremendous amount of water throughout the year, will turn the ground beneath them into a veritable desert, starving all but the weediest and most tenacious plants adjacent to them. They are vegetable leeches.

The next questions to be answered are, first—under what circumstances should these aforementioned trees be planted, and second—what trees should one choose if he passes these by? Perhaps both can be answered by the stating of a rule: one should choose trees with both the *purpose* or *use* of them and the *situation* which they will occupy in mind. The Norway Maple is one of the densest-foliaged trees in existence. It is also handsome in a broad, expansive, and spreading kind of way. It should be planted where it has lots of room to spread and where there is nothing but grass or tough ground-cover beneath it.

WHAT TO PLANT?

Buying Trees? Think: purpose, use, situation.

    Silver Maples should be planted only where one wants a quick screen or windbreak, since these trees really do not last long. They should not be planted near anything frangible and valuable (whether it be plant or building) since sooner or later storms will send heavy trunks and branches crashing down.

    The Chinese Elm also is best suited for a quick-growing windbreak.

It grows rapidly, is not so brittle, and is really perhaps the best of the four mentioned here. It withstands the conditions of the Midwest well, being much used there for windbreaks. However, gardeners in more favored climates simply do not need to use it. There are better trees. This goes also for the London Plane, whose main claim to fame lies in its resistance to smog. So boring a tree is it, however, that it ought to stimulate all of us to eliminate the smog if for no other reason than to eliminate the tree. In regions where nothing else will grow, perhaps its use is justified. It certainly is more resistant to the anthracnose which attacks the new foliage of the native Sycamore.

Other native trees are desirable but have certain drawbacks. *Liriodendron tulipifera*, the Tulip-tree or Tulip-poplar (yellow poplar of the lumber trade), is a fine, straight, black-barked tree which reaches enormous proportions. Its fantastic green and orange blossoms betray its relationship to the magnolias, though these are usually displayed at such a height on mature trees that they can hardly be seen. It is deep-rooted and long-lived. A major problem, however, is that it is one of the favorite hosts of the multitudinous aphids which secret "honey dew." Anything under a Tulip-poplar—plant, building, automobile—is soon covered with a sticky film which turns blackish as it ages.

The American Beech, *Fagus grandifolia*, is another fine forest tree, its smooth gray bark, so dear to those who carve initials in trees, distinguishing it the year around. Its drawbacks are precisely those of its more widely planted European relative: voracious roots. Almost nothing will grow under a beech tree.

Black Locust for fragrance.

Black Locust (*Robinia pseudo-acacia*) is a big, handsome tree with light brown furrowed bark and fine, compound leaves which turn a delicate yellow in autumn. Young trees and younger branches of old trees are annoyingly thorny. It bears in May drooping clusters of white flowers (similar to those of its close relatives, *Laburnum* and *Wistaria*) which have a fragrance of almost unparalleled sweetness. It is one of the few big trees that flowers conspicuously, and its shade is so light that many shrubs and herbs will grow luxuriantly beneath it. A huge specimen in full flower is impressively beautiful.

The Black Locust has one very real drawback, though: it suckers prolifically from the wide-ranging roots; one tree will soon produce a veritable grove of what appear to be seedlings but are in reality root-suckers. If the tree is planted in the middle of a lawn, little difficulty will result, for the suckers are constantly mowed off, but if it grows near the foundations of a building, a shrub planting, or perennial beds, the suckers are a constant nuisance. Still, the perfume of the flowers is so sweet that one should grow the tree somewhere. Incidentally, these clusters of flowers, dipped in batter and deep-fried, then sprinkled with powdered sugar, are delicious eating.

There are clones of the species in commerce that are allegedly sucker-free. There is also a golden-leaved variant called 'Robinia Friesia,' which is quite showy in leaf. I know nothing about the quality of its flowers. Black Locust was originally native only on the western slopes of the Alleghenies from West Virginia to Georgia, and sporadically west to Arkansas. It has spread from cultivation throughout much of the country, and is a fairly common denizen of roadsides and abandoned fields (though seldom of true forests) in my area. To walk through a grove of flowering locusts is a wonderful experience, by the way, so fragrant are their flowers. It was introduced into Europe hundreds of years ago and is a great favorite there, many cultivars being offered.

Two locust relatives which also hail from west of the Appalachians are cultivated in the East, but, though both are desirable trees, neither is widely known at present. *Gymnocladus dioicus*, Kentucky Coffee-tree, is a tall (to a hundred feet in the wild), striking, and magnificent tree with a straight trunk and finely divided leaves. Its bark is rich brown and very rough and ridged, as are its coarse branches. These contrast with the extreme airiness of the fernlike foliage and lend much interest to the tree in winter. Its flowers are not conspicuous, but its large pods are showy throughout much of the summer, being quite noticeable as they hang heavy and silky sea-green in August and even more so as they ripen to a rich, polished mahogany. The seeds are large and germinate readily, so that the plant tends to self-sow in amenable locations. These seeds incidentally were allegedly used at one time as a substitute for coffee, hence the common name. I hasten to add that I have never tried them brewed, so cannot vouch for the accuracy of the statement. Kentucky Coffee-tree grows very rapidly and should be planted only in small sizes, since its deep, fleshy roots prevent easy transplanting of older plants. Its ferny leaves give a light, dappled shade in which many herbs and shrubs grow and blossom freely.

Yellow-wood: a tree with no faults.

More closely allied to locust is the second of our trans-Appalachian plants under discussion here: Yellow-wood, *Cladrastis lutea*. Here is a plant with no faults that I can see. It becomes a medium-sized tree, seldom over fifty feet tall even in age, with a heavy, buttressed trunk and spreading, branched crown. Its bark is smooth, light gray in color, as pleasing as that of Beech. Like many pea-family plants, Yellow-wood has compound leaves, larger and somewhat coarser than those of the locusts. In June comes the crowning glory of the plant: foot-long clusters of creamy white, fragrant pea-blossoms hang from the tip of every twig on the tree. In the wild the tree is a rare inhabitant of Kentucky and Tennessee. In cultivation it thrives: a tree at Winterthur, for example, planted sometime around the time of the First World War, now has a girth of ten feet three inches and a height of seventy feet, is in perfect health, and is a major display of the gardens each year. It is believed to be the largest Yellow-wood in Delaware. The specific name *lutea*, yellow, alludes to the color of the fresh wood, a bright sulfur yellow. An older discarded name, *tinctoria*, alludes to its use in the dye trade, the wood, according to authorities, yielding a "rich yellow dye."

Trees that are most desirable for yard planting are those with deep roots. Unfortunately these are also trees which do not transplant easily, precisely because of these deep roots, and thus most commercial nurserymen prefer to handle more easily moved but less desirable surface-rooted trees such as Silver and Norway Maples. Our native hickories fall into the deep-rooted and desirable category, as do the Black Gum and the oaks. Nearly all oaks are beautiful. It has been claimed that they are slow-growing. This is not true; once established their rate of growth is as rapid as that of the average shade tree.

The most readily available oak from nurseries is *Quercus palustris*, the Pin Oak. It turns out that this is the one oak which is most shallowly rooted—need one say more? Unfortunately it is not the most ornamental. In fact, from observation of the two fair-sized specimens growing in my yard, I have come to the conclusion that it is one of the least ornamental of the genus. Its leaves are attractive —very deeply cut, more so than perhaps any other oak—but its other features are not particularly outstanding, and its habit renders it a difficult plant to use in the landscape. As the tree grows, its lower branches droop downward. If these are cut off, the next tier bends downward until it nearly touches the ground, and so on. This would not be so bad, though it renders the tree impossible to sit under and a nuisance to the mower of lawns, were it not for the fact that the lower branches die off as they sweep the ground, so must be pruned constantly in order to keep the tree from becoming unsightly. Pin Oak also, in my garden, is very susceptible to atmospheric pollution, the symptoms of this susceptibility being discolored leaves. I understand also that a fungous disease is attacking the species on an almost nationwide scale.

OAKS

For general planting, there are superior oaks. The Red Oak (*Quercus borealis*) and the Black Oak (*Q. velutina*) are two widespread and adaptable members of the group which would be preferable to Pin Oak for general planting. Very similar to each other when mature, they differ considerably when young, in that the Red Oak's leaves are much larger and its trunk conspicuously striped black and whitish gray. Both have leaves which are deeply cut, though not so deeply as those of the Pin Oak. The common name Red Oak is somewhat mystifying: its autumn color is not particularly brighter than that of its relatives—mainly warm bronze or brown, not "red." "Black" Oak is perhaps named for its dark bark.

Red and Black Oak for general planting.

Few of the oaks are particularly valuable for autumn color; most have none at all, but one species is an exception: the Scarlet Oak, *Q. coccinea*. During the growing season its virtues are of the quiet type which do not call attention to themselves by any single gaudy characteristic but, combined, produce a tree of singular excellence. It has finely cut leaves like those of the Pin Oak but does not grow with those low drooping branches that require constant mutilation; nor is it, in my experience, as prone to disease. It resembles also the Black Oak (though growing more symmetrically, making a wider, more spreading tree) and the Red Oak, but has none of the latter's huge leaves and near-tropical coarseness when young.

Simply, then, for beauty of habit and sturdy growth, it is a desirable acquisition. In autumn, however, it comes into its own with an explosion of color that is unrivaled in its genus. The color is usually more crimson than scarlet, often a deep, smoky crimson which is among the most beautiful of autumn colors. Not only is the Scarlet Oak one of the brightest of trees in autumn, but like all oaks it is reluctant to let its leaves fall, even when they are dead. Unlike those of other oaks, however, its leaves retain a good deal of autumn color. At Thanksgiving the tree is almost as bright as it was a month before. It is thus perhaps the latest spot of brilliant autumn foliage. This would certainly be one of the three or four trees—along with Black Gum, Red Maple, and Sweet Gum—that I would choose for outstanding fall color. It is furthermore desirable for the extreme lateness of its color, as the Black Gum is for its earliness. Plant one of each, and you will have bright red autumn color from October to perhaps December. *Quercus coccinea* (the specific name meaning, of course, "scarlet") has an enormous range: from Ontario and Maine south on the coast to Virginia, and upland to Georgia and Mississippi, west to Oklahoma.

The Water Oak (*Quercus nigra*) is a true component of the austral wood. In nature it is found only as far north as Delaware and, inland, Kentucky, Missouri, and Oklahoma. It is, however, hardy farther north, to coastal New York at least (Zone 7). In the South it occurs in swamps and on the edges of rivers and bayous. In southern Delaware it grows natively; one encounters it in wet tangles, where it reaches an immense size, usually festooned heavily by another southern plant, the high-climbing Muscadine Grape, or Scuppernong, *Vitis rotundifolia.*

If the common name of this oak is easily explained by its habitat preference, the scientific *nigra*, "black," is not—what is black about it is hard to see. What *is* distinctive about it is its foliage, small and rather willowy and very persistent leaves, almost evergreen in sheltered climates. The leaves on Water Oak bonsai wintered in a frame kept at 32–40° F. remain green and handsome throughout the winter. They are small for an oak (for which reason the tree makes a good bonsai plant) and narrow in shape, with usually three angles—not really points—at the tip.

In the South it is a truly noble tree, often planted in city parks and along highways. I have vivid memories of the biggest Water Oak I have ever seen, a giant which grew in the front yard of the house of a friend in coastal North Carolina. At one time the tree must have been a mere accent in the landscape, perhaps shading the front of the house, but now it *was* the landscape, its moss-draped branches stretching over and beyond the house and its associated buildings. In its abundant shade grew veritable thickets of camellias and bamboos, and on its vast limbs roosted a flock of peacocks kept by my friend, the prince of the flock being a pure white bird which displayed when one spoke to it. The cries of these birds echoing in the somber depths of the great tree where they roosted at evening were singularly appropriate, somehow in keeping with the exotic atmosphere produced by the great, overhanging, dominating giant.

One of the most distinctive of all oaks is *Quercus phellos*, the Willow Oak, another which, like the Water and Spanish Oaks, is a denizen chiefly of the southern Coastal Plain, although this species occurs as far north as Long Island and sporadically westward into Illinois and even Oklahoma, a range which would seem to indicate that it is an adaptable plant. The layman would never take this tree for an oak, at least from its leaves alone, for these are linear, very willowlike, two or three inches in length and a half inch or so broad. It does, of course, have acorns just like any other oak. The scientific name, like those of many oaks, is obscure. *Phellos* is the old name of the Cork Oak, *Q. suber*, of the Mediterranean region. How it came to be attached to this plant, which is neither more closely related to it nor resembles it more closely than other American oaks, is a mystery to me. Certainly the common name, Willow Oak, is far more descriptive and logical.

In the wild it inhabits more or less the same places as the Pin and Water Oaks—bottomlands, wet woods, swamp and river-edges, occasionally sandy pine woods. But it is very adaptable in cultivation, thriving in any good soil, whether it be dry or moist. I have noticed a minor boom in Willow Oaks among progressive landscapers during the past few years; more and more are being used as landscape trees, especially in large plantings, such as on college campuses, around industrial buildings, and so forth. This is quite commendable and encouraging.

The tree has no autumn color at all. The leaves simply drop after turning from their normal light green to a yellowish-brownish-greenish. They do drop late, however, hanging on and retaining their green color as late as Thanksgiving, so that the tree is a good landscape subject for a long period. Nor is it to be despised during the winter, for like any aristocrat it has good bones. It is a broad and round-headed tree, in age as broad as tall. This applies to most wild trees also, even those growing in fairly dense woodlands. The growth of Willow Oak is very rapid. It is hardy through Zone 6.

The holly and the pine are typical Coastal Plain plants. Their occurrence is a true indicator of both southern latitudes and proximity to the sea. But there are other plants, less obvious because less noticeably different, which are fully as southern in distribution, and which on my trips marked my arrival south just as emphatically as did the hollies and pines. Foremost of these is the Spanish Oak, *Quercus falcata*, a tree which grows sparingly in the Piedmont Province but competes with the pines on the Coastal Plain, becoming perhaps the commonest oak of all in southern Delaware.

It is a large forest tree, as grand in proportions as any of its northern relatives. One of its common names, "Southern Red Oak," must surely allude to its similar size and girth, for it is, to me at least, totally unlike the northern Red Oak (*Q. borealis*) in leaf and in "character." Two attributes of the Spanish Oak make it unique:

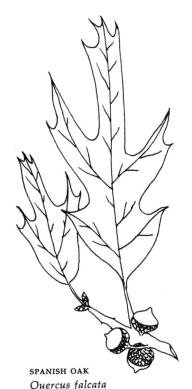

SPANISH OAK
Quercus falcata

the shape of its leaves and their color. Although cut in typical oak fashion, the leaves of this species are distinguished by the terminal lobe, which is always attenuated and somewhat curved, sometimes almost sickle-shaped (botanically "falcate," hence the specific name). Very often the side lobes are reduced to only two, the rest of the leaf tapering long to the base, giving the whole leaf something of the shape of an asymmetrical iron cross.

In color the leaves are a deep, somewhat olive but intense green, very glossy on the upper surface. They have an evergreen, leathery, persistent look to them. And they do persist long on the tree, though they turn brown with the autumn. The undersides of the leaves are densely woolly and reddish brown in color, totally unique among the common oaks native to the area. This pubescence I have found to be the major diagnostic feature of the tree, for when young it, like most young oaks, has leaves quite variable and different from those of mature trees. One rub, however, betrays the felty under-surface of the Spanish Oak. It is hardy in Zone 7, well beyond its native region. It really should be attempted by any gardener who can obtain it, for its glossy, almost magnolia-like foliage produces an effect very rare among the oaks.

IV

Woodland Wildflowers

There are many false starts to spring. Sometime in mid-February dawns a day when, after a week of warm rain, the sun rises clear and benign over a freshly washed and fragrant earth. Every depression has become a pond of clear water in which newly returned blackbirds splash and play before sunning themselves by the hundreds, looking from a distance like whistling, squealing black fruits hanging from my trees. I see that the tops of willows are golden, that maple twigs are red with swelling buds. The first snow crocuses push through along a sunny garden walk, and winter seems ended for good. But within a week the cold air masses from Canada sweep once more over a refrozen landscape, the formerly jubilant blackbirds undulate in silent, questing flocks over the fields, the crocus furls its flame-yellow petals tightly against the cold, and all the world waits out the temporary re-assault of winter.

So the year moves toward the equinox through freeze and thaw.

Subtle changes occur each day. Elm branches are beaded with buds in March which soon swell to flowers of filmy, gauzy, gossamery brown, so laden with pollen that each breeze shakes loose a cloud of it. In two months each of these flowers will be a waferlike brown seed which the wind will send skimming over lawns and down streets, and which attract all manner of arboreal seed-eaters. Many are the university commencements I have dreamed away listening not to the speaker but to the sweet warbling of goldfinches feeding on elm seeds above the rostrum.

In March the Red Maple flowers open in brilliant tufts like colonies of sea anemones on gray-barked branches. After the twentieth day of the month the northern hemisphere turns slowly and more fully each day into the path of the sun's warming and quickening rays, and though the earth will not immediately throw off her cold mantle, there are unmistakable signs that winter is vanquished.

On some mornings I drive at first light through spring mists, sweet, mild, fragrant, which roll dripping through the black trees on either side of me. The roads are wet and slick before me, though no rain has fallen. From every twig of every shrub and tree hangs delicately suspended a drop of water. The whole world drips, not with the cold moisture of winter, smelling of mold and death, but with sweet, warm, revivifying water, darkening the grays and browns of tree trunks, deepening the greens of willow and reds of maple twigs, running silently to roots and sending sap, the true *aqua vitae*, coursing back upward to every bud.

I know as I drive along that Skunk-cabbage is surely above ground in the swamps I pass, that Marsh-marigold blazes somewhere along the cold streams on my way, that on a rocky, sunny hill in the Piedmont I have just left, the first hepatica raises its pale lavender flower.

On a day in early April, mild, but with sun still pale and a wintry edge remaining on the breeze, I sped south through Sussex County toward my destination, down deserted back roads lined by miles of pine and holly forest.

BLOODROOT

*Bloodroot for adaptability
and beauty.*

Then I came suddenly on a beautiful sight—a stand of Bloodroot, hundreds upon hundreds of white flowers lying on a dark bed of pine litter, some half opened and chalice-like, others flat to the sun like gold-centered, gleaming white stars. For half a mile they graced the roadside, sprinkling the wood edge from shoulder to forest gloom in a great pale galaxy.

I could think of few cultivated spring flowers rivaling their beauty, and none eclipsing it. They were fully as lovely as drifts of daffodils and crocuses then opening in my garden farther north, and in addition there was that added charm in their being wildlings, of my discovering in so remote a place such sumptuous beauty.

And they had an added fascination for me this day. I never expected to see Bloodroot in such abundance so far south on the Coastal Plain, for I had always thought of it as characteristic of the rock-strewn slopes of the Piedmont, growing in company with Wild Columbine, Hepatica, Trillium, and Dutchman's Breeches. How exceedingly strange, then, to see it in such abundance in the acid sands and pine litter of these austral forests, stretching for hundreds of yards along the absolutely flat roadway.

Its presence here once more confirmed this plant's great adaptability, though as it happened I needed no proof, for I had been growing Bloodroot ever since I first collected it in the now vanished woodlands near my boyhood home. Though nearly thirty years have passed, the recollection of my first sight of that fragile white blossom with its attendant leaf half clasping it like a protective hand is as clear now as though it took place yesterday. I so treasured that plant that once, in anger at my mother (who, I assumed, valued it as much as I), I dug and presented it to my favorite aunt. I am ashamed to add that I compounded my spite with inconsistency, for once reconciled with my mother I reclaimed the precious Bloodroot and ceremoniously replanted it in her garden. Both the plant and my relationship with the women in my life thrived despite such treatment.

Sanguinaria canadensis is one of the easiest as well as (rare combination!) one of the prettiest of wildflowers. It can be transplanted at any time, in bloom or out, will grow in most soils, and will take a variety of light conditions from fairly deep shade to full sun. It must, of course, have adequate moisture if exposed to full sunlight. On the rocky, hilly Serpentine Barrens of northeastern Maryland it grows in the open among grasses and stunted bracken fern. Though the soil here is deficient in certain vital minerals, the plants seem to me to grow as luxuriantly as they do in the more benign environment of the Piedmont forest.

Both common and scientific (*sanguinaria* means something like "bleeding") names refer to the thick, succulent rhizome of the plant, which oozes a bright orange-red juice when injured. From this rhizome grows a single leaf almost the size and somewhat the shape of a man's hand, and a scape topped by a solitary flower of eight to twelve white petals surrounding a boss of bright golden stamens. The scape usually rises gracefully between the basal lobes of the leaf, so that it looks as if the leaf is half-cupping the blossom almost protectively. The leaf remains green well into summer.

Certain mutations of Bloodroot have been perpetuated in gardens. Two of these are a pink form known botanically as *colbyorum* and a really lovely double white form whose correct botanical title is *multiplex*. The latter is usually available (at a reasonable price for such an excellent plant) from wildflower nurseries under the erroneous name "flore-pleno." It blooms a bit later than the single form, its abundant petals making a perfect sphere of white.

In the garden I have found Bloodroot especially effective in combination with the deep blue forms of the Greek Windflower, *Anemone blanda*. If it is happy, the anemone attains the size of the Bloodroot, the two looking like so many blue and white stars when open in the spring sun. Like many spring flowers, both close at night and remain closed on especially cold or gloomy days.

Many millions of years ago, much of what is now called the Coastal Plain was under water. As oceans receded and volcanic upheavals farther west caused adjacent land to emerge from the depths, the plain rose a few feet above sea level. The rivers draining the mountains

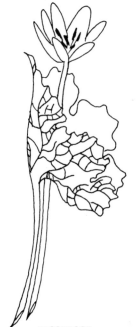

BLOODROOT
Sanguinaria canadensis

to the west now ran first through a gently falling Piedmont Plateau and then a broad, flat expanse of land indented by salt bays and tidal guts. With them these rivers brought both sediment, which built up new land on the Coastal Plain, and the seeds of plants from the mountains. The newly emerged plain, at first devoid of land plants, slowly grew to forests of trees and shrubs, immigrants from the higher lands farther west, all busy finding and occupying new niches here and, some of them, in the process of evolving into new races and species. Much more was to happen to this area: more volcanic upheavals caused parts to sink and new parts to rise; oceans advanced and fell back, and eternally the rivers drained the western mountains. Glaciers later marched down from the north, killing all they passed over. When they began to recede, restocking of the barren areas began again, this time from the south or southwest, rather than from the west. The strange distribution of some American plants can be traced to the geological phenomena just touched on. Many so-called Appalachian groups are just as abundant on the coast as in the mountains—the azaleas, for example, and their relatives the kalmias and leucothoes. Or the genus *Hudsonia*, which occurs (in two, possibly three species) from eastern Canada south to the shores of Delmarva and in the high mountains of North Carolina.

TRILLIUMS

Other groups were apparently unable to colonize the Coastal Plain. The genus *Phlox* is one such; in my area I can find just four species, and none is abundant. Contrast this with the fifty or so species which occur from the Appalachians west to the Pacific. Equally illustrative of this sort of distribution is the genus *Trillium*, unique and beautiful members of the lily family. Four species are listed in the manuals for the region, all strictly limited to the Piedmont, one very rare and not recently seen, one not collected since 1863, one limited to two colonies on the western edge of the peninsula at the edge of the Piedmont, and one (Nodding Trillium, *T. cernuum*) moderately abundant in the rocky Piedmont woods. All are abundant farther west, and indeed form one of the distinctive components, along with Hepatica, Spring-beauty, Trout-lily, of the hardwood-forest flora of Appalachia.

Our *Trillium cernuum* is unfortunately not especially showy, and until the spring of 1970 I was ignorant of the kind of display that the showier species make in the wild. I had some inkling, of course, since I had grown some of the species in my own garden and had come into contact with most of the others during my years as taxonomist at Winterthur. But even that magnificent display called the "Trillium Bed" at Winterthur did not prepare me for the sight of one of the rare colonies of *Trillium grandiflorum*, Wakerobin or Great White Trillium, which grow in Cecil County, Maryland.

In 1969, I heard of a discovery made by Helen (Mrs. Sydney) Glass, along the Bohemia River near her home, Strawberry Hill. It was a ravine (a "gulch," Mrs. Glass, a horsewoman, called it) with both sides covered by a profusion of trilliums. Some friends and I looked the place over and discovered several moderately rare or unusual plants for the area—among them great trees of Canadian Hemlock, carpets of Trailing-arbutus, thickets of Paw-paw. It was autumn, so we didn't see the trilliums, but the woods seemed extremely interesting to me, and I determined to explore them more thoroughly the following spring.

During April, Mrs. Glass kept us informed of the progress of the plants. When the plants were in full bloom, two friends, Dick Ryan and Jim Deeney, and I set off for Strawberry Hill, where we picked up Mrs. Glass and drove to the edge of the cultivated fields in order to conserve as much energy as we could for exploring. The fields here occupy a sort of plateau; this breaks and very quickly falls down to the tidal Bohemia River, which is really little more than an arm of the Chesapeake. The steep slope from plateau to water is sliced by great ravines running at right angles to the river and at least partially created by run-off from the upland. These ravines, rendering the land unfit for cultivation, have saved the remnant of forest which clothes the slope from total destruction (though it has been timbered at least once in the past few decades).

R. R. Tatnall's manual of Delmarvan flora gives an enthusiastic description of the two colonies of this plant. It reproduces a photograph in black and white, and in its caption describes the plant as

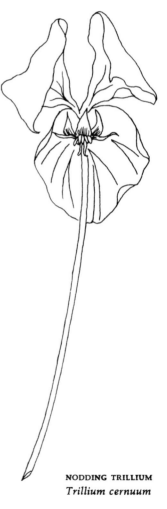

NODDING TRILLIUM
Trillium cernuum

"carpeting the forest floor with gorgeous bloom." But neither the description nor the photograph was adequate preparation for the sight which met my eyes the minute we stepped beneath the overhanging branches of beech and dogwood and looked down the slope. Pink and mauve flowers carpeted both faces of the ravine, grew down to the very bottom, where a ferny stream flowed, marched up the sides and into the ironwood and spice bush underbrush clothing the crowns of both the slopes. They bloomed even through the Japanese Honeysuckle at the edge of the field. There were literally acres of trilliums, a magnificent spectacle. I reflected on how seldom we see such awesome sights of natural abundance here in urbanized, commercialized, industrialized America, and my enthusiasm was somewhat tempered by sadness.

Since that day the woods have been timbered. I don't suppose many trilliums died as a direct result of the lumbermen's actions, though what loggers do to a woodland in simply entering and leaving is unbelievable. The problem will be that with the shade of the large trees gone, the dreaded Japanese Honeysuckle may creep down the slope, romp over the underbrush and in a short time smother the trilliums.

I give a great deal of credit to Mrs. Sydney Glass, who waged a heroic battle persuading the owner of the woodlands to prevent the lumber company from logging that ravine. He eventually gave in to her entreaties, but the loggers ignored his request to spare the ravine. Time will tell how the trilliums fare, but their fate is already for me a symbol of the criminal disregard we have for the beautiful, vulnerable, and tragically irreplaceable past. There are no more than two or three colonies of this plant on the whole Delmarva peninsula, and for a few board feet one has been gravely endangered, perhaps seriously injured. What will be the eventual fate of the others? The time may come when a nature-starved populace will pay for the sight of a spectacle like that of Mrs. Glass's "trillium gulch." Let us hope there will be one to salvage.

Trillium grandiflorum, perhaps the showiest and certainly one of the easiest members of the group to grow, is an excellent choice to begin a discussion of the various species in the genus. *Grandiflorum* means, of course, "large-flowered," and large-flowered the Great White Trillium certainly is. When conditions (a well-drained but moist situation in moderate shade, and humusy soil with pH slightly acid to slightly alkaline) suit it, it will grow to nearly two feet—a straight, strong stem surmounted by three oval, pointed, deep green leaves, and a lush, showy flower of three pink or white petals and three green sepals, nestled at the base of the leaves and looking out at the world. Its blooming season is long: those in Winterthur's Trillium Bed, which I once kept close watch on, sometimes last in flower from late April to late May. Most (perhaps all) specimens turn from white to pink or rose as they age. There is considerable variation in this: some become a really deep rose, and at least the Chesapeake Bay populations open pink—never *are* white. There is also variation in petal width. My observations would indicate that those plants which are deepest rose have the narrowest petals. This may indicate the possibility of introgressive hybridization with another species, most logically the narrower-petaled maroon *T. erectum*. A few years ago Michael Dodge mentioned this possibility in connection with certain plants at Winterthur, and I was skeptical. Now I am less sure.

In the March 1974 issue of *The Green Scene*, the magazine of the Pennsylvania Horticultural Society, Dr. Edgar T. Wherry asserts that the pink coloration of these Chesapeake Bay trilliums is a "pathologic" response to the unusually high iron content of the soil where they grow. He states further that these plants, transplanted into soils with lower iron content, bloom subsequently with white flowers. Dr. Wherry is probably the foremost authority on wildflowers east of the Rockies, and I would be the last to question his conclusions; however, my Strawberry Hill trilliums have bloomed pink in my garden for three subsequent years, while nearby blooms a snow-white clump of the same species purchased from a collector in North Carolina. Perhaps response to iron poisoning is not the sole reason for the different coloration.

Interesting as the pink variants are, my choice for beauty goes to

First choice: TRILLIUM GRANDIFLORUM—*showiest and one of easiest to grow.*

the pure white, not only because these usually have broad, overlapping petals, but because their whiteness, set off by deep green leaves, fairly gleams in the woodland setting which is their habitat.

The species is extremely variable. The normally staid Gray's *Manual of Botany* characterizes it as our "handsomest, most fickle and sporting species." Some forms have leaves and flowers in twos, fours, and fives, rather than threes. Others have flowers of green, or white striped with green. Horticulturally the most interesting form is that known botanically as *petalosum,* the "double" trillium with other floral parts metamorphosed into petals, the flower looking like a white gardenia or tuberous begonia, a really sumptuous woodland wildflower. Because its carpels are converted into petals, it is sterile and cannot be reproduced by any means other than by division (you orchid breeders who have practiced meristem culture—why not try something like this?); thus it is still a rare and comparatively expensive plant. It is most certainly worth growing in any garden, though. At least one major wildflower nursery offers it.

Second choice: Painted Trillium.

My choice for the second showiest species of *Trillium* would go to the elegant *T. undulatum,* Painted Trillium. It is indeed a hard contender for first place and, were it not for the difficulty experienced by some gardeners in growing it, might very well rank equally with *T. grandiflorum.* Its beauties are on a somewhat different order. For sheer *exquisiteness* it cannot really be matched: an ethereal white flower with a wine-red halo in the center, set in a cluster of three bronze-red leaves on a stem a foot or foot-and-a-half tall.

Its great drawback is that it is a boreal species, native to the cold, wet, acid forest of the North, found south only on the mountaintops. In temperate and lowland regions where summers are hot and dry, it languishes and dies. It also demands much more acid conditions than most trilliums do. To succeed with it, give it a bed rich in peat and leafmold, and water it copiously during the hot season. Growing it partially under a large stone might also help keep it cool and healthy.

The "halo" in the center of the flower is formed by an inverted "v" of crimson at the base of each of the three white petals. *Undulatum,* "wavy," refers to the gracefully fluted petal-margins. After flowering time, the leaves turn from bronzy crimson to deep green. In the fall the brilliant scarlet fruit is showy, brighter than that of any other trillium.

After the two foregoing beauties are discussed, the choice of third place might easily light on several species. Two very different but attractive trilliums are *T. erectum* (Purple Trillium or Purple Wake-robin) and *T. nivale* (Dwarf or Snow Trillium). The first is really maroon or mahogany-crimson in color, not purple, and is nearly as vigorous and tall as *grandiflorum*. It is native from the head of the Appalachian Chain on the Gaspé south in the uplands to Georgia, and like most widely distributed plants lends itself well to cultivation because it is adaptable. It resembles, except for color, *grandiflorum*, but has smaller flowers on longer stalks. It, too, is a very variable plant: there are forms with white, yellow, or green flowers, and forms with flowers and leaves in cycles of fours or fives. The white variants can easily be told from *grandiflorum* by their relatively narrower petals, as well as by more arcane botanical characteristics such as the width and shape of the stigmata. In cultivation it responds to exactly the same treatment which suits *grandiflorum*, and looks well growing with its showier relative. Other names for it are "Birthroot," "Stinking Benjamin," and "Wet-dog Trillium," the last two alluding to the allegedly evil smell of the flower. For years I tried to detect this foul odor in *Trillium erectum* and could not. In fact in the first draft of this chapter I stated that my nose was at variance with folklore—that this trillium had no smell at all. Moreover, I found myself in excellent company, for no less an authority than Elizabeth Lawrence says that she too cannot detect a bad odor. However, on a chilly day in late April in the spring of 1974 I crawled among the trilliums in the Azalea Woods at Winterthur, thrusting my nose into every *T. erectum* I could find. And there it was: the vilest smell imaginable coming from so attractive a blossom. Each smelled the way my greenhouse does after I have fertilized with fish emulsion. I would add, though, that it is necessary to get right down there on the forest floor to detect this odor. It is neither strong nor pervasive.

The color of *T. erectum* is very reminiscent of the colors of certain foul-smelling aroids and succulent African stapelias—a sort of dried-

Third choice: Purple Trillium or Snow Trillium.

blood or decaying-meat hue. Now, these plants certainly depend for pollination on flies which mistake their appearance and odor for real flesh. Can it be that the trillium does also? Perhaps like many plants it releases its "fragrance" only at certain times of the day or night, when its pollinators are active.

In contrast to the foregoing, all the names of Snow Trillium, *T. nivale*, are accurate. *Nivale* means "of the snow," and this epithet as well as its English translation may refer with equal force both to its pure white hue or its habit of blooming very early, often before the final snows have fallen. In my garden it is the very first native flower of the year, blooming with the snowdrops, species crocuses, and winter-aconites, and appearing two weeks before the first hepaticas or bloodroots open. In some years it shows color in February!

Snow Trillium is a tiny plant (hence its other common name, Dwarf Trillium). Manuals list it as growing to six inches in height, but in my garden it never exceeds two—a perfect little white trillium with a flower nearly as wide as its stem is tall. It is so tiny that it is likely to be crowded out by more robust plants; in fact mine has been threatened by seedling winter-aconites. I grow it under a rare dwarfish rhododendron, which may be the wrong place since the plant in the wild occurs on limestone formations and is listed in many manuals as a lover of lime. However, mine blooms each year for me, though it does not increase, and I find that when plants are happy it is well to let them alone. In the wild, *T. nivale* is found only west of the Appalachians, which would seem to indicate an adaptation to the limestone soils west of the mountains. All in all, this perfect miniature doesn't offer much more difficulty than *T. grandiflorum,* and it is certainly just as rewarding to grow.

There are about thirty species of Trillium, the center of the genus occurring in the southern mountains. All of these fascinating southern species are hardy and, fortunately, many of them are available from plant dealers in the South. The plants of Appalachia may be momentarily safer than those of the Northeast, but no species of plant is truly secure as long as the present trend of expansion continues. It would be well to establish these southern trilliums in our gardens.

But before going on to these, the real exotics of the clan, I want to discuss the most familiar trillium over much of the East: *T. cernuum*, the Nodding Trillium. Like all members of its genus, it grows from an underground tuber from which rises a straight stem which is topped by a whorl of three leaves and, nestling at the juxtaposed bases of these leaves, a flower which is composed of three green sepals, three colored petals, and the usual liliaceous formula of six stamens and a three-cleft stigma. This formula of threes or multiples thereof gives rise to the name *Trillium*, derived from the Latin root *tri-*, three. The specific names of the species, like those of all plants, are usually really not "names," nouns, at all, but are descriptive adjectives. Thus, *erectum* means "upright" (probably a reference to the flower stalk), *grandiflorum* "large-flowered," *undulatum* "wavy," *nivale* "snowy." *Cernuum*, "nodding," "modest," "hiding," is an excellent description of this species, for unlike many trilliums, its flower neither rises above nor nestles among its leaves but hides beneath their conjunctive bases on a down-curved stalk. Thus you cannot really see it unless you look under its leaves; it is more elusive and hidden even than the flower of the May-apple, and it is for this reason that I term it an unshowy wildflower.

Nodding Trillium the most familiar over much of the East.

It is graceful and pretty, but does not equal most of the other members of the genus in showiness. It simply lacks distinguishing characteristics, being a sort of minor-key version of its magnificent cousin, *grandiflorum*. When I see the two together I am reminded of Reginald Farrer's characterization of *Paradisea liliastrum*, St. Bruno's Lily, as an "understudy for the Madonna Lily." *Trillium cernuum* seems to be trying to become a Wakerobin but never succeeds. Nodding Trillium is nevertheless a pretty little species, as well as an easy plant in the garden. Its three white petals are strongly recurved; this characteristic, along with its often chocolate-colored anthers, gives the flower a martagon-lily winsomeness that is really charming. If only it did not hide its blossoms! I would like to have a steep hillside on which to grow it, so that it could be viewed from below. Unfortunately, my garden is flat as a table-top.

The southern mountains and Piedmont provide us with a bewildering array of trilliums. I do not use the adjective loosely. Harold Rickett's beautifully illustrated book on wildflowers of the southeastern states lists seventeen species besides those already discussed here. Unfortunately not all of these are illustrated; some of those which are resemble their northern relatives closely, but others are extremely distinct.

Trillium catesbaei (also known as *T. stylosum*) is somewhat like *T. cernuum* in appearance but more showy, with larger flowers of bright rose-pink which do not hide themselves so successfully beneath the leaves. It is a Piedmont species from the Deep South, but grows successfully at Winterthur, and is reported to do well in New England. The common name listed in books is Rose Trillium, presumably an allusion to its color.

There are two other southerners which I cannot help mentioning, although I admit that I have acquaintance with them only from literature. *T. simile* is very early and very beautiful, with cupped white petals and contrasting ovary of deep brownish black. According to Rickett, it may be a geographical form of *T. erectum*, although it looks very different in photographs at least. Rickett further states that this species lacks the "bad smell" of *erectum*. Odor or no, I would dearly love to get my hands on a plant or two of this intriguing species. The second beautiful southerner is also closely related to *T. erectum*: this is *T. vaseyi*, Sweet Beth or Sweet Trillium. It is the giant of the genus, looking like an enormous *erectum* with broad-petaled maroon flowers four to five inches across. The common name alludes to its sweet fragrance. Its flowers, which appear late in the season, often droop below the leaves, but are so large that they are not hidden.

Mottled-leaved Trilliums for showy foliage.

Not that trilliums, or any plants for that matter, need showy flowers to become desirable as garden plants: certain other trilliums have flowers of extreme insignificance, but nearly all of these have leaves which are very attractively mottled and marbled with dark green, silvery green, and chartreuse. They may be more interesting than beautiful, as the folk name for some of them, "Toad-shade," implies, but it must be remembered that foliage as a rule lasts longer than flowers, so that the garden value of these plants is great because they provide interest for a long period of time.

At the logical, if not botanical, heart of this complex is *Trillium sessile*. Considerable botanical confusion attends the species: one trusted manual gives its extreme northwestern range as Indiana, while another gives it as Minnesota; one states that the leaves are often mottled, the other that they are not mottled. We do not need to concern ourselves too much with this, however. Except for the leaf-mottling, other technical details do not make much difference in the garden. The plants I grow, those growing at Winterthur (and those offered by the major wildflower nursery dealing in southern plants) are mottled, and were collected in the heart of Appalachia, where the *sessile* complex is concentrated.

Whereas the "lines" of most trilliums are graceful and flowing, those of *T. sessile* are squat and rotund: stout, short, rigid stem; horizontal, stalkless leaves; flower with absolutely no pedicel or stalk at all, but jammed right down in the center of those leaves, and without the bright, spreading petals of conventional trilliums. What makes conventional trilliums so attractive is the similarity of shape between flower and leaf cluster; the former is a colored miniature of the latter. This seldom applies, however, to members of the *sessile* complex, which typically have smallish flowers with petals which remain upright and closed rather than spreading. Imagine the deep maroon ellipse of *Calycanthus*, the Sweet Shrub or Strawberry Bush (or just "Shrub," of old gardens), set down in the center of an especially stout trillium plant with marbled leaves, and you will get an adequate idea of what most *sessile* trilliums look like.

T. sessile has almost orbicular, overlapping leaves and deep maroon flowers with green spreading sepals. Its leaves are lightly mottled deep green on a grayish green ground. At Winterthur there grows a somewhat different type which was purchased from a reputable dealer as the "eastern form" of *sessile*. Its leaves are very broadly diamond-shaped and much more strongly mottled, and it is distinguished by rich maroon upright petals and spreading maroon sepals. I also grow a plant purchased at a local nursery which is similar but has less broad leaves (diamond-shaped but not overlapping) and maroon flowers whose greenish sepals are more spreading than upright. After careful research I have identified this definitely as *T. cuneatum*, a plant which occurs in mountains, Piedmont, and Coastal Plain from North Carolina and Tennessee south to Florida and Mississippi. The only common name I can find for this species is "Little Sweet Betsy." Two other scientific names appear to be synonymous for this species: *hugeri* and *underwoodi*.

Distinctively characteristic of my *cuneatum* and the very similar Winterthur eastern form of *sessile* is their scent—rich and cidery, very like that of *Calycanthus floridus*, the Sweet Shrub. It is perhaps no coincidence that these trilliums have flowers which resemble those of Sweet Shrub in size, shape, color, fragrance, and blooming time, or that the range of Sweet Shrub in the wild closely parallels that of *T. cuneatum*. Though the plants are not even remotely related, they must have evolved in response to the same pollinator, some insect which is attracted by the color maroon and a cidery perfume. Possibly the closed petals of both exclude unwanted insects.

A third member of this complex is yellow-flowered but otherwise resembles the "eastern form" of *T. sessile*. It is usually listed by dealers as *sessile luteum* or as a distinct species, *T. luteum*. Others list it as a variant of *T. cuneatum*. I suspect that they are right, and that the so-called eastern form of *sessile* mentioned above is also a form of *cuneatum*. Be that as it may, *luteum*, like the others, is a good woodland plant which is easy to grow. Its flowers open a pale lemon-chartreuse and turn green as they age, making a fine foil for the maroon forms. Its scent, interestingly enough, is quite distinct. It is rank and weedy, like the smell of bruised pokeweed or cooking asparagus. Again, though, one must get close to the plant in order to detect the odor.

I (and Winterthur) grow two others of this complex. *T. recurvatum*, the Prairie Trillium, seems to thrive in this area in spite of its name. This seems to be a misnomer anyway, for Rickett states that it grows in woods from Michigan to Nebraska, Alabama, and Arkansas. It grows about as tall (a foot or so) as the others mentioned, but is altogether more slender in stem and much narrower in leaf. Its maroon petals are touching at the tips and are contracted at the bases, and its sepals fold downward along the stem. The flower is obviously designed to be pollinated by an insect which crawls between the contracted petal-bases across the stigma. Interestingly enough, the six maroon-black stamens arch over the stigma exactly as the three petals do above them. It is an interesting plant, though not so showy as the others. Its leaves are marbled but, being narrower than those of *T. cuneatum*, are much less effective in the garden.

There are at least two trilliums of this alliance on the West Coast which are worth mention if only for the fact that one of them, surprisingly enough, thrives in the East. *T. chloropetalum* (also known as *T. sessile californicum*) is a robust species with green or slightly mottled leaves and showy white flowers. These are sessile (the botanical term for stalkless) but have more or less spreading petals. The plant looks exactly like what you might get from a cross of the ordinary Wakerobin with a *sessile* trillium, and in many ways combines the showiness of the former with the bizarreness of the latter. A specimen in my garden stands a foot tall at the leaf-whorl, with petals three inches long and an inch wide, and wavy, overlapping leaves four inches long and four inches wide at the broadest point. In color its flowers are white with a greenish tinge and are strongly veined. They are slightly pink at the petal-bases. The spreading sepals are light green and almost as long as the petals. This seems to be very easy to suit in the garden. It is reported as doing well in New England, and it certainly thrives in Delaware, clumping rapidly and presenting quite a show in a short time.

Another western trillium of the *sessile* group is *T. rubrum* (*T. sessile rubrum*). I have not grown this species but of course would like to. If the color plate in the December 1945 issue of that wonderful but unfortunately now-defunct garden magazine *The Home Garden* is at all accurate, this species is extremely attractive, with elongated petals curving outward like three maroon horns. I can find no record of its cultivation here, but in view of its white-flowered congener's success in the East, it is certainly worth a try.

West Coast Trilliums.

A third Pacific trillium, this of a very different type, *T. rivale,* Oregon Trillium, is the western counterpart of *T. nivale,* and like it very dwarf, the whole plant seldom exceeding three inches in height. That great grower of alpine and dwarf plants, the late Bertram Anderson, grew this species in England and had high praise for it. Judging from the illustration in his *Seven Gardens,* he had a very fine form of the species—or perhaps, which is more likely, the English climate suits it better than that of our American East. In any case, the Oregon Trillium succeeds in Delaware, but does not grow with abandon. Like the equally tiny *nivale,* it is easily crowded out by other plants, or smothered by too deep a covering of fallen leaves. In Delaware it blooms with the large species, fully a month later than *nivale,* and is thus rather eclipsed by the abundance of spring flowers around it. *Nivale,* which comes so early as to almost come alone, appears with much more of a splash. Except for size, the Oregon Trillium resembles *T. undulatum* more than any other. It has similar bronzy-green leaves with so bright a gloss that they appear lacquered, and its tiny white flowers are freckled with rose in such a manner as to form a faint pinkish halo around the ovary. Anderson states that it is dwarfer than *nivale,* but in Delaware they are the same size—about two inches in height, with flowers about an inch wide.

A final Pacific trillium, which I mention because it does very well in the woodlands at Winterthur, is *T. ovatum,* the Coast Trillium. This is a robust species, twelve or sixteen inches tall, with very much the same appearance as the ordinary Wakerobin. Its two-and-a-half-inch flowers have rather narrow petals and face skyward on opening. As they age, they turn from white to rose, become larger, and gradually incline to the horizontal.

Like so many of our more interesting woodland plants—Phlox, Trailing-arbutus, May-apple, and others—trilliums are found only in North America and in eastern Asia. Like most of these plants also, and like the deciduous azaleas, their evolutionary center is the Appalachian Chain, where many beautiful forms have evolved. They should certainly be appreciated by Americans as much as they are

12. A view of a portion of the cutting garden
at Winterthur, with a bed of Purple Loosestrife,
several plants of *Yucca filamentosa,* and a large specimen
of Bottle-brush Buckeye, *Aesculus parviflora.*

13. Sweet Azalea, *Rhododendron arbo- rescens.* A mountain species with glossy leaves and fragrant white flowers in the middle of June.

14. Cumberland Aza- lea, *Rhododendron bakeri,* blooming in mid-June. Brilliant color, abundant flowers, and a compact habit make this one of the best of the native azaleas for gardens.

15. Mountain-laurel, *Kalmia latifolia,* at the beginning of June.
Perhaps the most beautiful native evergreen shrub.

16. *(left)* An early-summer view of a stream at Winterthur, with Black-eyed Susans *(Rudbeckia serotina)* growing spontaneously on its banks.

17. *(below)* Blossom of the Tulip-poplar, or Tulip-tree *(Liriodendron tulipifera)*, a magnificent timber tree of the magnolia family.

18. Trumpet-vine, *Campsis radicans*. One of the showiest native summer-flowering vines.

19. A young plant of the rare "Red Bud" mutation of Mountain-laurel, *Kalmia latifolia*.

20. Goat's-rue or Devil's-shoestring, *Tephrosia virginiana*. This deep-rooted relative of the Sweet Pea is fine for dry, sandy soils.

21. Rose-mallow, *Hibiscus palustris*, in a swamp in southern Delaware. An excellent plant for either wet problem-spots or ordinary garden soils.

22. American Lotus, *Nelumbo lutea*,
and White Waterlily, *Nymphaea odorata*,
on the author's pond.

by Europeans. They are with few exceptions fairly easy to grow as long as they have a deep, humus-rich soil and some shade. The secret of success with them seems to be humus; they dwindle away in soils devoid of it. I have used everything from brown and black peat, evergreen needles, composted grass clippings and wood chips, and ordinary compost on mine, and have had them respond well to all. I chop fallen leaves (sycamore, mainly) with a rotary lawnmower and mulch with the finished product, which breaks down rapidly and does not smother as the unchopped leaves do. Many trilliums grow in limestone soils in the wild, and indeed Anderson found that, of the species he grew in his very alkaline soil, only the Asiatic *T. kamtschaticum* showed "a dislike of lime." My soil is quite acid, yet several species thrive in my garden. Probably most trilliums will adapt to either acid or alkaline soils, provided their pH is neither extremely high nor extremely low. Bonemeal would very likely be a valuable additive to the humus at planting time, though, especially in regions of acid soil.

The secret of Trillium success: humus.

All in all, trilliums with a few exceptions are probably plants for collectors rather than ordinary gardeners. Many species are interesting rather than showy, a great many are hard to find commercially, and the nomenclature of the southern species is a nightmare of confusion. Elizabeth Lawrence calls them an acquired taste, and I agree with her. (She writes beautifully, interestingly, and knowledgeably about the fascinating southern species in her *The Little Bulbs*, a book I would not want to be without.) Still, acquired tastes are often powerful and lasting, as well as gratifying. I know that trilliums exercise a fascination for me that few other plants do. Not the least of their interest lies in their folk names. Some are highly fanciful, like "Wakerobin." Others are descriptive, like the terms "Stinking" and "Wet-dog" describing *T. erectum*. Still others are interestingly obscure. What, for example, does "Benjamin" in "Stinking Benjamin" mean? ("Benjamin" is a colloquialization of the name of the Benzoin or Spice Bush, *Lindera benzoin*, but its application here is obscure, to say the least.) And what is the origin of the fanciful folk name for *T. cuneatum*, "Little Sweet Betsy"? Possibly it relates

Trillium nomenclature.

to "Sweet Beth," a name for *T. vaseyi* (though *cuneatum* doesn't look much like *vaseyi*, even though it is smaller), and possibly the element "Beth" is a variant of "birth" as found in "Birthroot," one of the names for *T. erectum*. *T. vaseyi*, then, which looks like a giant *erectum* and is allegedly sweet-scented, would be distinguished by "Sweet" as *erectum* is by "Stinking." But whence Beth or Birth? Are these terms metaphors of the birth of spring, along the same lines as "Wakerobin?" Or do trilliums possess obscure pharmaceutical properties—were they, perhaps, used in pioneer or Indian midwifery? The question may not be answerable, but it adds interest to an already very interesting genus of plants. Some other folk names for trilliums may be of further interest. *T. cuneatum* is known as Whippoorwill-flower. According to Harold Moldenke of the New York Botanical Garden, many different species are known as Trinity-lilies or Herb-trinity. *T. grandiflorum*, perhaps in allusion to its chaste whiteness, is called Bathflower or Whitelilies. (Or is "bath" a variant of "beth"?) *T. undulatum* is called Painted-lady in reference to its pink halo. The widespread *T. cernuum* has several names. One is White Benjamin, which probably connects it with *T. erectum* in the folk mind. Others are medicinal: Cough-root and Snakebite. Whether trilliums ever really were used against coughing or snakebite, I do not know. It is interesting to note that the closest European relative of these plants, *Paris quadrifolia*, was often used in herbal remedies in the days before modern medicine, as its common English name, "Herb Paris," signifies. Herb Paris is interesting from a plantsman's point of view in that it looks much like a trillium except that all its parts are in fours (not threes) or multiples thereof. Its flowers, unfortunately, are not particularly showy.

Trillium and several of its close relatives like Lily-of-the-Valley and Solomon-seal have been removed from the Lily family by some botanists, mainly on the strength of fruiting characteristics—true lilies produce a dry capsule; trilliums and their close kin produce a fleshy berry. Others, however, feel that this difference is not really significant. A plant which has always seemed to me to refute the splitters is Indian Cucumber-root, *Medeola virginiana*, for though

INDIAN CUCUMBER-ROOT
Medeola virginiana

it bears a berry and in many ways resembles *Trillium*, it also approaches the lilies, particularly the martagons or Turks-caps, in appearance. The plant bears a whorl of five or more polished leaves about halfway up its two-foot stem. These are very much like those of our native true lilies. At the summit of the stem a much smaller whorl of three leaves appears, and from these grow several small greenish yellow flowers, on stalks which nod below the circle of leaves precisely as *Trillium cernuum* does. The petals and sepals are not clearly different, as in *Trillium*, but are similar in shape and color, as in *Lilium*. Finally, they are strongly recurved, so that the flower resembles that of a Turks-cap lily in shape. One characteristic peculiar to the genus is that its stigmas are elongated into three threadlike branches which project far beyond the other parts of the flower. These are also recurved, less strongly than the petals and sepals.

The common name alludes to the taste of its rhizome, which supposedly provided food for the Indians. I confess that I have never sampled the plant, finding it too pretty to destroy (and also far too rare in these parts), but all the books say that it is edible. The scientific name derives from that of Medea, the celebrated sorceress of Greek legend. As with trilliums, there is an aura of folklore and legend about the plant. There is only one species in the genus. It grows in woodlands from Minnesota to Quebec south to Florida and Louisiana. Though not so showy as most trilliums, it is a valuable plant for the shady garden, graceful, pretty, and easy to grow.

Phlox, one of the most important genera in gardens, belies the generalization that American plants are not popular in America (though not disputing the generalization that they are *more* popular in Europe: probably more cultivars of *Phlox* have been produced in England than anywhere else). The genus is large and diverse, including prostrate, semi-evergreen, woody plants, soft woodland herbs, and strong perennials reaching four or five feet. In flowering time, too, they are varied, some being spring-flowering woodland plants and alpines,

Indian Cucumber-root.

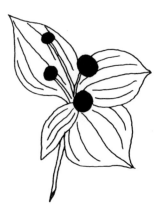

INDIAN CUCUMBER-ROOT
Detail of berries

PHLOXES

others summer-blooming prairie and meadow dwellers. In color, finally, they run the gamut from lavender blue through purples, pinks, reds, oranges, and pale yellows to white. So diverse are they that one could have a pleasing and long-lasting garden of phloxes alone.

There are some sixty species, all but the East Asian *P. sibirica* native to America, where there are two centers of distribution: the Appalachians and Alleghenies in the East and the Rockies in the West. Western phloxes are the delight of rock gardeners, but they are really not in the scope of this book (or my experience). The eastern phloxes may be divided into three horticultural categories: (1) mat-forming semi-evergreen sub-shrubs, (2) early-blooming woodland species, (3) tall summer phloxes. The first group is typified by the ubiquitous Moss Phlox or "Mountain-pink," *P. subulata;* the second by the widespread "Sweet-william Phlox," *P. divaricata;* and the third by the Tall Garden Phlox, *P. paniculata.*

Some of the commonest sights of spring in eastern gardens are patches of hot pink or strident magenta Moss Phlox growing with crimson azaleas or heavy yellow daffodils in a color combination the visual equivalent of the screech of chalk on a blackboard. Such careless use of the plant has rendered it objectionable to many gardening purists, particularly those of the rock-gardening persuasion. Many pleasing color forms exist, however; one is not limited to hot pink or magenta. The creeping, matted little plant looks as much like a high-mountain conifer as anything else and is always rather attractive. *Subulata* means "awl-shaped," a good description of the cylindrical, pointed leaves.

For ideas as to how to utilize Moss Phlox in the garden, one could do no better than to see it as it occurs naturally, in my region only in two widely separated sections, the Serpentine Barrens in adjacent Cecil County, Maryland, and Chester County, Pennsylvania, and at isolated spots in nearby New Jersey, where it occurs on exposed, barren outcrops and rocky banks. Witmer Stone in 1910 praised the beauty of the natural plantings of this and the all-blue form of Birdsfoot Violet along the railroad between Moorestown and New

Lisbon, in eastern New Jersey: ". . . a brilliant show . . . in alternating beds of pink and blue." The idea is a good one, provided you can grow Birdsfoot Violet with ease.

On the barrens north of Rising Sun, Maryland, I found the wild plant growing only on the steepest hillsides where the green serpentine stone had collected into the closest approach to an alpine scree that Coastal Plain or Piedmont will allow. Here it grew with two white-flowered endemics, a sandwort, *Arenaria stricta*, of most delicately lacy leaf and fine, matted stems, and a chickweed, *Cerastium arvense* var. *villosum*, with small oval, fuzzy leaves on prostrate stems. The three seemed delicate and tenuous indeed, creeping among the jade-green rubble of the hillside in full sun. Moss Phlox in its wild form is a soft and lovely pink, its flowers are sparser (at least as it grows on the barrens), and it is not at all overpowering.

I personally prefer it this way. To me it is much prettier as I grow it, planted in dry soil which supports a thin grass cover which is mowed sporadically through the summer. Here the phlox blooms as individual starry blossoms scattered through the grass, rather than as a brilliant blob. I once saw a most marvelous effect with *P. subulata* growing in the short grass of a sloping lawn beneath and extending beyond a weeping cherry, the scattered phlox flowers looking like cherry blossoms blown across the lawn. No subtle Japanese gardener could have planned a more enchanting picture. I actually changed my normal route to work so that I could look at it during the ten days or so that it lasted. Unfortunately the owners of the property did not share my enthusiasm. The next year the lawn had been leveled, and a low brick retaining wall built between property and road, and the phlox planting beefed up with whitewashed rocks and new clumps of the hot pink cultivar spilling over the brickwork.

Try Moss Phlox wild in grass cover.

An extremely delicate form of Moss Phlox occurs in the high mountains from Ontario to North Carolina, var. *brittoni*. Smaller in all its parts, it is further differentiated by the deep notches in the tips of all five "petals" (actually lobes of the corolla). The effect: like hundreds of minute Ragged Robins on the prostrate, tiny-leaved mats. There are white and rose forms of this variety, the white especially very lacy and pretty. The variety is so distinct that it is given the status of full species by some.

P. nivalis has woody, prostrate stems, needle-like leaves, and five-lobed, yellow-centered salver-form flowers much like those of *subulata*. Its scientific name means "snowy," presumably an allusion to flower color. All the forms I have seen were deep pink. It is the southern counterpart of *P. subulata* (though Dr. Wherry puts it in a different section), growing in sandy pinelands and barrens from Virginia south. Probably it does better in the extreme South than *subulata*. It is also one of the few Coastal Plain phloxes. The woody species, like those thus far discussed, root easily from cuttings or layers—in fact, all the true creepers in the family root as they creep and thus provide potential new plants.

Of the woodland phloxes far and away the best known, and deservedly so, is the Wild Blue Phlox (often called Sweet-william Phlox), *P. divaricata*. This is a Piedmont plant native from Canada to the Carolinas and west along the Great Lakes to Michigan and Illinois. Its masses of misty lavender-blue flowers on foot or foot-and-a-half upright stems are indispensable in the spring woodland garden. I cannot think of any spring wildflower with which I would be more reluctant to part than the Wild Blue Phlox. With the yellow and orange Wild Columbine of the East it is beautiful. It is very fine planted among evergreen azaleas, its color binding and toning down their bright pinks and reds, or with red primroses. In my garden it mingles with pale yellow English Cowslip and magenta Honesty (*Lunaria*) in a pleasing effect. With white *Trillium grandiflorum*, and rose-red tulips (like the old 'Clara Butt') it makes a splendid display also. The color goes with just about any other, which makes the plant very useful. The species has naturalized itself in woodlands in the north of Delaware. At Winterthur it is a carpet of blue in the woodlands. The typical form is a soft, powdery blue with a touch of rose that makes it close to but not quite lavender. It varies in depth of color, some forms being quite rosy, some very blue, some almost or quite white. Like most Piedmont plants it does best in a humus-rich loam which tests close to neutral in pH. My soil

Combine Wild Blue Phlox with yellow and orange Wild Columbine, evergreen azaleas, red primroses.

is quite acid, however, and it thrives for me in shade with plenty of leafmold. *Divaricata* means something like "widely forked." Gray tells us that this refers to the way the inflorescence branches. *Phlox divaricata* grows from a slowly creeping rhizome, making a spreading clump of dark green lanceolate, evergreen leaves. The stems and undersides of leaves are usually rich purple, rather showy in wintertime. After flowering, the stems often arch outward from the center of the clump, taking root where they touch ground. The species may be rooted from stem cuttings.

The third of this triumvirate of common garden plants is *P. paniculata*, the Garden Phlox. It has a typical phlox distribution: New York to Georgia west of the Coastal Plain, penetrating into, but not beyond, the Mississippi–Missouri river system. As a wild plant it reaches five or six feet in the woodland glades and open river bottoms where it grows, bearing in late summer and fall a large compound cluster (which is at first flat-topped but later elongates) of muddy rose-purple blossoms.

I am not one of those gardeners who flinch at the word "magenta." True magenta is a bright but pleasing color in proper context. In fact all the combinations of red and blue which go by the names of mauve, lavender, maroon, purple, and magenta are attractive in gardens (and easier to use than, say, some yellows) as long as they are clear, not muddy and grayed. Ordinary *P. paniculata* is not clear, and it is only really attractive seen from a distance with lots of green behind it. What plant breeders have wrought with the species is, however, incredible. Cultivars now occur in white, rich true purple, pink, salmon, crimson, true scarlet, and coral-orange. Flower size is often larger, and, in some cases, height considerably reduced (though most garden varieties stay around three feet). These are mainstays in the perennial border. In wild gardens they are often lovely, though some of the neon reds and corals are rather difficult to reconcile with nature. If you are planting a summer wild garden, use cultivated forms in place of the ordinary wild form. Some of the soft lavenders and pinks are very nice naturalized. Beware of self-sown seedlings, though, since these very often revert to type in height, flower color, and, unfortunately, vigor, and choke out their lovelier but sometimes weaker parent. Take time to cut the flower heads off just as soon as the final floret drops.

Few plants are easier to grow than Garden Phlox. It propagates easily by division of the clumps or by cuttings. It will grow in almost any soil, but to grow *well* it must have moisture during the hot weather, as of course its natural habitat would suggest. In dry or impoverished soils the leaves yellow, the plant becomes stunted, and red spider attacks it fiercely.

There are several other phloxes which recommend themselves. In my garden I have one called *Phlox pilosa* var. *ozarkana*—a gift whose origin I do not know and cannot trace, for it is listed in none of the American garden books I have consulted, though Edgar T. Wherry described the variety many years ago. It is a vigorous and broader-leaved form native to the Ozark region. Downy Phlox (as the species itself is called) is native west of the Coastal Plain from Ontario to the Gulf. It looks much like a larger and somewhat later *divaricata*, except that its usual color is rose-purple. *Ozarkana* grows strongly from a creeping, stoloniferous crown, its two-foot stems bearing pairs of narrow, glossy deep green leaves and surmounted in mid-May by clusters of large flowers of a true, soft pink. This phlox is exceedingly showy in bloom. It comes into flower just as *divaricata* is going out.

Like the latter, it is evergreen (or nearly so) in my climate. Since it is larger in every way, it is much more noticeable in a winter landscape, having the value, really, of a dwarf evergreen shrub. In every way but one it is a magnificent and desirable garden plant. Unfortunately, it is invasive. One rooted cutting set out from a two-inch pot in spring of 1969 was two feet across and smothered with bloom the following year, and by 1971 consisted of a dozen clumps covering an area of about sixteen square feet. Since I had planted it among choice wild plants and tiny spring bulbs in the wild garden, I had to remove it to a more remote spot where its neighbors are able to compete with it. Young plants are still sprouting from buried rhizomes in the original spot. They seem nearly as persistent as couch grass!

In plants as in people, what are in one context vices become virtues in another, and *pilosa ozarkana*'s invasiveness is translated to healthy vigor where it is now planted—in a remote corner of the wild garden and along a wire fence behind shrubs where the lawn mower does not reach. In these places its flowers are welcome in late May and June. I have envisioned this plant also as a tall groundcover beneath trees, perhaps mixed with pachysandra and vinca. Its vegetative parts are handsome and persistent enough to recommend it in such a role, and its flowers are certainly beautiful. It blooms for about a month.

PHLOX PILOSA OZARKANA *as a ground cover.*

Up until the spring of 1974 I had never found a reference to this variety (or cultivar) in a garden book. Then I read *Seven Gardens*, by Bertram Anderson, and found one (predictably by an Englishman). It may be worth quoting, since comments on the plant are as yet sparse. Anderson grew it in a rock bed, with the "usual run" of rock plants. He says, "good . . . but beginning to run— visitors do not mind this—is the pink nine-inch *Phlox pilosa* 'Ozarkana' that blooms for months on end."

I wonder how long the plant had been in place, or if the different climate of England reduces its growth. This would seem to be indicated in his notation as to height, for the plants in my garden are twice nine inches at the very least. Then, the comment on long blooming season. Apparently the different climate again affects the plant, for here the bloom season is long but hardly months on end, though plants do re-bloom in summer. It is interesting to notice that he treats it as a mere cultivar, 'Ozarkana,' rather than a true botanical variety, as Dr. Wherry does.

A much better known and very different little woodland phlox is Creeping Phlox, *P. stolonifera*. Imagine a *divaricata* with almost round leaves, which instead of growing in normal clumpy manner lies flat on the ground and runs like a Periwinkle or Creeping Jenny, and you have a reasonable picture of this native of woods from the slopes of the Alleghenies in Pennsylvania south (in the uplands) to Georgia. It is an amenable little plant, easy to grow. In early May flowering stems rise six to twelve inches high from the basal rosettes of spoon-shaped leaves, opening to rounded heads of showy flowers of lavender or mauve, each bloom with a conspicuous orange point in the center, the tips of the anthers protruding from the tube. There are named forms in soft lavender and deep rose which are very pretty. The plant is evergreen. In the wild it grows on partially shaded slopes; I have found that it will not succeed in deep shade and summer drought (as when planted beneath beeches). In high shade with some summer water it thrives. Like all creeping plants, however, it is easily killed by deep accumulations of leaves (which is why it frequents windswept slopes in nature, I suppose). If your garden is level, rake off at least part of the year's leaf fall before spring. In hilly gardens, Creeping Phlox will find its own favored spots.

Use wild phlox with Wood-hyacinth and Polemonium.

The plant creeps extensively, rooting at each node and forming there a basal rosette and flowering stem. These can be detached and moved elsewhere with absolutely no problem. Sections of the stem (with leaf nodes, naturally) may be rooted with no difficulty. Unlike *pilosa*, this species doesn't grow rampantly enough to smother or crowd out delicate neighbors. Snowdrops and squills bloom through its mats in my garden, and Wood-hyacinths (*Scilla campanulata*) accompany it in bloom. I find that a really pretty spring picture can be created with the latter bulbs in pink, blue, white, with the pale blue *Polemonium reptans*, with *P. divaricata*, and with color forms of *P. stolonifera*. There is the same shifting, elusive quality about the color of the Wood-hyacinth and Polemonium, pinks that are not quite pink and blues clouded by mauve, as about the phloxes. In my garden *stolonifera* begins blooming a little later than *divaricata* but doesn't last quite as long. It makes a good groundcover for azalea beds.

P. buckleyi, Sword-leaf Phlox, is a relative of *stolonifera* which differs principally in shape of leaves, these being long and very narrow. Its flowers are usually rose. It looks to me to be precisely what you'd get if you crossed *stolonifera* with *subulata*. Buckley's Phlox is rare in cultivation, unfortunately.

Two species which I have never grown but are worthy of mention are *P. ovata* and *P. glaberrima*. *Ovata* looks a little like *pilosa* and a little like *stolonifera*. It forms a mound of foliage from which stems rise to a foot or so and bear mauve or purple flowers. Its rather sparse leaves are very large. *Glaberrima* (the name means "very smooth") rather resembles a large *pilosa*. It and a group of related species (*carolina, maculata*) are more or less intermediate in habitat, height, blooming time, and general appearance between woodland phloxes like *divaricata* and the tall Garden Phlox. They are three of the few phloxes which occur naturally on the Coastal Plain. In fact, it is often supposed that at least some of these species may have entered into the ancestry of some of the cultivars of Garden Phlox. The old white cultivar 'Miss Lingard,' with its elongated inflorescence, lower stature, and earlier blooming season, is most likely one of these, though the vast majority of these cultivars are pure *paniculata*.

The most widespread of these three Coastal Plain species is *P. maculata*, called in most manuals Wild Sweet-william (and thereby being confused with Blue Phlox), a rather slender, upright plant, much like a Garden Phlox scaled down by about one half. Its rose-pink flowers are arranged in elongated or cylindrical clusters quite different in effect from the umbels of, say, *stolonifera* or the pyramidal inflorescences of *paniculata*. The green stem is speckled maroon, hence the Latin *maculata:* "spotted." I have found it growing in roadside ditches near the Fall Line, blooming in June. Transplanted to a sunny spot in my wild garden, it bloomed and did quite well in rather dry soil among native shrubs like Chokeberry and Spice Bush. It begins blooming a month before *paniculata* and its cultivars.

Nearly all thrive under the same conditions: rich soil that is near neutral or slightly acid is best for them, with at least partial sunlight and with plenty of moisture during the growing season. The creeping, needle-leaved species take more sun, though they will grow in partial shade, as do the taller summer-flowering species. The latter will often grow in quite wet places. The needle-leaved species, which are adapted to rocky hillsides in the wild, will not tolerate damp conditions at the root but can become very dry during summer.

CULTIVATION OF PHLOXES

The woodland species do well under the sort of care given most wild-flowers from the woods.

I mentioned earlier that it is possible to have a garden colorful from spring to fall using the genus *Phlox* alone. If anyone should be interested in specializing so intensively, the following information may prove useful.

PHLOX

SPECIES	BLOOM TIME	COLORS	HABIT, ETC.
subulata	April–May	red, pink, blue, white	mat-forming, sunny spot
subulata brittoni	April–May	mauve, white	same as above
nivalis	April–May	lilac, pink, white	same as above
divaricata	late April	blue, white	clumping woodland plant (some sun)
stolonifera	April–May	blue, mauve, pink	creeping woodland plant (some sun)
pilosa	May–June	lavender	clumping woodland plant (some sun)
pilosa ozarkana	May–June	clear pink	clumping woodland plant (some sun)
maculata	June–July	pink, lavender	upright perennial (sun or part shade)
paniculata	July–Sept.	many colors	upright perennial (sun or part shade)

The species *ovata, glaberrima, carolina* bloom about the same time as *maculata,* the latter two resembling it in habit. If one wants to cheat a little bit, he can tuck plants of the dwarf annual Texan *P. drummondi* in sunny spots of the garden to provide summer-long bloom in many bright colors. Some of the reds are marvelous. This little species has been exploited as extensively as has *paniculata;* it reminds one of the Garden Phlox in color and flower except that its cultivars are far dwarfer and, of course, only last one season.

Some cultivars of other species: 'Blue Ridge,' 'Pink Ridge,' and 'Lavender Lady' are three clones of *stolonifera* worth growing. The blue clone especially is lovely. 'Camla,' a named clone of *nivalis*, is a good pink often available. A selection of *ovata* called 'Pulchra' ("beautiful") is in the trade, though I have not seen it yet. Donald Wyman describes it as carrying "beautiful, dark-veined, fragrant, pink flowers" in late May and early June. Dr. Wherry regards this as a distinct species (*P. pulchra*), but agrees on its great beauty.

There are also some interesting hybrids available: the afore-mentioned 'Miss Lingard,' a floriferous early white with elongated flower clusters, is a fine plant (though somewhat fugacious with me) much resembling the species *carolina*. It is probably a hybrid of *paniculata* or *maculata* with *carolina*. It sets no seed. A hybrid group of *paniculata x divaricata*, known collectively as *P. x arendsi* has been produced in Europe but thus far is difficult to obtain here. They bloom in early summer, as might be expected, and the best apparently combine the best of both parents. Another hybrid group is *P. x procumbens (stolonifera x subulata)*, usually sold as a true species. It is available from rock garden specialists, and is highly recommended by expert rock gardeners. All the treasures of the genus have been by no means tapped through hybridization. Some of the little phloxes of the western mountains, difficult to grow in the East, are exceedingly lovely and provide great potential for breeding with our more adaptable easterners. This is only one avenue to pursue; little hybridizing has been done even among the easterners. Unlike many American natives, phloxes have become common in gardens, but only three, or at most four, of the sixty-odd species have been developed to anything like their full potential.

In May blooms what is not only beyond doubt the showiest of the violets but one of the showiest of all American wildflowers: the Birdsfoot Violet, *Viola pedata*. With finely cut leaves like buttercup or anemone and showy, flat, pansy-form flower (one of its common names is "Pansy Violet"), it is the glory of the roadsides in the sandy, more or less barren areas where it habitually grows. I have

VIOLETS

already described how Witmer Stone lyricizes on the beauty of this plant growing with *Phlox subulata* in great patches of pink and blue along railroad embankments in southern New Jersey.

Because it is limited in its habitat requirements, the Birdsfoot is perhaps not so widely known as some other violets. It is also rather difficult to grow under ordinary garden conditions. These two factors combine to make it less common in gardens than others, a situation which is unfortunate. But this beautiful plant is as easy to grow as any member of the genus, once its rather peculiar requirements are met. It does *not* want deep shade, rich soil, a mulch of humus-rich material, and abundant moisture. No combination will kill a plant more quickly than this will a Birdsfoot Violet. In nature it is found in full sun (or only light shade), on sterile, usually acid, sandy or stony soil. In the garden its most exacting requirement is soil: no humus, above all no manure or other source of organic nutrients, no chemical fertilizer. Given the right sort of soil, it will endure a considerable amount of shade, although it really does its best in full or nearly full sun.

For infertile, quickly draining soil: Birdsfoot Violet.

I am not absolutely sure, but I think that extra watering in the summer will encourage it to bloom beyond what is normally considered its natural blooming season. Plants in a very well-drained acid section of my garden which were watered copiously last summer (I was attempting to establish some difficult heaths nearby) bloomed heavily in May and rebloomed through the summer and autumn right up to the last of September! I kept most of the dying flowers picked, however, on *all* my plants, so this may have been an added factor. Even with no extra care, Birdsfoot Violets bloom sporadically until fall.

My first plant of the species was of the botanical variety *pedata*, with the two upper petals a deep velvety purple. It was given me by a friend and planted with my other violets, where it bloomed beautifully and promptly died. Later I was to see the all-lavender var. *lineariloba* in bloom by the thousands in southern New Jersey and to observe the semi-arid conditions under which it thrived. These I am fortunately able to emulate in my present garden.

My plants are growing in three separate localities: with other acid-soil plants in a sterile, stony silt beneath two *Pinus virginiana;* in a sterile, acid field; and in the cinders and gravel on the edge of my driveway. In all three they are doing well, though in the last position they tend to be crowded out by other plants—notably *Phlox pilosa.* In the first situation they grow with wintergreens, teaberry, mountain cranberry, sand-myrtle, ericas, dwarf rhododendrons, galax, shortias, dwarf asters, and choice low-growing milkweeds. The pines above them are high-branched, and they receive full sun in morning and afternoon. In order to keep the ericaceous plants alive in this infertile, quickly draining soil, I water very frequently (the heaths are also planted with a pad of humus and well mulched with the short needles of the pine, but the violets, milkweeds, and *Aster depauperatus* are not). Here the Birdsfoot Violet has grown to large, flat clumps of leaves that are simply covered with showy flowers in spring, blooming on, though not so heavily, throughout the rest of the season. They have also seeded themselves, which is always a good indication that a plant is happy. In the dry field the plants have taken longer to establish, but seem to be taking hold even better. This position is closest to that in which one sees them grow in the wild. The soil is so poor and so acid that they have little competition from other plants—two species of dwarfish goldenrod (*Solidago nemoralis* and another low species, possibly a hybrid, whose exact identity I cannot determine), Flowering Spurge (*Euphorbia corollata*), *Liatris graminifolia,* and a few others. Large patches of the ground here are almost bare—covered by mosses and lichens, or by various sparse grasses. The sun beats down all summer long, and the little violets appear to thrive. Here they also bloom during summer, but our summers have been wet for the past few years. More important, they have begun to seed themselves.

Another locality for growing these plants should be mentioned: at a friend's summer place in the coastal pinewoods of southern Delaware. Here they grow in the filtered light of the pines, in acid sand (the "sassafras" soils of the lower peninsula: sand with a layer of very acid humus, underlaid by a high water-table which helps prevent drying out), and have succeeded in seeding themselves lightly. It would appear, then, that the crucial factor in growing the plant is the sterility and acidity of the soil.

I have really not described *Viola pedata* adequately. It has finely divided leaves, but so do other violets. It has large, showy, flat flowers, but so again do others. It is difficult to convey the effect the plant gives. Its crown is tight and upright—it does not run across the ground like more common violets, thus could never be considered an invasive plant. Its leaves never overtop the flowers as those of some other violets do; instead they lie low and spreading, a kind of green ruff encircling the cluster of up-facing flowers which grow from the crown in a kind of natural bouquet. Finally, it differs from other native violets in the kinds of flowers it produces. In others, flowers are of two kinds—normal, with five showy petals, and flowers which lack the colored petals completely, called "cleistogams." These are borne later in the season than the showy flowers and are hidden down in the crowns beneath the leaves. Unlike the showy flowers, they do not depend on insects for pollination but fertilize themselves. Thus, no matter what happens to the showy flowers when they bloom in spring, most violets mature an abundant crop of seed each year. But not so the Birdsfoot. It has no cleistogams and must depend on its petaled flowers for seed. Perhaps this accounts for its extreme showiness (it *must* attract insects, or die as a species)—I am not sure. But I am sure that it accounts for the plant's willingness to bloom beyond its normal season, like many other perennials, if some agency prevents the spring flowers from setting their normal crop of seeds.

The flowers of this violet vary enormously in color, shape, size, pattern, proportions, and other more subtle characteristics. On a special trip to the southern fringe of the New Jersey Pine Barrens to photograph this plant, Dick Ryan and I found dozens of variants— some with almost orbicular, overlapping petals creating a large flower of perennial-border magnificence, others with narrower, rolled upper petals that gave the flowers a two-lipped, faintly orchidlike effect; some flowers of bright, deep lavender, others of pale mauve or silvery blue, others which paled to whitish at the center, still others

For a noninvasive violet: the Birdsfoot.

which varied from blue-white to mauve-white to pure, pristine white, all with the central tuft of orange stamens characteristic of the species, a dart of flame at the flower's center.

We stopped at a small frame house whose "lawn" was a sheet of these plants, showing endless variation. Each plant was slightly different from its neighbors, yet the darker variants seemed to occur with other darker variants and the pale with the pale, the result being that the entire lawn shifted in color from dark lavender through pale blue and even a mauve-rose which approached pink, on to white and back through the pale shades to the deeper tones again. It was a splendid spectacle.

All these belonged to the botanical variety *lineariloba*, whose most obvious distinction is what orchid growers call a "concolor" flower—all the petals similar in color. The other variety, *pedata*, is a "bicolor"—distinguished by its two upper petals being a dark velvety purple (and causing the flower to look even more like a pansy than does the concolor variety). To my acute disappointment, true *pedata* does not grow in this area. It is abundant elsewhere in the East, however, though not so widely distributed as the concolor variety. One hardly dare speculate on the variation likely to occur in a comparable colony of it! I have up until now attempted the bicolor only once. Unfortunately I killed it with the rich diet that I lavished on comparable beauties. It is reportedly no more difficult to grow than *lineariloba*.

Other native members of the genus *Viola* are common in the wild and showy in gardens, though few match the Birdsfoot Violet. One which comes close is also a plant of barren places rather than woods. I found it colonizing the sterile red clay subsoil left after a digging gang had cut a sewerage line through a nearby wood and bulldozed into oblivion a swath, two hundred feet wide and several miles long, of plants, leafmold, topsoil, and all the organisms living in that rich earth. The Woolly Blue Violet, *V. fimbriatula*, was the only cheering note in this grim business, for in a few years' time it had covered the raw, red scars left by the machines. It was shaded out itself in a few years by the River Birches which colonized the cut. So

Second choice: the Woolly Blue Violet.

goes the fate of plants which spring up on disturbed soil. But while it lasted it was a very pretty little thing.

I have also found the plant growing in the cinder banks along railway lines, and on steep roadside banks where other vegetation grows sparsely. In my garden it grows well in acid soil and partial sunshine, with no encroachment from other plants—precisely the conditions under which the Birdsfoot grows.

V. fimbriatula is a small plant, growing only a few inches tall and never making great clumps like those of the dooryard violet so common everywhere. The round flowers, large for the size of the plant, are a deep, smoky blue, and the showy leaves are deep, glossy green, densely woolly on their undersides. The petioles are often highly pigmented, almost purple. Also distinctive is the shape of its leaves—long and oval, rather than heart-shaped. There are several similar, related species which differ mainly in leaf shape: *V. emarginata*, whose common name, Triangle-leaved Violet, explains itself, as does that of *V. sagittata*, Arrow-leaved Violet, and a trio, *V. triloba*, *palmata*, and *brittoniana*, with leaves varying from three-lobed to as finely dissected as those of the Birdsfoot. These are all pretty little violets, not so showy in my opinion as *V. fimbriatula*, but delicate and attractive. They will grow well if given poor soil and a bit of sun, but they will not long endure woods conditions.

Other blue violets are more amenable. The Common or Dooryard Violet, *V. papilionacea*, is a weedy species which will grow anywhere. Admittedly lovely when in bloom, it later in the season allows its leaves to grow to twice their size and height at flowering time and produces so many seeds that it soon takes over every available inch of space, killing and crowding out anything not rank or robust enough to compete with it. It has no place near delicate plants, but is beautiful if allowed to colonize moist meadows or waste places where it can do no damage to other plants. I have a white variant of it which is possibly a hybrid. This has pure white flowers and a much less weedy disposition, possibly because it is an albino. It came to me from a friend who got it from a friend, so its origins are forever shrouded in mystery. It is as excellent a plant for the woodland garden as the blue form is undesirable. One other form of the

For moist meadows and waste places: Common Violet.

Common Violet deserves mention, *albiflora* (or *V. priceana*), the Confederate Violet, with flowers of a pale blue-white with dark blue veins. It is a pretty plant and one about which I have always been sentimental, but is unfortunately as robust as the ordinary purple form.

The Blue Bog Violet, *V. cucullata*, is very similar under cultivation to the Common Violet, but it lacks that species' aggressiveness. In the wild here, it is found only in woodland bogs and swamps and along shaded stream banks, where it grows right in the muck and is often inundated. In May it lifts its light violet-blue flowers on long stems, perfect for picking, to the filtered sun. It will grow in much drier soil in the garden and in brighter sunshine seems to make larger clumps. Since its flower stems are so long its flowers are always beautifully displayed. Its leaves do not expand after the blooming season, nor is it invasive.

Most of the violets so far discussed have been plants which have thick, horizontal, rootlike stems at ground level, from which leaves and flower-stalks spring. There is a group of dwarf white species which are similarly "stemless," but propagate themselves by means of slender runners. In my area the two commonest species are *V. primulifolia*, Primrose-leaved Violet, and *V. lanceolata*, Lance-leaved Violet, both of which have descriptive enough names. They grow naturally in wet ground, but unlike some other bog violets do not adapt easily to drier conditions. I have had them linger for a few years in my wild garden, but eventually die out. As companion plants to such things as trollius, candelabra primroses, and similar damp-soil plants they are, however, excellent, forming mats (but never becoming invasive) of fresh green foliage topped by tiny, purple-striped white flowers on long red stems. All one needs is perpetually moist soil to grow them. Two other well-known species with rounder leaves are the Sweet Violet, *V. blanda*, and the Pale Violet, *V. pallens*. All these have the special charm associated with very tiny plants.

A final group is the stemmed violets, which by contrast respond so well to cultivation that they often double or triple their size and propagate themselves extensively by seed. In these species the stem is upright and branching rather than forming a kind of squat root-

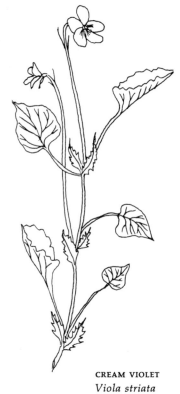

CREAM VIOLET
Viola striata

stock, and as a result plants of this section become quite tall, two feet or so in some species. Most begin blooming when the stems first begin to elongate, and at this time look much like the stemless species. As spring wears on, however, the stems elongate and form dense clumps, topped by the flowers. By the time the blooming period is over, we have an attractive bushy clump of stems which stays good through the summer but does demand a bit of room. These plants are very much worth growing if only because in this section are contained the only yellow and white (barring albino forms of the blues) native violets which grow easily in the East. They are plants of the rich upland slopes, doing beautifully under conditions which suit trilliums, bloodroots, hepaticas, and woodland phloxes, all of which are their companions in the wild. Of the whole group, I would recommend four very highly. *V. canadensis*, the Canada Violet, native from Quebec south in the mountains to the Carolinas, makes a clump about a foot and a half tall when mature, blooming with showy white, yellow-centered flowers. *V. striata*, the Cream Violet, is similar but often taller, and an extremely easy plant to grow in the garden. Two species with yellow flowers, otherwise similar to the preceding, are *V. pensylvanica* and *V. pubescens*, the Smooth and Downy Yellow Violets, respectively. To complete the picture are two stemmed violets with blue flowers which make an interesting contrast with the foregoing: *V. conspersa*, called the American Dog Violet because it is closely related to the European Dog Violet, *V. canina*, is common in woods, easy to grow, and quite showy. The more northern *V. rostrata*, Long-spurred Violet, is similar but has somewhat more showy, or at least more interesting, flowers with straight, elongated spurs protruding backward.

There is often considerable variation in violets, so one's best course is to select plants in bloom. Not mentioned here are several species which are less showy (in my judgment) than those discussed, difficult to grow, or with which I am not acquainted. There are some real beauties in the West, for example, but they are beyond the scope of this book.

For yellow and white violets: use the Canada, the Cream, the Smooth and the Downy Yellow species.

DETAIL OF *Viola striata*

V

Wild Azaleas

The azaleas of the East are difficult to associate with any specific time or season. Even in Delaware, which has only about three of the dozen-and-a-half wild species, May, June, and July are blossoming months for wild azaleas. Three months of flowers is quite a long time, but if species from other parts of the country are brought into the garden, that time is nearly doubled—beginning with New England's Rhodora in April and ending with Georgia's Plumleaf Azalea and Florida's Hammocksweet Azalea in August and September. This amounts to nearly half a year of flowering.

Wild azaleas for blossoms from April through September.

Why is it that American azaleas are not better known, more widely grown? Well, you say, first of all, blooming season isn't everything. Plants must have showy flowers, attractive growing habits, good foliage, and must be fairly easy to handle in cultivation. At least *some* of these considerations are important. In answer to that, let me ask you to imagine a low, dense, deciduous shrub covered with spheres of lacy white or lavender flowers, each individual bloom shaped like a tiny butterfly, in full flower on leafless branches the third week in April. Or imagine a tall, rounded, tiered-branched bush with smooth, pale green leaves, bearing at each branch tip, truly magnificent in the dull heat of August, clusters of up-facing trumpets of glowing cinnabar red, blotched garnet. These, the early *Rhododendron canadense* and the late *R. prunifolium*, are only two of the many beautiful native azaleas which, beautiful as they are, are no more so than most of the other species.

In fact, species for species, the American azaleas are probably unparalleled for sheer beauty. There is not an unpleasing member of the group. As for ease of cultivation, all grow very well under conditions which suit other acid-soil plants. Many may even be easier to grow than garden varieties of azaleas, because they are adapted to local conditions. It is almost universally true that a plant native to a given region is more easily grown there than one which is not native, simply because the former has become adapted to regional climatic quirks while the latter has not. Some difficulty may be experienced in growing the northern Rhodora (*R. canadense*) in the hotter parts of the East, and conversely the southern lowlanders *R. prunifolium* and *serrulatum* may prove sensitive to cold in the North. Generally speaking, though, the native azaleas are extremely easy to grow under the same conditions given cultivated azaleas and their relatives.

For green, unblemished foliage: wild azaleas.

One other advantage they possess: clear green or glaucous foliage that remains unblemished until fall, when it turns bright yellow or orange before falling. Those who, like myself, have rejoiced in the giant flowers of the Exbury Hybrid azaleas and then lamented their brown-blotched and mildewed foliage for the rest of the season will know just how desirable a trait good foliage on azaleas can be.

In passing, I should perhaps insert a botanical note on why azaleas in this book are called *Rhododendron* in Greek. The problem is that today botanists agree that what we call azaleas are just one section of the enormous group botanically known as *Rhododendron*. Horticulturally, we can still distinguish azaleas from rhododendrons (except in the case of intermediate plants like *R. mucronulatum*, the Korean Rhododendron, which is not an azalea though it looks like one and is often called one), but botanically they are now *Rhododendron*.

American natives are usually colloquially called "honeysuckle," especially in the South. A glance at any of their flowers will explain this, for each is longer-tubed, more trumpet-shaped, than the flowers of evergreen azaleas, and each has five long stamens and an even longer pistil protruding from the trumpet's throat. I would guess that hummingbirds are primary vectors in the pollination of these plants, judging from the number of red and orange flowers among them (the favorite colors of these birds).

Colors and shades of colors vary greatly within the group. The range is from purest white to deep scarlet or crimson red. Interim shades are yellows, oranges, pink, salmons, corals, and all sorts of combinations. Many have flowers of yellow with red tubes, or of orange with a yellow blotch. Others are pure white with carmine filaments, or with hairline streaks of carmine down the center of each lobe of the corolla. The common Pinxterbloom Azalea often has pink trumpets with vivid carmine tubes. The Alabama Azalea often has white flowers, very sweetly fragrant, each with a lemon-yellow blotch on the upper lobe.

Size and form vary also in the group. Two of the species are rather remote from the others, and these (the northern *R. canadense* and the southern *R. vaseyi*) are totally different in flower shape, having short-tubed, saucer-form flowers which have the side lobes elongated, so that each flower looks like a butterfly. The rest are characterized by trumpet-shaped flowers. Variations on the basic trumpet shape are, however, endless: some (such as *R. canescens*) have small, narrow flowers tightly packed into a spherical head, the exserted stamens of each flower projecting at first downward and then outward and upward in a graceful curve. Others (like *R. calendulaceum*) have wider, shorter-tubed trumpets in a more lax cluster in which the individual bloom is the unit of beauty, these often having a contrasting blotch on the upper lobe. Still others (like *R. prunifolium*) have crowded clusters of large flowers with long tubes all curved upward and inward so that the flower cluster is flat-topped and the long stamens of each floret sweep up and inward.

PINXTERBLOOM

Each May I am impressed as I travel through southern Pennsylvania, northern Delaware, and eastern Maryland on Interstate Route 95, by the brilliant display of the Pinxterbloom, *R. nudiflorum*. Not that those in charge of planting and maintaining the highway have anything to do with this display; they are far too busy trying to grow exotics which either look out of place or will not grow along the freeway banks. The wild azaleas have been there, blooming sparsely in the dense shade of the woods until the cutting through of the road provided more light for them to flower profusely, which they now do in the underbrush between wood-edge and graded slope.

This is by far the most abundant azalea through much of the East. It is very abundant in the north of Delaware, less so, though still common, on the Coastal Plain. Like many widespread plants it is variable in habit, color, form of flower. This fact is of importance to the gardener who decides to use it, since some individuals are far more attractive than others. I have, in the course of a morning's exploration, found plants with large, open flowers of a pink so deep as to seem lavender, in large but few-flowered trusses; or plants with small, narrow-tubed flowers of blush pink, nearly white, in many-flowered globular heads, and every extreme between the two. Some of the paler specimens had tubes of bright pink; others had both filaments and tubes of deep carmine. I have also seen the species growing with every habit from that of a two-foot colonial shrublet carpeting the forest floor in a sheet of pink and green to that of a tree fifteen feet tall with four-inch trunk and tier upon tier of blossom-laden branches.

The Pinxter's apple-green leaves are fresh and bright as they unfold at blooming time, but they are not particularly distinctive. They do make a good contrast with the flowers. The common name of the plant was given it by the Dutch who settled so thickly in the Middle States. If it has anything to do with flower color, always some shade of pink, this meaning was added afterward, for "Pinxster" is Dutch dialect for Whitsunday, the seventh sunday after Easter, the word itself deriving from Greek *Pēntekostē*. The reference is apparently to blooming time. In Delaware it blooms during the first or second week in May.

The best way to acquire good forms of such variable plants as this is to search them out in bloom. The plants can then be marked and dug in the fall, or, if there is danger that the locality will be destroyed before then, transplanted when in bloom. There are certain rules to follow when transplanting wild azaleas which will make the difference between success and failure. First of all, many species are stoloniferous; this means that unlike their evergreen relatives they can be propagated by division. If plants are not growing in condemned areas, it is good conservation to take only a piece, rather than the whole plant, if this is at all possible. This does not harm or unduly disturb the parent plant, and the divisions, for reasons which I will shortly discuss, reestablish as quickly as full plants do. Second: all azaleas are plants which will not tolerate having their roots stripped clean of soil or dried out. This means that you must leave at least some of the soil in which the plants are growing on the roots, and must wrap them quickly in some material such as plastic or wet burlap—to prevent their drying out. Third: no matter how large a root ball you dig with wild plants, there will be an imbalance between top and root after the digging. The only safe way to transplant wild azaleas is to cut them back severely, to about a foot, after they are dug (or before, which makes them easier to handle while digging). Cut-back plants can be plunged in a peat bed or nursery for a year and then planted out as compact new plants in their permanent positions. Many people naturally balk at cutting back the plants so severely, but the importance of it cannot really be overemphasized. While plants *can* be successfully transplanted without cutting back, they often languish for years without making either much new growth or many flower buds. All deciduous azaleas quickly recover after pruning and bloom within a year or two. The new growth is much more vigorous and floriferous than old wood. Once, when an invading sewer line cut through a local woodland, my friend Dick Ryan and I decided to rescue a fifteen-foot Pinxter which had been uprooted by the bulldozers. We cut away an enormous pad of soil with the tree and hauled it home, where we planted it with bushels of peat and braced it with guy wires and iron pipes. The following year the tree put out tentative leaves and blossoms.

Search for and mark Pinxters during blooming time.

Transplanting Pinxters? Take only a piece.

The second year it sent up a stout new shoot from the base and the top died. It was a good lesson.

SWAMP AZALEA

For summer bloom:
Swamp Azalea.

The second most abundant azalea in Delmarva is different in every way from Pinxter. Called Swamp Honeysuckle by local people, and Swamp Azalea by azalea specialists, *R. viscosum* blooms a month after *nudiflorum*, with glistening white flowers. Even out of bloom it is a pleasing shrub with deep green to glaucous, smooth, and very lustrous leaves which are not persistent (they turn a good red in the fall) but look as though they are. One finds the Swamp Azalea in every swamp, streamside, wet hollow on the Coastal Plain, where its small, starry, long-tubed blossoms are conspicuous among the dense vegetation of early summer. I associate it in particular with a mill-pond in southern Delaware, where it grows on an earth dam across the water with Sweet-bay, Wax-myrtle, and towering, dark White-cedars. Its flowers gleam white among the dark foliage, reflected in the peat-laden brown waters of the pond all through early summer. It is extremely fragrant: one often locates it by scent rather than by sight in the bogs and wet tangles where it grows. To me the scent is cloying, faintly sickening—like the fragrance of the Gold-band Lily, *Lilium auratum*. But many people whose judgment I respect find the scents of both these plants delicious. It is more pleasing to me from a distance, when diluted by air. I once had near my bedroom window a plant whose fragrance very delicately perfumed the room in June and early July.

Although it grows in swamps in the wild, in cultivation it needs little more water than other azaleas. I have several specimens growing among other shrubs, and seldom have to worry about watering them. They are, however, growing in acid, humus-rich soil.

R. viscosum is less variable than the Pinxter. Forms with larger flowers occur, and these should be searched out; forms with pink flowers also rarely occur, and there is a form with bluer leaves than the type. Much of its variation has to do with blooming time. I have seen plants which bloom consistently in June, while others nearby do not begin until early July. With careful selection, one can have this species in bloom for two months.

The forms I have seen in Delaware are always rather tall, stately shrubs, seven feet or so high. In the South dwarf stoloniferous forms occur. The major fault with the shrub is that its flowers are not especially large or showy (although some forms are larger; I have a young plant with flowers twice the size of the usual form). It flowers so late, however, that it is valuable for summer bloom alone. Its fall foliage is also very fine. One of my plants is a pink-flowered form. Its individual blooms are rather small, but the clusters are of adequate size. In late June, it is a seven-foot mass of coral trumpets.

The colloquial names Swamp Azalea and Honeysuckle are, incidentally, far preferable to the manufactured name of some manuals, "Clammy Azalea." This, a translation of *viscosum*, refers to the fact that the tubes of this species are covered with minute viscous glands which make the whole flower sticky. The Coast Azalea (*R. atlanticum*) has this feature also. It is of more than botanical significance since it means that dead flowers have a tendency to cling to the flower cluster instead of falling away, which may be objectionable to neat gardeners.

COAST AZALEA

I first met the third member of the Delaware flora, *R. atlanticum*, under cultivation, in the native azalea collection on Oak Hill at Winterthur, where it forms an admirably rounded low shrub covered with pale bluish gray leaves and, in late May, large clusters of white flowers with the faintest pink blush. A superb shrub in every way, I thought. In addition, I soon found that it could be propagated rather easily from stem cuttings (unlike many deciduous azaleas). Why wasn't it better known? To this day I have never found out.

My second encounter with it was along roadsides in coastal Virginia and North Carolina, on a visit to my friend of the giant Water Oak and peacocks. Here there were occasional foot-high plants blooming with bright pink flowers—from blood of the Pinxter, perhaps, but good *atlanticum* in growth, stature, and leaf. Later I read Henry Skinner's classic paper on American azaleas and discovered that he had found the Coast Azalea at a place in Delaware called Sandtown.

Late in May of 1970, Dick Ryan and I set forth to find (or to see if there were any left) Coast Azaleas at Sandtown. We drove southwest into territory unfamiliar to either of us, passing through wide fields and pastures, occasional hamlets, and stretches of oak woods. The rain which had been threatening most of the morning was by this time streaming down. On we drove, and I began to despair of the whole purpose of the trip when suddenly, in a patch of roadside woods, I glimpsed an azalea looking out, or so it almost seemed, at the road. It was large-flowered, blush white, no Pinxter or early Swamp Azalea, I knew, but a true *atlanticum*. We stopped, backed up, got out in the pouring rain, and entered the woods. The ground was carpeted with Coast Azalea, two feet high, blue-leaved, and in full flower. From there on for the next several miles the azalea grew thickly wherever the ground was not cultivated or grazed. At one spot we collected several variants—a bright pink, an extreme dwarf, and several large-flowered clones. A few miles in either direction and the plant suddenly disappeared. I have yet to discover reasons for this strange distribution.

The Coast Azalea— flawless.

   The virtues of this little plant are many; I do not know that it has any flaws. It is a very heavy bloomer. A healthy plant in sun will seem simply covered with flowers. It is low and dense, rivaling the evergreen azaleas, and can be used as a pleasing contrast with them in foundation planting. Its foliage is superb; perhaps no native azalea has so fine a leaf as this species. Its flowers in addition are very fragrant (like *viscosum*'s, they are sticky at their bases). Although it is deciduous, its framework of bright brown twigs, each bearing a fat, lacquered, scaly bud like a tiny pineapple at its apex, is interesting in winter. One caution if you grow the plant: like several other azaleas and rhododendrons, it is inclined in cultivation to set far too heavy a crop of seeds each year, which, if allowed to mature, will cause it to bloom sparsely the following year (the strength of the plant going into the current crop of seeds rather than into next year's flower buds). Bloom clusters must be removed, then, shortly after the flowers fade. This may be done with the fingers or with shears. It is almost never necessary to prune or shear *atlanticum*, but if it must be done, this is the time to do it. The same applies to *all* azaleas and rhododendrons, as well as flowering cherries, crab-apples, forsythias, spireas: in fact all flowering shrubs which form their bloom buds by autumn. One must prune them early enough so that next year's buds will form on the current year's growth.

The distribution of other American azaleas can very nearly be summed up in one word: Appalachia. True, there is one West Coast native, (*R. occidentale*), one native to the western Gulf states (a southwest relative of the Swamp Azalea called *R. oblongifolium*), and one or two southern species which leave the mountains to venture out on the Coastal Plain (such as the Florida relative of the Swamp Azalea, the Hammocksweet Azalea, *R. serrulatum*). By and large, though, the rest of the azaleas to be discussed are confined to the uplands, if not the mountains proper.

Those discussed in detail so far have all been members of the azalea subseries known botanically as *Luteum* ("yellow") or *Pentanthera* ("five stamens"). This is a very homogeneous group, differing essentially only in color and minor details. The form of flower —the long-tubed trumpet with five pointed, flaring lobes and five long, curving stamens—is very distinctive. Two American species, however, belong to the section *Canadense*, visibly distinct in the form of the flowers: these have no tube to speak of, but open flat, with two large side lobes which make the flowers look like butterflies on the tips of the leafless branches. This seems like as good a place as any to part company for a moment with the *Luteum* subseries and consider these two different species.

They certainly merit consideration. One, the Pink-shell Azalea native to southern Appalachia (*R. vaseyi*), is highly regarded even in this country. Britain's Royal Horticultural Society gives it a four-star rating, the highest possible. It makes a graceful, spreading shrub, covered in late April and early May by clear pink flowers lightly speckled darker on the upper lobe, with short, curling stamens. Its leaves are just beginning to unfurl when it blooms. Although a native of the South, it is perfectly hardy through most of New

Four-star rating: 'Pink-shell' species.

England and should be grown by all lovers of beautiful plants. It has absolutely no drawbacks except those usually associated with azaleas—it needs acid soil and it will not tolerate prolonged drought. There is a pure white variant called 'White Find' which is also very handsome.

The second native member of the *Canadense* group is *R. canadense* itself. This is the Rhodora, immortalized by Emerson, and though it is a plainer plant than its glamorous cousin from the South, it has its own virtues. It is, for one thing, extremely hardy, being found wild from Newfoundland down through the Appalachian Chain into Pennsylvania. It blooms early—the first, really, of all native azaleas to bloom, beginning in Delaware not too long after the middle of April, and following just on the heels of the very early *R. mucronulatum* from Korea. Its flowers are smaller than those of *vaseyi*, but they are more numerous in the cluster, and so deeply cleft are the segments that they look like lace. There is a pure white form, *albiflorum*, which is perhaps more desirable than the mauve-lavender type of the species. In Delaware, at least, it grows slowly and never becomes a large shrub. Its major drawback is that being a boreal plant, it will not take too much heat in the summer, so probably it should not be attempted much farther south on the Coastal Plain.

Very hardy early bloomer: CANADENSE.

There are about ten eastern *Luteum* azaleas yet to be discussed. Five of these are early (May) bloomers, and five are late (June–August); two are pink, three are white, and five fall in the yellow-orange-red range. I have either grown all of them in my garden or observed them growing at Winterthur, and I can say with honesty that all of them are desirable garden plants.

In the yellow-to-red range the earliest to flower are two from the Deep South, *R. austrinum* and *R. speciosum*. *R. austrinum* is a glandular, sticky plant with flowers of bright yellow, each with usually a red tube. It is not so ornamental as some others in this range of color because the flowers are rather small. They are abundantly borne, however, and this is the earliest yellow to flower—about the 18th of May in Delaware, just a few days after the Pinxterflower. A week later the Oconee Azalea, *R. speciosum*, comes into flower;

Other desirable garden species: AUSTRINUM, SPECIOSUM, CALENDULACEUM, BAKERI.

in the forms I have seen a bright scarlet and extremely beautiful. It well merits its Latin description *speciosum,* "showy." Its flowers are rather small but, like the preceding, are abundantly borne. It is a smooth plant throughout, both in leaf and flower, and a really gorgeous spot of color in late May.

The third azalea in this color range to bloom (in early June) is perhaps the showiest of all—an Appalachian native that is one of the best known of the group: *R. calendulaceum,* the Flame Azalea. Introduced into cultivation in the latter part of the eighteenth century, and confusingly called *Azalea lutea* by Linnaeus, the plant has held its own in gardens of Europe and America ever since. What really distinguishes the Flame Azalea is not so much its color, which ranges from pure yellow to bright scarlet, but its size. The flowers of some specimens are over two inches in diameter. In my experience, the larger flowers are inclined to be paler in color—the oranges and yellows, rather than the reds. Whether this is due to hybridization with some other species (such as *R. speciosum*) with smaller, red flowers, I do not know.

A robust plant, in age becoming ten or more feet tall and as broad, the species makes an excellent lawn specimen. It takes a good while to reach its mature height, so don't be deterred from planting it by fears of its outgrowing your garden. It can be kept permanently shorter by pruning, also. (This applies to all azaleas of the *Luteum* group, whether they be native or exotic.) The Flame Azalea is big and showy in both plant and flower, and one of the reasons for its showiness and size is that it has twice the number of chromosomes in its cells that the other species have. It is, in other words, more or less to its orange-flowered relatives what the tetraploid "Gloriosa Daisies" are to ordinary Black-eyed Susans.

Which is not to say that the "ordinary" azaleas in this color range are to be despised. Altogether there are about five of these species, which conveniently stretch out the season of bloom for about four months here in Delaware, beginning with the previously discussed species *austrinum* and *speciosum* in May, and *calendulaceum* in early June, and continuing with *bakeri* in late June, and *prunifolium* flower-

UPLAND AZALEAS

RHODORA
Rhodora canadense

ing sporadically through July, August, and even into September. The Cumberland Azalea, *R. bakeri,* is a little-known denizen of Appalachia that deserves far wider cultivation than it now enjoys. Its flowers, somewhat smaller than those of the Flame Azalea, but showy nevertheless, are of a bright orange, varying somewhat (as the flowers of all these species do) in depth of color but always very attractive. They are borne in abundant clusters during the latter half of June, sometimes remaining in good condition into early July. The plant habit is often very dwarf and spreading. Indeed, I have heard it referred to, under the name "Baker's Honeysuckle," as a groundcover in the South. It is a plant whose taxonomic status is still somewhat uncertain. At first regarded as a subspecies of *calendulaceum,* it was later separated as a species under two names, *R. cumberlandense,* and the name it presently carries. It may be that botanists one day will find the population known as *cumberlandense* different enough from *bakeri* to be considered a distinct species. In the meantime, we all should grow it, whatever its taxonomy. Appalachian plants have usually been protected by the remoteness of their habitat, but as population grows, and distance closes, plans to bring "progress and prosperity" to impoverished Appalachia will probably affect plants as adversely as they benefit the pocketbooks of people. *Rhododendron bakeri* is currently not easy to find. It is, however, offered by a few people who specialize in azaleas.

PLUMLEAF AZALEA

Most beautiful, most unusual: Plumleaf species.

R. prunifolium, the last member of the yellow-to-red native azaleas to bloom, is a species so distinct and unusual that it merits space in every garden in this country where it will grow. It is native in a highly restricted area of the Deep South: Southwest Georgia and adjacent areas of Alabama, where Henry Skinner, on his famous search for American azaleas, found it growing along the banks of the Chattahoochee River in southwestern Georgia in 1951. It is especially ironic that what is probably the most unusual (and very possibly the most beautiful) of all the American natives is also the rarest and therefore most endangered species in the wild.

The most unusual characteristic of *R. prunifolium* (the specific name means "plum leaf," so called because naturalist John Kunkel Small, who named it, saw some resemblance between its leaves and those of a plum) is its blooming period. Not in May do its blood-red flowers brighten the banks of the Chattahoochee River, nor in June, but well into July and even later. And this late-blooming habit is retained wherever the plant is grown. At Winterthur, where *prunifolium* has thrived for over fifteen years, the average date of full bloom lies somewhere in the final week of July or the first of August, but I have found flowers on isolated plants in pristine condition on the first of September. And what flowers! I have described in the beginning of this chapter their general aspect. They are usually some shade of orange-red (although occasional plants have flowers of paler orange), quite large, very gracefully formed and held. The foliage, if your soil is sufficiently acid, is of a pleasing apple-green, the habit rather open and tall. The plant is slow-growing, at least in Delaware, after it reaches blooming size, and responds like all deciduous azaleas to pruning. Plumleaf Azalea is an especially graceful shrub for woodland conditions. As a young plant the growth is quite rapid. In 1970, plants which I raised from seeds sown in 1964 were three feet tall and had set their first bloom buds, opening their gorgeous red blossoms in July of that year. The species is one of the most valuable plants for American gardens, for blooming period alone.

For the summer shade garden: Plumleaf Azalea.

In all fairness, its few faults should be mentioned. Because of its southern distribution, it is unfortunately not as hardy as many of its relatives. In northern Delaware it may lose flower buds during exceptionally cold winters, though the vegetative portions of the plant are seldom injured. This location is on the northern edge of Zone 7. Its second drawback is that it is not so adaptable as to soil and location as other native azaleas, needing acid soil and plenty of moisture in summer. It transplants with less ease than many of its relatives, and seems to need more time to reestablish itself. And, finally, it withstands less exposure than most native azaleas, its thinnish, pale, smooth leaves becoming blotched and brown-spotted in too much wind and sun, or pale and chlorotic in dry or alkaline soil. However, its rapid growth, the vibrantly colored and elegantly shaped flowers it produces so late in the season, and its tolerance for shade are virtues that far outweigh its faults. Plumleaf Azalea is an excellent choice for the summer shade garden.

OTHER SPECIES

The remaining species duplicate to a certain degree the characteristics of those already discussed; each, however, is sufficiently unique to be worthy of inclusion in our gardens, especially if the best expressions of each are obtained. *R. canescens*, the Southern Pinxter, is to the Southeast what *nudiflorum* is to the North—widespread, abundant, extremely variable. It tends to bear smaller, paler flowers than the northern Pinxter, but otherwise resembles it outwardly. In some of its forms the flowers are tiny but very numerous, borne in perfect spheres like balls of pink fluff at the tips of the many branches. These are very showy. It blooms early in May, a few days ahead of *nudiflorum*, and thus is one of the earliest of all to come into flower.

Related to *canescens* is the Alabama Azalea, *R. alabamense*. It is somewhat intermediate between that species and *R. atlanticum* in blooming season, habit, color, and flower form—a compact shrub with white or pale pink flowers, often yellow-spotted, which appear in the middle of May. Like many white-flowered azaleas, it is fragrant. It hybridizes with other species, especially with *canescens*, in the wild, and pure forms of it are often difficult to obtain. It is valuable as a low-growing, large-flowered, fragrant, early white.

Roseshell Azalea: the hardiest in the pink range.

R. roseum, whose "accepted" common name, Roseshell Azalea, always seems forced and literary to me, is another very close relative of the Pinxterbloom. In nature it is found from Quebec to Virginia, replacing the lowland *nudiflorum* in the Piedmont and mountains. Like *canescens* it often intergrades with *nudiflorum*, but in its typical form is rather more attractive, with large flowers of a uniform deep pink. Many experts rate this as the finest wild azalea in the pink range. It is probably the hardiest, also.

The Swamp Azalea, discussed earlier, has two close relatives which resemble it in nearly every way—that is, they are glossy-leaved, late-flowering whites with small, fragrant blossoms. These are *R. oblongifolium*, called variously Texas or Oklahoma Azalea, and *R. ser-*

rulatum, the Florida Swamp Azalea or Hammocksweet. Neither offers an improvement on the true Swamp Azalea, but either should probably be grown in place of it where native (Texas, Arkansas, and Oklahoma, and Florida to Louisiana, respectively). Neither is hardy in the Northeast. I have not grown *oblongifolium,* but the Hammocksweet grows at Winterthur, where it loses flower buds in very cold winters. It is distinct only for its blooming season here, August and even into September. Mary Henry, who collected extensively in the South, crossed this species with *R. prunifolium* many years ago to obtain a late-flowering group of hybrids in shades of pink. These are known as *R. x gladwynense* and are very attractive plants, about as hardy as *prunifolium.*

Possibly the most beautiful of the white-flowering natives is the Sweet Azalea, *R. arborescens,* native in the mountains from Pennsylvania to Georgia. It blooms in mid-June, slightly before *viscosum,* with quite large, broad trumpets which are usually pure white. Often the flowers are marked or striped with pink, or have bright pink filaments and styles. The smooth leaves are glossy, deep green. It is rather larger than most natives in size, although perhaps not so large as its specific name, "treelike," might imply. The manuals give it a maximum height of twenty feet. The blooms, like those of all the white species, are deliciously fragrant. This is another extremely desirable species.

Most beautiful of late white-flowering natives: Sweet Azalea.

The hardiness of native azaleas varies according to range. Those native to the southern Coastal Plain, like *serrulatum, prunifolium, speciosum,* are less hardy than wide-ranging northerners like *roseum* and *viscosum* (which are hardy to southern Maine) or mountain species like *arborescens* and *calendulaceum* (which do well in northern Massachusetts). As I have pointed out, all do well in Delaware, only *serrulatum* and *prunifolium* losing flower buds during especially cold winters. If you live in areas of extremely low winter temperatures, it might be well to find out which species are native in your area and try them. In any case, the hardiest (*arborescens, bakeri, calendulaceum, nudiflorum, roseum,* and *viscosum*) will do well through most

HARDINESS AND HYBRIDS

of the North. Conversely, the remaining species might well be tried if you live in sections of the country with hot summers and mild winters which discourage commercially available azaleas like the Exburies and Ghents.

The famous Biltmore Estate in North Carolina and the Callaway Gardens in Georgia both have excellent collections of native azaleas on display. Fred Galle, the director at Callaway Gardens, has done much hybridizing with *prunifolium* in an attempt to bring the rich color and late blooming season of this species into combination with the good points of others.

Other breeders working with the wild azaleas have named a few hybrids or selected forms of the species. One of the oldest of these is the red clone of *calendulaceum* introduced by the Arnold Arboretum called 'Smoky Mountaineer.' More recently, the National Arboretum introduced a selection of *bakeri* made by Henry Skinner which is called 'Camp's Red.' It is tall for *bakeri*, which is usually a compact shrub, with inch-and-a-half flowers of blood-red in June. David Leach, the rhododendron authority, has named at least two interesting clones of *bakeri*: 'Pink Fire' is described as having pink flowers flushed orange; 'Scarlet Salute' as brilliant red. Each has flowers about two inches wide in late June.

Leach has also produced some hybrids which sound very good to me. These are so new that I haven't yet seen them, but reproduce excerpts from their printed descriptions. There are five advanced-generation hybrids of *bakeri x arborescens*: 'Chamois' has two-inch flowers of bright yellow in late June; 'Coloratura' bears slightly larger flowers of bright rose with yellow blotch in early July; 'Cream Puff' is bright yellow with orange blotch, with two-and-one-quarter-inch flowers in late June or early July; 'Pink Puff' has orange-spotted salmon flowers over two inches wide in late June and early July; 'June Bride' bears two-inch flowers of white with a yellow blotch in late June. 'Maid of Honor' is a primary cross of *bakeri* and *arborescens* which is deep pink with an orange blotch, one and three-quarter inches wide, in late June. Finally, 'Tang' is a descendant of *bakeri* which has brilliant scarlet blossoms, nine to eleven per truss,

Native Azaleas

Color and Blooming Season

Note: Spring-blooming species tend to flower profusely for shorter periods of time, while summer-blooming forms flower sporadically over a long period and also vary individually as to the date at which they begin flowering.

April	May	June	July	August	September	
	canadense					Lavender-Mauve
	canadense*·· vaseyi †··· atlanticum alabamense	arborescens ······· viscosum ···········		serrulatum ········		White
	vaseyi canescens nudiflorum roseum	bakeri x arborescens‡ bakeri x viscosum	x gladwynense§ ·········			Pink
	speciosum calendulaceum ·· bakeri ·	prunifolium ·················				Red
	austrinum calendulaceum bakeri	prunifolium ·················				Orange
	austrinum calendulaceum ··					Yellow

* forma *albiflorum* ‡ natural hybrids, some in shades of salmon
† *album* 'White Find' § hybrids of *prunifolium* and *serrulatum*

that measure two and three-eighths inches across. It is listed as blooming in "mid-season," which I assume means late May and early June.

It may perhaps seem inconsistent of me to advocate the use of hybrid plants in a book dedicated to the salvation of species, but I certainly do not advocate the use of species alone, or even native plants alone. There are far too many beautiful exotics and man-made varieties for that. What I do say is that native plants have a place in our gardens that they are too often denied. They should complement rather than replace exotics. (For example, these hybrids provide June-blooming pinks with large flowers, whereas nearly all the wild species with pink flowers appear in May, and none of the exotic hybrids blooms in June at all.) No one, furthermore, can deny the sheer fascination of new hybrid combinations. They are often more ornamental than their parents. In addition, being derived from parents native to this country, they should possess the adaptability which is one of the strong points of all natives. I should add that all of Mr. Leach's creations, being developed either in northwestern Pennsylvania or eastern Ohio, are exceedingly hardy.

VI

Shrubs in the Woodland

April is the month of water, of flooded marsh and stream, swollen river, swamp and estuary, of shad running, waterfowl in pairs on every pond and bay, Skunk-cabbage and False-hellebore showing great green leaves in black bogs; of soft rains warming the ground, calling up pink Spring-beauties, shattering white Bloodroot, and opening the buds of one of the earliest of native trees or shrubs, the Shad Bush, Shad-blow, or Service-berry.

When shad run upstream to spawn, so runs the old legend, the Shad-blow flowers, and indeed when the plant blooms you may be sure to find shad in the rivers of the East—at least you could in the days before all our major streams were polluted. The old word "blow" (as in "full-blown rose") derives from Indo-European *bhlo*, "to spring up," from which we also get "bloom" and "blossom" (and, by way of Latin *flos, flor,* with change of initial *b* to *f*, "flower" and the names Florence and Flossie).

SHAD BUSH

There are some twenty-five species of Shad Bush in the world, the majority in North America, with a few in southern Europe and Asia. In my travels I came across three, one (*Amelanchier stolonifera*) a three-foot colonial shrub of bog-edge and wet barren with upright spikes of white flowers in early spring, and two woodland species with flowers at about the same time but much taller and more tree-like in growth.

A. arborea is a veritable tree, as its name implies, growing to seventy feet in height, a pillar of white flowers when in bloom. Such huge specimens are always in open woodlands and are, of course, very old. It has light gray, handsome bark and makes a delicate and graceful tree. *A. laevis* is similar but less tall, and its bark is less handsome. Its drooping racemes of large flowers are made even showier by the distinct maroon of the unfolding leaves.

All shad bushes bear elongated clusters of white blossoms early in spring, just as the leaves unfold. Those of the shrubby species are upright; those of the arborescent species tend to droop more, in keeping with their generally more graceful habit. In June or July they bear edible fruits (another name is Juneberry) which are eaten by birds and animals, including man. The genus belongs to the apple subfamily of the Rose family, as a close inspection of its flowers and fruits indicates. The fruits of *arborea* are by far the best of the species mentioned here.

AMELANCHIER *the first to bloom.*

Amelanchiers are the first white-flowered native shrubs to bloom, coming into full flower long before the dogwoods with which they commonly associate. Their flowers are short-lived, but so early (Witmer Stone calls them "pioneer flowers") that they are worth growing. In addition, of course, their fruits are pretty and beneficial, their orange autumn coloration is excellent, and their habit always pleasing. That their flowers are so fugacious almost enhances their charm for me—they are like Bloodroot, so fragile-looking that one wonders how they can endure the rain, wind, and cold of early spring as long as they do.

They offer little difficulty under cultivation, being adaptable to most soils of moderate moisture and fertility. I have transplanted many sizable plants from the wild and never lost one. There are a few variants of the species with pinkish rather than white flowers. A cultivar called 'Robin Hill Pink' has flowers which open pink and fade white. Flowers of the arborescent species are about an inch wide, with five oblong white petals. These are disposed in terminal elongate clusters of eight or ten, each cluster subtended by several bright pink or rose bracts which contribute materially to the showiness of the plant before they fall. *Amelanchier* is a genus well worth growing for ornament and its fruit. Birds of all sorts love the soft, juicy fruits. One species has been widely advertised by a major nursery as "Sarvis Tree."

Closely related to *Amelanchier* is a genus of three species found only in eastern North America: *Aronia*, the Chokeberries. The commonest species, Red Chokeberry (*A. arbutifolia*), is also the most ornamental. It is an upright, bushy shrub six or eight feet tall, with leaves green above and whitish below, flat corymbs of white flowers in mid-May, handsome red autumn color, and bright, crimson-red fruits which persist well into winter. It is a shrub with several seasons of interest which might well be grown more than it is. A cultivated variety which is offered by several nurseries is named 'Brilliantissima.' Its growth is reputedly more upright than that of the type.

CHOKEBERRIES

Chokeberries for year-round interest.

The fields and woodlands of this country are filled with beautiful woody plants that are occasionally but not often enough used as ornamentals. There seems to be no tradition associated with most of them, as there is with the hydrangeas and syringas of our grandmothers' gardens. Most of us pass them by with hardly a glance, in spite of the fact that some are extremely ornamental. The question which haunts every person who begins working with wild plants is "Why?" Why do we ignore our natives and pay court to exotics?

To be perfectly honest, one must ask also another question: do they really compete with the forsythias, syringas, hydrangeas grown in our gardens? The answer must be equivocal: it depends. Some do—in my opinion, surpass these plants—and some do not. We should not forget that the old garden shrubs have been around so long not only because they are hardy and tolerant but because they are beautiful in bloom. No native shrub, for example, can in mid-April give the *blast* of golden yellow that *Forsythia x intermedia* gives. On the other hand, quite a few native shrubs are more interesting over a far longer period of time than forsythia. I might cite Mountain-laurel, for instance, beautiful the whole year and only more beautiful when in flower, but such a comparison may seem unfair to forsythia. Take *Aronia arbutifolia*, the Red Chokeberry, then. If a chokeberry and a forsythia were planted side by side, chances are that everyone passing them would notice the latter when it was in bloom, while a much smaller percentage would pay attention to the flowers of *Aronia* (since they are less profusely borne, are not so colorful, and appear in the late spring, when many other flowers compete). In autumn and winter, however, the chokeberry would be much more noticeable. Forsythia shoots its wad, as it were, in April. Its foliage is not bad but not remarkable in summer, and its autumn color is not particularly bright. *Aronia*, however, has flaming red autumn leaves and clusters of equally red fruits which remain long after leaves have fallen (and attract winter birds). The difference between the two shrubs, then, lies in the manner in which they display their charms. Forsythia expends nearly all in one flash of blinding intensity. Chokeberry husbands its attractions, parceling them out over the year. It seems obvious that we need both types of plants in our gardens.

DOGWOOD

There is one native flowering shrub (or small tree) which gives the lie to everything I have said about our neglect of wildlings—one of the commonest of all our native woody plants and one of the most beautiful, *Cornus florida*, the Flowering Dogwood, which grows wherever there are woodlands from Ontario and Michigan south to Florida and the mountains of northern Mexico. In the East it occurs in every woodland (and in nearly every front yard) where its beautiful white or pink flowers make a fine show in April and May. So widely known and grown is it that many of us treat it in cavalier fashion. But in England, whose "soft" climate doesn't suit it, it is regarded as the finest of the genus, and many an English garden writer has lamented the fact that it will not bloom well in his garden.

Flowering Dogwood is one of those woody plants adapted to growth in the understory of the forest, occupying the space beneath the branches of the tall oaks and tulip-poplars but above the true shrubs like viburnums and spice bushes which form the underbrush. Here in the filtered sun it becomes a slender tree sometimes as high as forty feet but usually lower, with an umbrella-like crown of spreading branches. Few sights are more beautiful than a forest of dogwood in bloom.

Where it occurs away from woodlands, it forms a bushy little tree branched to the ground, often multiple-trunked, which in the abundant sunshine of such positions blooms profusely. This is the way the species is seen in most of our gardens, though it really is prettier as it grows naturally, a slim, airy tree of the woodlands.

Dogwood blossoms are no more single flowers than daisies, but are really flat clusters of tiny blooms surrounded by modified leaves (the white "petals") which render them attractive to pollinators and gardeners alike. Like many plants whose "petals" are really modified leaves or bracts (florists' poinsettias, for example), its flowers last a long time, not unfolding from a calyx-covered bud like a rose but growing slowly like the leaves they truly are and assuming color as they enlarge. In early April the flower heads of dogwood are nickel-sized, still pale green, but fully formed, growing to three or four inches in diameter by the last week of the month and fading to white or changing to pink as the tiny true flowers mature, and finally dropping the showy bracts in mid-May. They are showy for a full month.

Like all really choice plants, this species is of interest at other times of the year. It is, for example, one of the most effective of berried plants in autumn, its branch-tips adorned with clusters of half-inch ovoid fruits of glistening red. These, providing that the birds do not eat them, last in good condition until at least Christmas.

*Dogwood excellent for
autumn foliage and
berries.*

A dogwood in fruit (or flower, for that matter) is doubly effective
with a background of evergreens like conifers or hollies, against
which the pale blossoms or bright fruits really show to advantage.
I have seen magnificent winter effects from dogwoods in combination
with American holly. The autumnal foliage of Flowering Dogwood
also recommends it. It is deep purplish crimson, and it turns early
in the season.

The usual color of Flowering Dogwood blossoms is white, with
each of the four bracts touched brown at their notched tips. The
form usually designated "rubra" is a rich pink, rather on the coral
side. Some clones are quite deep, others only tinted pink. Many of
these have been named and introduced, often with extravagant claims
by the introducers. It is well to visit arboreta or botanical gardens
and see plants growing—and blooming—before succumbing to ad-
vertisements about them.

Flowering Dogwood is surprisingly unvariable for such a widely
distributed species. Some cultivars with which I have had experience
are: 'Pendula,' with drooping branches and flowers, more curious
than beautiful; 'Welchi,' with variegated foliage, a rather weak clone;
'Pluribracteata,' with semi-double but rather untidy flowers which
last longer than the normal type; 'Prosseri,' a very dark pink selection; 'Pygmaea,' a dwarf clone; 'White Cloud,' a floriferous white;
'Cherokee Chief' and 'Sweetwater Red,' both dark pinks; and 'Apple-
blossom,' a floriferous and lovely pale pink. A yellow-fruited form,
'Xanthocarpa,' is listed in all the manuals. The ordinary wild white
form, like its frequent neighbor *Trillium grandiflorum*, fades to pink,
at least during certain years, as the flowers age.

Dogwood easy to grow.

As might be expected from a plant which grows from the coast
to the summits of mountains throughout much of the continent,
Flowering Dogwood is very easy to grow. It seems rather indifferent
to soil pH, plants growing beautifully in the neutral soil of the
uplands and with equal abandon in the acid pinewoods of the Coastal
Plain. Like many woody plants its floriferousness decreases in direct ratio to the amount of shade it receives, so that if you grow
it in deep woodland, you should not expect it to be smothered in

bloom each year. I have found that it behaves like fruit trees under certain conditions, during good years blooming and fruiting phenomenally but blooming sparsely the following. This is called "biennial bearing" among fruit growers. It comes about because the plant one year puts most of its energy during the growing season into setting fruit, rather than into forming flower buds for the next season, while the following year, with few flowers to provide fruits, and lots of excess energy, it devotes much of this to setting a larger than normal amount of flower buds for the next season, when the cycle starts again. In the fruit industry this is uneconomical, since one year provides a sparse crop while the next provides such an abundant one that it gluts the market. With flowering plants we needn't worry about economics, of course, but we can correct biennial flowering/fruiting as fruit growers do, by pruning. The plant should be sheared lightly just after blooming, so that about half of the faded flower heads are removed. This will cut the fruit crop by about fifty percent and allow sufficient energy to be channeled into next year's blooms. Never prune a dogwood in late summer or fall unless you want to lose all or part of the next season's flowers. Like most spring-flowering shrubs and trees, dogwoods form flower buds on wood of the previous year. The only safe time to prune and still have a full crop of flowers for next season is just after flowering. This applies to many other woody plants—azaleas, rhododendrons, lilacs, forsythias, mountain-laurel, hollies, andromedas, and many others.

Flowering Dogwood's deficits as a garden plant are two: it does not transplant with ease in large sizes, and it is somewhat surface-rooted and voracious as a feeder, so will rob less vigorous plants. The solution to the latter problem is placing; to the former: plant in small sizes, buy well-rooted nursery stock which has been several times transplanted, or severely prune collected stock. I have established six- or eight-foot willowy plants taken from woodlands by pruning all side branches from the plant immediately. It takes a year to establish the plants, but thereafter they grow well and soon bloom. In my estimation the best time to plant in my latitude is very early in the spring. Where summers are hotter and winters milder, fall planting is perhaps better.

On the West Coast is a relative which is perhaps even more beautiful—*Cornus nuttallii*, the Western Dogwood. It is very similar, but becomes a larger tree (Sargent says that it sometimes grows to one hundred feet—a statement which boggles the imagination!). Its flowers are larger, with up to six (rather than a maximum of four) bracts, and its fruits are joined in dense, berrylike aggregates, rather than arranged in clusters of free-standing individual drupes like those of its eastern cousin. (In this characteristic *nuttallii* approaches the Oriental *Cornus kousa*.) *Nuttallii* is one of the common plants of Yosemite Valley, where it is gorgeous in the spring. Unfortunately it does not do well in the East, but a fairly new hybrid with *C. florida* is more amenable and possesses some of *nuttallii*'s showiness. This is known in the trade by the graceless name of 'Eddie's White Wonder.' It was introduced a few years ago with much ballyhoo as a combination of the beauty of the western and the hardiness of the eastern species. Anyone lured by such publicity should be aware that it is quite difficult to transplant except in very small sizes and is considerably less tolerant of extremes of heat or cold than is *C. florida*. With some care, though, it does succeed in the East, and it is certainly an approach to the spectacle that is *C. nuttallii* in bloom.

A frequent companion of Flowering Dogwood, though on the whole a much rarer plant, is the Wild Crab-apple, *Malus coronaria*. I occasionally come upon a specimen of this tree in some remote woodland corner when it is in full bloom, a sheet of clear pink, and never fail to marvel at its beauty, which far surpasses that of the exotic species so common in parks, around public buildings, and in private yards. Our Wild Crab is never planted, and the reasons for this are not hard to discover. It is, first, a *tree*, not a shrub. It attains forty feet in the wild. It is also not particularly easy to transplant except when very small. The roots of specimens I have attempted are invariably large, few, and go straight down to China. (These have been wild plants; it is quite probable that nursery-grown stock,

WESTERN DOGWOOD
Cornus nuttallii
Flower

were such to exist, would have a more fibrous root system.) Its fruits are not tiny, abundant, bright red or yellow, as are those of many exotics, but are sparse, quite large, and pale green-yellow, nor is its foliage reddish or purple. Finally, like all American *Malus* it is susceptible to fire blight (as are many exotic *Malus* also, though some are relatively resistant to it). All these facts add up to the sort of plant not greatly admired by nurserymen, and I suspect that the reason it is almost never seen is that nurserymen just will not grow it and landscape architects will not specify it in their plans.

It is very much worth growing, though, along with exotic crabs, for it does not really compete with them at all, mainly because it blooms later than they do, not till the middle of May. And it holds its own with any of them as to beauty, for its flowers are very large and are a true, good pink, not the muddy rose-purple that passes for pink in so many highly publicized crab-apple cultivars.

Harold Hillier calls it a "beautiful, strong growing American Crab" with "large fragrant flowers of a delightful shade of shell pink." He also offers 'Charlottae' ('Flore Pleno'), a double-flowered variety. The species was introduced into England in 1724—a long time ago!

The large, abundant foliage of *Malus coronaria* is more or less apple-like on mature branches, but on young, vigorous growth it becomes lobed almost as much as a maple, most unapple-like. It turns a good orange in autumn.

A southern counterpart is *M. angustifolia,* similar except that the mature leaves are very narrow. In the Midwest another species, *M. ioensis,* occurs. This species is sometimes cultivated, and in its double form 'Plena' (usually sold as 'Bechtel's Crab') is fairly often planted. Hillier states that this form at its best is "perhaps the most beautiful" crab-apple, but adds that it is not a strong grower in England, unfortunately. Here it does well enough. Like the other American species, this blooms late, after the leaves have unfolded, and thus does not give quite the overpowering effect that the early-flowering exotics do. Native crabs look best to me in their natural surroundings—woodlands—where they introduce a note of welcome color at a critical time, as the dogwoods fade and the woods begin to take on a late-spring, tired look.

WILD CRAB-APPLES

WESTERN DOGWOOD
Cornus nuttallii
Seed head

With the passing of the flowers of Wild Crab in late May, spring passes, though nearly a month will elapse before the solstice and the ensuing long, hot days of summer. The days of late May and early June are progressively longer, hotter, sultrier, dustier, in spite of an occasional ghost of winter in a cold night or sudden storm. In woodlands the trees have assumed their full canopy of leaves, shading the ground and preventing the development of flowers. The trout-lilies and trilliums that bloomed there a month before now begin to go dormant. What bloom there is moves up into the understory of the forest, into trees and shrubs, or along streams or roadsides, openings in the canopy of leaves through which a bit of sun enters.

HONEYSUCKLE

Trumpet honeysuckle for a non-takeover flowering climber.

In such places one may encounter the rare and elegant Trumpet Honeysuckle, *Lonicera sempervirens*, twining in restrained fashion through roadside or streamside viburnums, elders, and coneflowers, its beautiful scarlet trumpets and large bluish leaves immediately distinguishable among the tangled vegetation through which it grows. This is one of the most desirable of flowering climbers. It begins blooming in late spring and continues for much of the summer (the hummingbird season, for its flowers are perfect examples of adaptation to pollination by these tiny birds). Its handsome foliage is evergreen and attractive both summer and winter. And it has none of the vices of its much better known relative Japanese Honeysuckle, *L. japonica*—that is, it does not grow so thickly or spread so rapidly that it smothers other plants. That it lacks Japanese Honeysuckle's unsurpassable fragrance is a pity, but one would not expect a hummingbird flower to smell sweet.

In my old garden, I grew a plant at the base of venerable French lilac, allowing it to twine freely through its upright host. The relationship seemed beneficial from an aesthetic point of view, for the honeysuckle began producing its flowers after the lilac had ceased blooming, and gave color during a period when the lilac, with its mildew-prone foliage, was at its worst. Hummingbirds were at the honeysuckle blossoms constantly.

The berries of Trumpet Honeysuckle are red (unlike those of the

Japanese species, which are black) and are attractive in themselves. Many sorts of birds feed on them, also. I have called the flowers of the species "trumpets," as indeed all the manuals do, but I am afraid that this noun does not adequately describe them. They do not flare widely as the "trumpets" of petunias or nicotianas do, nor are they short-tubed and two-lipped like the flowers of the moth-pollinated Japanese Honeysuckle. They seem all tube, with a narrowly flaring mouth, and much of their distinctive elegance derives from this extreme attenuation. They most resemble the flowers of the unrelated Cypress-vine, *Ipomoea quamoclit*, and Scarlet Morning Glory, *I. coccinea* (hummingbird flowers from the tropics), an obvious case of convergence. I believe that the reason Trumpet Honeysuckle never is covered with a sheet of flowers at one time but instead blooms with fewer flowers over a long period is a further adaptation to its pollinator. In eastern North America hummingbirds are never as abundant as insects. They are also a more constant vector of pollination in that a single bird tends to visit the same plants throughout the season. Therefore, a moderate number of flowers opening in succession throughout the whole season provides both sufficient food and ample incentive to return to the source for the hummingbird and sufficient fertilized seeds for the plant.

The species has one fault: like all the smooth-leaved vine honeysuckles it is susceptible to aphids, which may distort new growths. This has never deterred me, since I grew my plant in a semi-wild setting in the first place, and thought moreover that the aphids no doubt supplied extra food for the hummingbirds. In a more formal setting one could tip the plant with shears if he has, as I do, an aversion to poisonous sprays. The plant otherwise never needs to be pruned.

Growing in the same sort of locations as Trumpet Honeysuckle is *Itea virginica*, the Tassel-white, Virginia-willow, or Sweetspire, a deciduous shrub of six feet or so. Its elliptic leaves are somewhat willowlike (hence one common name) but remind me rather more of those of Wild Cherry. Its slender branches are terminated in

TASSEL-WHITE

mid-June by spikes of fragrant white flowers three to six inches in length. Its foliage turns a good rose-red in the autumn.

Tassel-white is a plant of the Austral Zone, occurring from Florida no farther north than Pennsylvania. I have only seen it in the southern Pine Barrens of New Jersey and in the woodlands of southern Delmarva. It nearly always grows near water, and is an excellent plant for wet problem spots in the garden. Though not extremely showy, it is graceful and unusual-looking in flower. Its effect somewhat resembles that of Sweet-pepper Bush (*Clethra*), with which it often grows, though the latter blooms a full month later and is somewhat coarser. *Itea virginica* has no close relatives in this country. The genus, like so many in the Southeast, has representatives in North America and eastern Asia.

Tassel-white good for wet problem spots.

LAURELS

Should any reader doubt that nature provides splendors which are unrivaled by any that man produces, I would advise him to drive along New Jersey routes 70 and 72 east from Marlton during the last week of May and the first of June when the endless forests of stocky White Oaks and rugged Pitch Pines rising from the sandy plain are abloom for mile on mile with pink and white billows of Mountain-laurel. The sight is breathtaking, and because we are after all in the midst of the famous Pine Barrens, where vegetation is sparse and spare, the blooming laurels never become overly sumptuous and cloying, but maintain a rich balance against the gnarled trees above them.

Kalmia latifolia is one of the most beautiful flowering shrubs in the world, rivaling its near relatives the rhododendrons. Yet it is not often grown in its native country except by specialists. Every suburban yard in America has at least one Japanese azalea or hybrid rhododendron. Few have Mountain-laurel. Why? It is hardy—at least as hardy as the "ironclad" rhododendrons, certainly hardier than any evergreen azalea. It is easy to grow; in my garden, in fact, it withstands summer drought better than any exotic rhododendron (as well it should, after millennia of adaptation to this climate!), and better than most evergreen azaleas. It is beautiful in flower and leaf,

Four-star rating: Mountain-laurel.

and makes a dense, rounded, evergreen shrub, just the sort beloved by the average gardener. The reasons, to parody Shakespeare, are found not in the kalmias themselves, but in our nurserymen, who seldom handle these plants because they are hard to propagate by cuttings.

One must look to specialist nurseries for them, and specialist nurseries are, alas, fast dying out in this country. Or one can collect his own plants. I have found that, to do this successfully, one should select small plants which are, preferably, growing in full sun. Plants growing in deep woodland, even apparently small ones, have a heavy, woody crown and few fibrous roots, and will not transplant well.

Mountain-laurel's clusters of bowl-shaped blossoms are usually bright pink in bud, opening paler. They vary in intensity of color, many opening almost white, others much deeper. There are growing at Winterthur two young plants from an unknown source which are labeled 'Red Bud,' and red-budded they indeed are—their keeled pyramidal buds a glowing cerise-scarlet which fairly vibrates in the landscape. The flowers are pink after opening. This form is still sparingly distributed among nurseries, but hopefully it will become commoner in time. One problem with Mountain-laurel which works against it from a nurseryman's point of view is that it is difficult to propagate except by seed. This is the main reason that often the only plants offered by the trade are collected from the wild.

Besides 'Red Bud,' another interesting form is 'Fuscata,' with pale pink flowers the inside of which is decorated with a band of deep maroon-brown. This form is decidedly prettier close up; from a distance it seems dirty. There are several other variants listed in manuals.

Kalmia, with about eight species in North America and Cuba, is a distinctively American genus. Only three of its members occur north of the Carolinas, and of these only one besides Mountain-laurel is at all common. This is *K. angustifolia*, Sheep-laurel or Lambkill, which is found growing in the same region as Mountain-laurel, though usually in drier, more barren habitat. It is a much less showy plant, of smaller stature, leaves, and flowers. Its leaves are not glossy like those of its relative, but soft olive with a dull gray finish. Its flowers are in lateral clusters along the stem, rather than terminal, so that the flowering effect is quite different. They are commonly a rather muddy rose-purple (a color which nevertheless contrasts nicely with the grayish leaves). Selected forms, however, are better in color. There is also a very pretty white form ('Candida') to be found.

Sheep-laurel grows in great abundance in the New Jersey Pine Barrens, usually in drier, sunnier sections away from the pines where Mountain-laurel occurs. Here it forms part of the undergrowth with huckleberry, chokeberry, scrub oak as a leggy, suckering shrub of very limited ornamental appearance. In very open, barren areas, however, I have seen it growing as a dense, dwarf shrub of decided ornamental value. It transplants with no difficulty. Those who climb Cannon Mountain (and many others) in New Hampshire will see Sheep-laurel growing in great dwarf thickets at the summit. It seldom, under any conditions, exceeds three feet in height, while Mountain-laurel with age may become a tree to forty feet (this usually in dense forest, however). Sheep-laurel's common names both allude (one far more directly!) to its poisonous properties as far as livestock is concerned. *Latifolia* and *angustifolia* mean, respectively, "broad-leaved" and "narrow-leaved," and refer to the width of leaf of each species in comparison to the other. *Kalmia* commemorates Peter Kalm, a Swedish botanist who explored America in the eighteenth century.

A close relative to *Kalmia* is Rose-bay or Great-laurel, *Rhododendron maximum*, found in mountain ravines from Canada to Georgia along the Appalachians and occurring in isolated situations west to the Great Lakes region of Ohio and east to the New Jersey Pine Barrens. This is the species which formerly was collected by the millions for estate planting, and in many parts of the East enormous cultivated specimens may still be seen. It has long, dark green leaves and a rather open habit. Its flowers are small, even insignificant for a rhododendron, opening white from soft pink buds. It has a great advantage over many of its kin, however, in that it blooms long after the majority of them, in late June or early July, and thus is quite valuable for late color. One waits patiently for rhododendron specialists to cross it with larger-flowered species or hybrids and produce cultivars with enormous, showy, colorful flowers in July, but as yet few have done so.

The species is valuable, though, in itself. It is no plant for foundations because of its open, rangy habit, but it will take much shade, and is excellent in woodlands or as a sort of evergreen screen or loose hedge. It is possibly the most adaptable rhododendron as far as its ability to withstand extremes of heat, drought, and cold is concerned, and I know of few plants which will grow in denser shade. If one uses it in deeply shaded locations, incidentally, he should be prepared to forgo its flowers, since no rhododendron (or kalmia or any flowering shrub for that matter) will flower profusely in deep shade. Some very old and very large wood-edge specimens of Rose-bay at Winterthur are today extremely handsome plants throughout the year. Like all rhododendrons and kalmias, this species becomes more ornamental as it grows older and its vegetative growth slows, for its flower clusters tend to be hidden by the rampantly growing new shoots on young plants. Old specimens are neatly studded at branch tips with globes of pink and pearly white.

Dense shade? Try Rose-bay.

Every gardener knows some form of viburnum—the fragrant early *V. carlesii* (or its coarser hybrid, *V. x carlcephalum*), the dogwoodlike *V. plicatum tomentosum*, the evergreen *V. rhytidophyllum*, in aspect like a great, quilted-leaved rhododendron, the graceful, red-fruited *V. setigerum*, or one of the snowballs: Chinese, Japanese, or European. All these are Asiatic or European, but several of this large genus are American, and some of these equal the best of the exotics for ornamental qualities.

VIBURNUMS

One of the most beautiful of all in flower is the Hobble-bush, *V. alnifolium*, a native of woods and swamps from Canada to North Carolina, mainly in the mountains. Unlike many viburnums this will not usually thrive in full sun and dryish situations; it demands woodland conditions. As a woodland plant, then, it is of value to those gardeners who have too much shade and don't wish to part with their trees. An open shrub of six to ten feet, it has large, nearly orbicular leaves arranged along its arching branches, and in mid-

Hobble-bush for shady areas.

spring, white "lace-cap" flowers (flat clusters consisting of tiny, unshowy fertile florets encircled by a ring of large, showy sterile florets). Its vernacular name refers to its arching branches, the lower of which tend to strike root where they touch the humus-rich ground of their native woodlands and thus trip unwary walkers. This species apparently requires acid soil.

Five species comprise the purely American section *Lentago:* Nanny-berry, *V. lentago;* Black-haw, *V. prunifolium;* Southern Black-haw, *V. rufidulum;* Withe-rod, *V. cassinoides;* Smooth Withe-rod, *V. nudum.* All have blue-black berries, cream or white flowers which lack the showy, sterile ring, and dark, glossy foliage. All are ornamental. Nanny-berry, native from Hudson Bay to Georgia, becomes a tree of thirty-five feet, with large rather drooping leaves. *V. prunifolium,* probably the commonest of this section in the East, makes a large, treelike shrub (which can easily be trained to tree form) with very distinct growth—rigidly horizontal branches and spurlike twigs give it a superficial resemblance to hawthorn, hence the common name. Although the creamy blossoms are not individually showy, in early May the plant is smothered with them and is then quite showy. The bloomy blue fruits are also showy in fall, but are quickly taken by the birds. It is an excellent conservation plant for this reason. The berries are edible, though too insipid for my taste. The leaves, glossy green turning wine-purple in fall, resemble those of wild cherry, hence the name *prunifolium:* leaves of *Prunus.* It is fast-growing and extremely adaptable. The southern counterpart of this plant is *V. rufidulum,* like it but growing twice as tall, larger in all its parts, and more abundantly clothed with the rufous fuzz on twigs and branches which is the hallmark of this group of viburnums. This species is not easy to get. It is hardy to Massachusetts.

In the withe-rods we have a pair of related species which are similar and yet very different. Native in swamps of the East, they are shrubby, not treelike, the sort of shrub which in the wild tends to become a formless, stoloniferous mass in the understory of woodlands. No one seeing the average withe-rod growing naturally would picture it as the shapely bush it becomes under cultivation. Both withe-rods (so called because their supple, wandlike branches were used for caning, basketwork, and similar industries in earlier times) have glossy leaves, flat heads of creamy flowers in ordinary viburnum fashion, and blue fruits. These turn at random from green to white to pink to blue as the anthocyanin pigment in them develops, and since all these colors are often represented in a single cluster, they make no mean display in autumn.

In many articles on viburnums, *V. nudum* is dismissed as merely a more southerly growing counterpart of *V. cassinoides*, but differences between the two are considerable. Both grow in the wild hereabouts, *nudum* frequenting really wet woods and *cassinoides* appearing as stoloniferous underbrush in low but not necessarily wet woodlands. Ten years ago I collected two plants of each species for the viburnum collection at Winterthur. Today all four plants stand between five and seven feet in height, with the two *cassinoides* somewhat larger and rounder in habit. The general appearance of each of the two species is very different. In foliage, *cassinoides* looks much like the Wild Black Cherry, *Prunus serotina*. In fact, while collecting these plants I often had to ascertain that the leaves were opposite, as in all viburnums, rather than alternate as in *Prunus*, in order to avoid collecting a young cherry.

Nudum, in contrast, looks nothing like a cherry. It is quite distinct, but in its untoothed, glossy leaves, somewhat resembles a young Black Gum, *Nyssa sylvatica*. The leaves of *cassinoides* are of a medium green, not particularly glossy, with a prominent pale midrib. They are minutely wavy-toothed along the edges and come to an attenuated point. Those of *nudum* are, in botanical parlance, entire—completely untoothed on the edges—and of a deep lustrous green, with impressed veins that give them a quilted look. They are very rich leaves, which look as though they are more thick and evergreen than they really are. One common name, Shining Viburnum, pays tribute to these lustrous leaves. They are blunt or very short-pointed at the tips.

Both plants of *nudum* in the Winterthur collection are more vase-shaped than *cassinoides*, with shorter more gnarled branchlets that attract attention. I consider it much more ornamental than *cassinoides,* simply because it has more "character."

The differences between these four individuals of two species illustrate once again the advantage of judicious selection in collecting native plants. There is considerable difference between the two *cassinoides* in size, one being a good two feet taller than the other and generally more robust-looking. There is even more difference between the two specimens of *nudum.* One is far more compact and well furnished with foliage, widespreading in habit, abundant in flower and in fruit. It is spectacular throughout the month of October with its long-lasting berries which, after their characteristic and colorful changes, remain a bloomy damson blue against the shining foliage, green going to wine-purple. Harold Hillier, the famous English plantsman, was so enthusiastic about this specimen when he visited Winterthur that we decided to name it *Viburnum nudum* 'Winterthur' and disseminate propagating material of it.

I should mention one other difference between *cassinoides* and *nudum:* the former blooms with prunifolium in May; the latter blooms much later, toward the end of June. It is one of the latest-flowering of the genus, in fact, and is valuable for this reason as well as for others. Possibly the difference in blooming times serves to keep the two species from hybridizing themselves out of existence, though how such an adaptation occurs is unclear to me. Like *alnifolium,* these two species need an acid soil, which in eastern North America is usually easy to provide.

Hillier mentions a form of *cassinoides* called variously 'Nanum' or 'Bullatum,' which is "remarkable, slow-growing," with "large, peculiarly-formed, wavy leaves which color richly in the autumn." One excellent characteristic of both *cassinoides* and *nudum* is fine autumn color, a sort of pinkish crimson in the former and a deeper wine in the latter.

Very different from the foregoing (and belonging to a different section of the genus) is Dockmackie or Maple-leaved Viburnum, *V. acerifolium.* It is common in upland woods as weedy underbrush that may cover acres in extent with hardly a flower or fruit and no character at all. As it grows in its native haunts, it is most unprepossessing, but given space, good soil, and some sunlight it makes a tall, vase-shaped bush with good foliage (lobed, very like the leaves of the European sycamore-maple), dark blue berries in fall, and in spring flat clusters of cream flowers. These are not particularly showy, though some plants have flowers with a decided pink tone which are more so.

In the same section, but quite different in appearance, are the Arrow-woods, a complex of species (or varieties) which have plagued taxonomists since Linnaeus named the first "dentatum" in the early 1700s. The arrow-woods are probably the commonest viburnums in my part of the country, inhabiting dense woodlands, swamps, marsh-edge, meadows, bogs, and roadsides throughout the Piedmont and Coastal Plain. In woodlands they tend, like all plants denied sufficient light, to straggle, but in the open they make fine, robust, densely furnished and tall shrubs which, though they give no period of exceptional color or interest, nevertheless are good plants throughout the season, with frothy creamy blossoms, good bright green foliage, and fruits of quite a bright, deep blue.

Arrow-wood good all-round plant in open areas.

All arrow-woods are distinguished by an abundance of straight, wandlike twigs (presumably good for arrow shafts, though whether the name originates from Indian experience or botanist fancy is unclear), which are clothed with roundish to oval leaves strongly and regularly toothed along the edges. The abundance of botanical names given to various members of the group is confusing: *V. dentatum, pubescens, rafinesquianum, recognitum, venosum, molle* are some of the names which have been applied to various forms. There is much individual variation in habit, leaf form and color, showiness of flower, and blooming period. I see two distinct species in my area: one is a perfectly smooth plant, flowering in mid-May, which is rare near the coast but commoner in the Piedmont, and the other is downier in all its parts, flowering profusely a full month later than the preceding, and is common through the whole state. The first I call *V. dentatum;* the second *V. pubescens,* in accordance with Rehder's *Manual of Cultivated Trees and Shrubs.* The latter plant is of great value in the landscape, for it blooms well after the great spring burst of color, when comparatively few shrubs are in flower. Its striking blue fruits are unfortunately soon eaten by birds.

A final American viburnum, one probably more familiar to readers from the northern part of the country than to others: *V. trilobum*, the "High-bush Cranberry." This species belongs to the section *Opulus*, which is distinguished by lobed, maple-like leaves, red fruits, and flower heads which, surrounded by a ring of sterile flowers, are quite a bit showier than those of most others. Exotic species in this section include such well-known plants as the Asiatic *Viburnum sargenti* and the European *V. opulus*, one form of which, with flower heads composed entirely of sterile florets, is known as Guelder-rose or European snowball and is as ubiquitous as forsythia in old gardens.

V. trilobum is similar to these, though considered by some a better garden plant than its European counterpart because it is more resistant to the aphid damage which so often distorts young shoots of the latter. It forms a shrub of about fifteen feet, and is very attractive in mid-spring with snow-white blossoms and in autumn with pendulous clusters of translucent scarlet berries. The plant has a decided economic value also, the acid fruits being collected and used for jellies (hence the common name). A variety (considered by some a distinct species) equally valuable for edible fruits but not so ornamental, being lower and more straggly, is *edule:* Mooseberry, Squashberry, or Pimbina. *V. trilobum* has, collectively, a very wide range, inhabiting the cooler part of the continent from Labrador to Alaska, south to New York, the mountains of Pennsylvania, Ohio, Illinois, Indiana, Michigan, Wisconsin, South Dakota, Wyoming, Colorado, and Oregon on the Pacific Coast. It appears to do well in warm climates, though I haven't much information about its adaptability in the South. A selection named 'Wentworth' is in the trade. This is said by Donald Egolf of the USDA, an expert on the genus, to be "a vigorous, spreading bush with large, somewhat drooping clusters that matures fruit early."

High-bush Cranberry aphid-resistant.

HIGH-BUSH CRANBERRY
Viburnum trilobum
Flower

To many gardeners the term "hydrangea" conjures images of "florists' " hydrangeas, with their enormous heads of pink or blue flowers as lush, overblown, and hot-housy as cyclamen, cineraria, or football mum. To others, the term may evoke the old-fashioned 'Peegee,' *H. paniculata 'Grandiflora,'* a common standby in the average suburban garden and no mean summer-flowering shrub, though rather overused. Fewer gardeners picture the American species when the term is mentioned, though two of them are rather widely grown, and one is fairly common as a "snowball."

This last-named species is *H. arborescens*, in its cultivated form 'Grandiflora,' called also 'Hills of Snow.' It is a spreading bushy shrub with pleasing if rather unimpressive foliage and habit, covered in early summer with enormous heads of florets which equal florists' hydrangeas in size but are creamy white in color. Hydrangeas, like many viburnums, bear two types of blossom in each flower cluster—fertile flowers, which are small and unshowy, and sterile flowers, much larger and showier, which usually surround the cluster and serve as signals to pollinating insects. This type of cluster is popularly called the "lace-cap" type, and is often very attractive. Many cultivated hydrangeas and viburnums, however, are cultivars which have been selected because by some freak of nature all their blossoms have become sterile (and very showy). Such mutations as these would, of course, die out in the wild, but since a head of sterile flowers is much fuller and larger than a naturally mixed cluster, man has selected these and propagated them by shoots and cuttings. The result is that sterile-flowered viburnums, like the Japanese, Chinese, and European snowballs, and hydrangeas like the various florists' cultivars and the 'Peegee' and 'Hills of Snow,' are better represented in gardens than the less spectacular if more graceful species from which they derive.

'Hills of Snow' for a colorful summer shrub.

'Hills of Snow' is a valuable though somewhat garish summer shrub, blooming as it does in June and July when any flowering shrub is at a premium. The great heads cut well and are excellent in massive bouquets. One undoubted advantage of sterile flowers over fertile is that the former, because they never go to seed, last

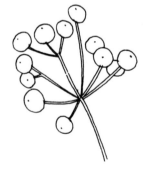

HIGH-BUSH CRANBERRY
Viburnum trilobum
Seeds

far longer on the bush. The business of the fertile flower, after all, is to become fertilized and perpetuate the species. The business of the sterile flower is to attract insects to the whole cluster; thus those which last longest will insure that insects are attracted over a longer period of time and that even late-opening fertile flowers are pollinated. 'Hills of Snow' is colorful for a long period, the flower clusters turning from bright green through chartreuse, greenish cream, and ivory as the flowers mature, and turning again greenish in age, then pinkish bronze, and finally drying a pale beige on the plant. This was what I erroneously called "Snowball" as a child. The dry flowerheads add a nice touch to the bleak winter landscape, and are excellent in winter bouquets. A recent cultivar of the species which has appeared on the market is called 'Annabelle.' It is reputedly larger and showier in bloom even than 'Hills of Snow.'

In nature, *Hydrangea arborescens* is found in woodlands, usually rocky and hilly, in the uplands from New York south to Florida. The species itself, though less showy than its previously mentioned cultivars, is worth growing for its dainty white lace-cap blossoms in June and July. These vary from four to six inches in width and consist of up to two hundred minute, cream, fertile florets surrounded by a dozen or so inch-wide sterile flowers. It will grow and bloom in considerable shade, where most summer-flowering shrubs tend to languish. A particularly attractive stand of this species grows about the fish pools in the "Glade" at Winterthur, arching their graceful, cinnamon-barked branches, each tipped with a creamy blossom head, over the rockbound, cool waters. This species is hardy throughout much of the United States (Zone 5). Closely related species which might be attempted locally: *H. radiata* (North and South Carolina), and *H. cinerea* (North Carolina and Tennessee, to Alabama).

At Winterthur also, I met my first representative of another very different native hydrangea, the Oakleaf (*H. quercifolia*) from the Deep South. A glance at a nonflowering plant of this species would lead one to suspect that it *was* an oak, perhaps, but certainly no hydrangea, for the leaves closely resemble those of the Red Oak. It is a robust, upright shrub, unlike the preceding, which is more spreading and "bushy." The fawn or light reddish brown exfoliating bark, very attractive in winter, is very distinctive. The new branches are rusty-felty, and the leaves, deep green above and whitish below in summer, are reddish bronze when unfolding and deep orange in the autumn. There is about the plant a suggestion of red pigment behind the green and white throughout the year.

Flowers of the Oakleaf Hydrangea are in elongate panicles, some a foot and a half in length. The starry, cream, fertile florets are clustered in bunches of a dozen to three dozen along the main axis of the panicle, each of these bunches crowned by a long-stemmed sterile floret, an inch and a quarter across, which consists of four overlapping petals. Because the sterile florets are on such long stems, the effect is that of a cloud of white butterflies around a spike of flowers.

As the fertile flowers go to seed and develop into green, jug-shaped capsules (*hydrangea* is Greek for "water jar" in allusion to these capsules), the sterile florets turn to a deep bronzy rose (with some sun) or soft apple-green (in shade), thus remaining colorful for quite a long time. The plant will grow in deep shade, and bloom sparsely. In sun, it blooms more abundantly, and the color of its autumn foliage and sterile florets is much more bright. It grows naturally in areas of rather acid soil, but seems to thrive in most ordinary garden soils under cultivation. It is hardy in climates comparable to that of coastal New York and eastern Pennsylvania. Hillier states that this shrub was introduced into Britain in 1803. It received the Award of Merit from the Royal Horticultural Society in 1928.

Hydrangeas may quite rightly be regarded as summer shrubs rather than spring bloomers, but since the two species discussed here really begin blooming around the time of the summer solstice, I see them as bridging the gap between the seasons. At Winterthur, certain individuals of *H. arborescens* begin blooming as early as the first week in June. That these are not all genetically the same variant is obvious because some have flowers of the lace-cap type while others have snowball flowers. Perhaps location is responsible. One stand grows in a sunny clearing in the middle of the woodlands. In any

Buckeyes and horse-chestnuts bridge gap between seasons.

case, these are joined within two or three weeks by the main body of their clan.

A totally unrelated genus which also bridges the gap between spring and summer is that of the buckeyes and horse-chestnuts, *Aesculus.* In fact, it is an even better example, for the first members of the genus to bloom (the exotic horse-chestnuts) begin in the middle of May when most spring flowers are at their height, and the last (at least among those I have grown), the Bottle-brush Buckeye, blooms in July.

There are several American species, most of them shrubs, or trees of medium size. In my view none of the taller species approaches the Common Horse-chestnut from Europe (or related species from the Himalayas or Japan) in beauty, though some are showy enough. There are at least two, however, in the South which are unique in their bright red flowers. These are excellent garden plants in their own right. In addition, one has produced a hybrid with the Common Horse-chestnut which combines vigor and flower size of the latter with red coloration of the former. The hybrid, known as *A. x carnea,* is fairly widely grown and a showy tree in May. Various named clones are on the market, most with flowers ranging from deep pink to coral red. The commonest is probably one called 'Briotti.'

Aesculus pavia, Red Buckeye, is native on the Coastal Plain from Virginia to Texas and Missouri. It is the other parent of the hybrid described above, and differs from its progeny in being smaller in stature (fifteen feet or so) and bearing smaller, more tubular flowers of a brighter red. Closely related to it is *A. splendens,* Flame Buckeye, native to the Deep South. It is supposedly showier and lower in stature, a shrub rather than a small tree. In the trade there is a great deal of confusion between the two. Plants sold to Winterthur by a respectable rare-plant nursery as *A. pavia humilis* (a dwarf form listed in the manuals) invariably turned out to be identical to plants received elsewhere as *A. splendens.* These are now about fifteen years of age, and are large, rounded shrubs of about ten feet, extremely attractive when they raise their upright panicles of soft red flowers in May. Plants which I bought simply as "Red Buckeye" at another nursery a year or two ago seem nearly identical to me. They begin to bloom at the height of three feet. Judging from my experience, I would say that one is safe in buying any native red buckeye species, in spite of nomenclatural confusion. They are all good garden plants.

As in all buckeyes and horse-chestnuts, the foliage is large and palmate (arranged in five to seven leaflets which radiate from a central point, like the spread fingers of one's hand). The color of these species is a good deep green, the prominent veining giving a somewhat quilted effect. The petiole of each leaf is often reddish. One great fault of all members of the genus is that they are susceptible, here at least, to a leaf-blotch disease which makes them very unsightly by late summer. The three species under discussion here seem not so susceptible to this disease.

The flower of the red buckeyes merits discussion on more than aesthetic grounds. It is tubular in shape but, unlike many flowers so formed (Cardinalflower, azalea, phlox, honeysuckle, and morning glory, to name a few), does not consist of petals fused into a true tube. Instead, it consists of four (rarely five) distinct petals which roll and overlap into a reasonable facsimile of a tube. The stamens protrude beyond the mouth. On the bases of shape and color, it seems reasonable to conclude that *A. pavia* and *A. splendens* are hummingbird flowers. That the petals of the Old World species are spreading rather than tubiform, are white, yellowish, or pinkish, and appear usually during the bee season in mid-spring, seems further evidence of the adaptation of our red species. The color of the latter, incidentally, though often called "scarlet" in manuals, is a softer, blander color, with a suffusion of pink slightly grayed. It is actually quite close to that of the Trumpet Honeysuckle. It is very pleasing, bright but not at all garish.

Another buckeye native to the Southeast warrants discussion here: *A. parviflora*, Bottle-brush Buckeye. It is different in almost every way from the foregoing; indeed, except for similarities in foliage and fruit, it would not be taken for a buckeye at all by the average gardener. The flowers are small, white, with very long pinkish stamens, disposed in great numbers on upright spikes a foot or more in length. The common name derives from the spike's resemblance to a white bottle-brush. These appear in early July, a period when comparatively few shrubs are in flower.

In habit the plant is a shrub reaching six or eight feet in height, which spreads rapidly from suckers and soon forms a dense colony. In sun, the individual stems cluster together and all attain the same height so that the effect is of a huge green flat-topped mass punctuated by the pointed flower spikes like white candles. In shade, the effect is altogether different. The plant becomes taller, slenderer, more wide-ranging, with stems contorted in strange, angular, often grotesque shapes, a long panicle of bloom lifting here and there toward the sun. There is an old specimen growing like this in the woodland surrounding one of the ponds at Longwood Gardens, and it is most interesting and ornamental. Since this buckeye is stoloniferous, it propagates with ease by division. I have read of a form with pink flowers, which sounds extremely interesting. Unfortunately, I have yet to see it.

THE TEA FAMILY

Stewartias superlative garden plants.

Few shrubs are more desirable or more coveted by knowledgeable gardeners than stewartias. There are perhaps seven species in cultivation, most of them from the Far East. All are superlative garden plants—tall, graceful shrubs or small trees with small, ovalish leaves and white flowers like a single camellia, with five petals and a central tuft of (usually) yellow stamens. Their habit is attractive. They are well clothed throughout the summer with good foliage which turns yellow, orange, or bronzy wine in autumn. The richly colored and flaking or peeling bark of many species is of interest in winter, as are the rich brown pyramidal seed capsules. There is little unattractive about any of them, and in addition most bloom after the main flush of spring bloom is past, thus giving color to the garden at a time when it is relatively scarce. They are members of the Tea family, *Theaceae*, an assemblage of plants so choice that each seems to have inspired its discoverer with the urge to commemorate a relative, a friend, or a colleague by naming it for him. We find few purely descriptive names in this family: instead, we encounter *Franklinia, Gordonia, Camellia, Ternstroemia, Cleyera,* all named after famous men, usually plantsmen. *Stewartia* honors John Stuart, Earl of Bute. Whether he was kin to the pretender to the English throne, the manuals do not say. The generic name was originally spelled as it is today. Later workers attempted to bring it into harmony with the way the earl usually spelled his surname, with a "u," by emending it to *Stuartia.* According to the rules of botanical nomenclature, however, the original spelling stands, but in some manuals the emended spelling is used.

Two stewartias are American, and excellent though the Asiatics may be, our natives in my view excel them. The Asiatic species usually met in cultivation are:

S. koreana (Korea): flowers to three inches wide; leaves ovate; habit upright, tall; bark flaking. Blooms late in June.

S. monadelpha (Japan): flowers about one and a half inches wide; leaves very narrow; habit upright. Late June.

S. pseudo-camellia (Japan): flowers two to two and a half inches; habit upright, tall; bark flaking. Blooms late June.

S. serrata (Japan): flowers about two inches wide, pendant; habit upright, treelike. Blooms early June.

S. sinensis (central China): flowers about one-and-a-half inches wide, the small overlapping petal and its opposite strong claret-pink; buds, bracts, and calyces bright pinkish maroon, showy; habit spreading or rounded rather than upright. Blooms early June.

Except for the last species, all these more or less resemble one another, differing mainly in flower size and relative width of the leaves. According to the literature, all attain a height of thirty to eighty feet in nature, though I have not seen any taller than twenty-five feet or so in this country. *S. sinensis* is quite distinct by reason of its different habit and red-pigmented flowers, as well as by its early blooming season.

The two American species are even more different. Neither is so tall, *S. malacodendron,* the Virginian Stewartia or Silky-camellia, seldom exceeding fifteen feet, and *S. ovata*, the Mountain Stewartia or Mountain-camellia just a little taller. Both are shapely small trees, often shrubby in cultivation. Both have glossy, bronze-tinted leaves that appear quilted by reason of their deeply impressed veins. Those of *ovata* have a lovely pubescent bloom on them, and have tips which attenuate to very long, sharp points.

A must for southern gardens: Silky-camellia.

The flowers of the Silky-camellia are spectacular, great white cups three inches across, with a prominent pale greenish conical pistil in the center, surrounded by myriad bright purple filaments tipped by pale blue anthers. The effect, though truly showy, is incongruously like a tiny sea urchin against a bed of white sand. In the plants I have seen, the petals tended to be marked with bright pink center stripes. This may have been due to weather conditions, but the result was beautiful.

The species is a native mainly of the Coastal Plain from lower Delmarva to Florida and Louisiana and, as might be expected from such a range, is not very hardy. According to Mrs. Henry, it grew well at her home near Philadelphia as long ago as 1938. A young specimen which was part of a collection of *Stewartia* species attempted at Winterthur died, but I do not think winter cold was the culprit. There is a fine young plant, a shrubby specimen about eight feet tall, in the nursery of Private Gardens, Inc., near Newark, Delaware. I would say that it is hardy in areas where temperatures do not go much below zero. In such areas it certainly should be attempted, and every garden in the South should grow it. One final distinction: it is the very first Stewartia to bloom, the flowers beginning in late May in Delaware.

The Mountain Stewartia complements its lowland relative in almost every way. It is one of the latest species to bloom, in July in Delaware. In typical form it has two-and-one-half-inch flowers which are white with yellow centers, reminiscent of the Asiatic species. In the form *grandiflora*, however, the centers are purple and the flowers are larger. There is a magnificent specimen of this form in Valley Garden Park northwest of the city of Wilmington. One July I wrote this description while standing in front of the tree:

Flower of *Stewartia ovata grandiflora:* more than four inches wide, the width of the widest of the five petals two inches, the flower a great white cup around a central puff of yellow-tipped deep violet stamens. In the very center is the white five-parted pistil. The stamens are of an electric purple, deep and glowing, a marvelous contrast to the petals. The petals are crisped and fluted, almost fringed, on the edges. The only comparison I can think of is the single white rose 'White Wings.'

The plant described is growing beside a brook which meanders through an open valley between densely wooded hills. It is a tree some ten feet tall, with a trunk about four inches in diameter. As it happens, this plant is difficult to measure because a vigorous Sweet Birch is growing with it, now dwarfing it by some ten or twelve feet. The stewartia is growing out and away from the birch, which will probably eventually kill it.

S. ovata is native in the mountains, not on the Coastal Plain except in a small area in Virginia. It may be found in the Blue Ridge and the Appalachian Plateau from Kentucky and Virginia south to Alabama and Georgia. It is hardy as far north as Ohio, Pennsylvania, and coastal Massachusetts.

A word on the nomenclature of this species. On the basis of some very important botanical differences, the botanist Cavanille in the eighteenth century proposed the genus *Malacodendron* for it, as distinct from *Stewartia* proper. He gave it the name *pentagynum,* "five-styled," on the basis of its most obvious distinguishing feature, its five-parted pistil. I do not know whether the other American species was named before or after this one, but apparently it never occurred to the botanists involved that they were compounding confusion for the layman. Here were two related and closely similar plants, both often known as stewartias (sometimes spelled stuartias), one sometimes called *S. ovata* and sometimes called *S. pentagyna,* or sometimes called *Malacodendron pentagynum,* not to be confused with the other species, which is always called *Stewartia malacodendron.*

The botanical differences cited above do provide an excellent means

MOUNTAIN STEWARTIA
Stewartia ovata

of telling the two species apart, especially the two purple-stamened forms, for the pistil of malacodendron is a perfect cone, with a single point, while that of *ovata* is divided into five very obvious segments. The seed capsule of the Silky-camellia is squat and hemispherical, whereas that of the Mountain-camellia is egg-shaped and prolonged into a distinct point or break. Either of these two native shrubs is desirable and beautiful, though neither is at all common in gardens here. In England they are more popular. According to Harold Hillier, *S. malacodendron* was introduced in 1742 and given a First Class Certificate by the Royal Horticultural Society in 1934. *S. ovata*, being a native of the less rapidly settled uplands, was not introduced into England until around 1800. Hillier makes no mention of the F.C.C. for this species, though I fail to see how the discriminating English could fail to grant one to the variety *grandiflora*.

There always seems something magnoliaceous about stewartias to me, in their foliage, bark, habit, and of course in their large, white cup-shaped blossoms. In most genealogies of the Plant Kingdom, the Tea and Magnolia families are placed far apart; nevertheless, many botanists consider the two families to derive from a similar ancestor, the "primitive" magnolias changing little through millions of years and the camellias and stewartias following a line of evolution leading toward "advanced" plants like rhododendrons and azaleas. Relationships between all these plants may be hypothetical, but cultural similarities are not. All members of the Tea family, like those of Magnolia and Heath, grow naturally in woods, thickets, bottomlands, moors, or swamps, where the soil is either humus-rich or very acid, and where they find abundant moisture throughout the growing season. Their requirements in cultivation are essentially the same. If you can grow one of these groups, you can grow them all.

Two close relatives of *Stewartia* native to the southern part of this country are, like members of that genus, beautiful flowering trees or shrubs. *Gordonia lasianthus*, the Loblolly-bay (also called Tan-bay, Black-laurel, and, erroneously, Red-bay) has much the same range as *Stewartia malacodendron* except that it does not cross the

Chesapeake. It is a magnificent evergreen tree which bears three-inch white flowers throughout the summer. As already mentioned, the Tea alliance has more than its share of commemorative names— a phenomenon which I have always thought attests to the ornamental qualities of the plants therein. One naturally assumes that Messrs. Gordon, Franklin, Stuart, Kamel, Cleyer, Ternstroem, et al. would be more greatly honored by having named after them genera of showy flowering plants rather than insignificant grasses or mosses. Gordonia, named for an eighteenth-century English nurseryman, is one of the most spectacular of all.

Like *Stewartia*, the genus occurs only in our Southeast and in eastern Asia. Our single species has large, glossy, evergreen leaves (as might be inferred by the occurrence of "bay" and "laurel" in its common names). It reaches seventy feet in the wild. Its one deficit is that like most southern broadleaved evergreens it is not very hardy. Just how hardy, or rather tender, it is, I am not sure. Very little is written about it in garden literature, and this is the one plant in this group that I have not grown—principally because I cannot find it! Wyman gives its hardiness as synonymous with its range— to southeastern Virginia. Since plants usually survive north of the areas in which they grow naturally, chances are that *Gordonia lasianthus* is somewhat hardier than it is listed. Another "bay," Bull-bay (*Magnolia grandiflora*), an evergreen tree with a similar range, thrives in central Delmarva, does very well in my garden in northern Delaware, and, in isolated hardy individuals, stands as far north as New York City.

GORDONIA *as spectacular as* MAGNOLIA GRANDIFLORA.

The great mystery to me is that this *Gordonia* has not become popular like *Magnolia grandiflora*, which is now grown throughout the world, or even like its relatives, the Stewartias. Typically, more has been written about it in modern times by Englishmen than by Americans. Hillier's manual calls it "a beautiful but tender, magnolia-like species attaining small tree size." His catalogues list it at a high price, which I assume means that it is highly coveted and therefore expensive, as, say, *Davidia*, the Dove-tree, is here. I was astounded to see in Mr. Hillier's manual that this plant was introduced into the

British Isles in 1768, doubtless by the agency of the Bartrams. For William Bartram wrote of it eloquently in his *Travels* (1791), and at this point I think it appropriate that this earliest of friends of the American flora describe it:

> The tall aspiring Gordonia lasianthus, which now stood in my view in all its splendour, is every way deserving of our admiration. Its thick foliage, of a dark green colour, is flowered over with large milk-white fragrant blossoms, on long slender elastic peduncles, at the extremities of its numerous branches, from the bosom of the leaves, and renewed every morning; and that in such incredible profusion, that the tree appears silvered over with them, and the ground beneath covered with the fallen flowers. It at the same time continually pushes forth new twigs, with young buds on them; and in the winter and spring the third year's leaves, now partly concealed by the new and perfect ones, are gradually chang- ing colour, from green to golden yellow, from that to a scarlet, from scarlet to crimson; and lastly to a brownish purple, and then fall . . . to the ground. So that the Gordonia lasianthus may be said to change and renew its garments every morning throughout the year; and every day appears with unfading lustre. And moreover, after the general flowering is past, there is a thin succession of scattering blossoms to be seen, on some parts of the tree, almost every day throughout the remaining months, until the floral season returns again. Its natural situation, when growing, is on the edges of shallow ponds, or low wet grounds on rivers, in a sandy soil, the nearest to the water of any other tree, so that in drouthy seasons its long serpentine roots which run near or upon the surface of the earth, may reach into the water. When the tree has arrived to the period of perfect magnitude, it is sixty, eighty or an hundred feet high, forming a pyramidal head.

The last of the native *Theaceae* is beyond doubt the most popular, probably owing as much to the mystery shrouding its discovery and introduction into cultivation as to any superiority over the others. This is the Franklin Tree, *Franklinia alatamaha*. It was found near the Georgia–Florida border by the naturalists John and William Bartram in 1765, observed and described a few times thereafter by William, the son, and then it disappeared. It has not been seen in the wild since 1803. Fortunately, the Bartrams had collected from the wild material which they grew in their Philadelphia garden. All the plants in cultivation today derive from these plants. It was named by the younger Bartram for another famous Philadelphian, Benjamin Franklin.

Franklinia has more to recommend it than an interesting history, however. It forms a small, graceful tree which may be grown with a single trunk or allowed to become a multiple-stemmed, tall shrub. Its light green, glossy leaf is broader toward the tips than the base, five or six inches long, narrowing to an inch-long pink petiole. The prominent midrib is also pinkish, as are the young leaves. The leaf-edges are shallowly sawtoothed. The smooth bark is dark brown, almost chestnut on the supple, upright branches. In July globular apple-green buds appear near the tip of each branch, developing slowly and by early August opening into beautiful three-inch white blossoms. The plant continues blooming into October.

FRANKLINIA *for late summer and fall blossoms.*

Like its relatives, *Franklinia* has flowers which are white, five-petaled, with a showy central bunch of stamens. The five petals overlap in bud, the uppermost forming a sort of protective cap for the others. This petal never develops as fully as they do, but remains a little smaller and more concave, thus making the flower somewhat asymmetrical in appearance. Most *Theaceae* have a similar flower. The species is probably unique as a flowering shrub—I can't think of anything remotely similar blooming at the same time—and is invaluable for the garden. Some of my most enjoyable moments have been passed on cool, dewy September mornings in front of my small Franklin Tree, marveling at the fresh, *vernal* appearance of these blossoms which appear just as the year begins its dark decline into winter. The boss of golden stamens in the center of each is especially beautiful. Bartram apparently found this feature as attractive as I, for in a quaint mixture of science and poetry he writes that the flowers are "ornamented with a crown or tassel of gold coloured refulgent staminae in their centre."

Franklinia, like *Stewartia* and *Gordonia*, grows naturally in locations of acid soil, and does well under cultivation in humus-rich or peaty soil. I think that it is quite adaptable, for it does well in my soil (admittedly acid) with no preparation, and has grown for years in the rather barren upland, neutral soil at Winterthur. From its range one would expect it to be quite tender, but it is not. In fact it is as hardy as *Stewartia ovata*—standing as far north as southern New England. I have seen some fine specimens in Westchester County, New York. If treated like an azalea, it is sure to survive. If subjected to extreme drought, it drops its flower buds, then its leaves.

The single species in this genus has been placed by some botanists in *Gordonia*, where it becomes *G. pubescens*. It really differs from *G. lasianthus* outwardly in only a few ways—in possessing deciduous leaves, in blooming later, and in bearing flowers on much shorter stalks. Because it is unknown as a wild plant it has nothing similar to the multitude of interesting folk names of Loblolly-bay. One southern manual gives only one, clearly literary but particularly poignant: "Lost Camellia." The specific name *alatamaha* refers to the Altamaha River, along whose shores the plant once grew. Whence the extra "a," I do not know.

A shrub native to the Coastal Plain from Virginia to Florida which is surprisingly hardy, valuable for late summer bloom, and of surpassing botanical interest is the Swamp Cyrilla or Leatherwood, *Cyrilla racemiflora*. It makes a shapely bush, at times a tree to thirty-five feet, well furnished with rather small and narrow leaves of deep glossy green, and white flowers in numerous three- to four-inch spikes in August. The flowers echo those of *Itea* or *Clethra*, both of which share its habitat and, perhaps, its pollinators. In the North, Cyrilla is only partly evergreen, a proportion of its foliage turning bright red or yellow in autumn and falling. In the South it is quite evergreen.

The plant belongs to a small family with only three genera, these in North and South America. Swamp Cyrilla has a surprising range: southeastern United States, the West Indies, and eastern South America. A plant of this species has stood for many years at Winterthur, blooming each summer. It is hardy in Zone 6. The family may be related to the hollies, and indeed Cyrilla resembles in many ways one of the smaller-leaved evergreen hollies. Cultivation given hollies suits it perfectly also. At present it seems to be limited mainly to gardens of connoisseurs, a pity. It roots easily from cuttings and transplants easily when small, two qualities which should endear it to nurserymen.

My experience with the plant is limited to specimens grown at Winterthur, where I have seen it flower but never fruit. *Gray's Manual of Botany* (which lists its common names as He-huckleberry and Black Ti-ti as well as those already given) says the following about the plant: "Autumnal foliage scarlet or orange, gorgeous when mingled with the bright yellow fruit."

MAGNOLIAS

The name magnolia surely ranks with lily, rose, gardenia, and jasmine as evocative of both beauty and as sweet a fragrance as any in the floral kingdom. One thinks of feminine complexions—creams, lotions, bath salts, and colognes, which give the cheek that creamy color, that delicate bloom that the magnolia petal alone possesses. It is ironic that the commonest magnolia in the United States, the Saucer Magnolia, *M. x soulangeana*, is neither particularly fragrant nor soft in color. In fact, its petals are usually suffused with a magenta-pink which no woman would want as a skin tone. *Magnolia x soulangeana* is a hybrid, developed in France, of two Asiatic species. It blooms very early in spring and is admittedly gorgeous (better at a distance than close up, except in its white and softer pink variants). Many American species are as beautiful, however, and more interesting in foliage and habit, thus more valuable. It is to these one must turn, also, for the true tone of white underlaid peach and gold which we know as "magnolia."

Sweet-bay excellent small tree for landscaping.

The only magnolia truly native in my immediate area is the Sweet-bay, *M. virginiana*, and, since this species has perhaps the widest distribution of the genus, it seems a good one to begin with. In the wild it is often seen as a straggling swamp plant, though some specimens become trees fifty feet tall or more. Under cultivation, however, it grows usually as a bushy and densely furnished small tree, an excellent landscape subject which will grow happily in ordinary soil. In May and all through June it is starred with three-inch flowers of creamy color and texture and delicious fragrance. All summer long its glossy green leaves, with striking blue-white undersurfaces, are attractive. They fall very late in the season, and in some variants remain throughout the winter. The manuals say that plants in the north of the species' range lose their leaves in winter while those in the south do not. I notice a great deal of individual variation, some plants in my area being almost evergreen while others are quite deciduous. Plants in more protected spots seem to retain their foliage longer than those in exposed locations, also, and young plants seem more nearly evergreen than old ones. The botanical variety *australis* ("southern") is quite evergreen even in cold climates. Its leaves last for twelve months, turning yellowish and falling in June, just after the first flush of new growth has hardened. This variety is also botanically separable on the basis of the thick silky fuzz on new growth. Plants I have observed at Winterthur, at the U.S. National Arboretum, and in my own garden have slightly more deeply colored leaves with undersides of a really brilliant blue-white. Their most obvious distinction, though, is in habit: they are all single-stemmed, tall, upright, narrow, almost fastigiate in growth. Ordinary *M. virginiana* tends to become an irregular, many-stemmed shrub, at least in sun.

It used to be that one had to go to the swamps to see Sweet-bay. Now, however, it is increasingly used in landscaping, and is sometimes even available at garden centers. It is remarkably drought-resistant for a plant of wet soil. In the drought and record-breaking heat of August 1973, I watched a planting of various shrubs which included Sweet-bay, in front of a hospital in Chester, Pennsylvania. By September every tree and shrub in the group had either yellowed or discolored leaves except the Sweet-bay, which remained as fresh-looking as June.

The species is sometimes called *Magnolia glauca*, especially in older books. This name, though now invalid, is more appropriate than *virginiana*, for the leaves are certainly glaucous (silvery-gray), at least underneath, while the plant can hardly be called Virginian, native as it is from Massachusetts south to Florida and east to Texas. To early European botanists, Virginia meant the eastern United States in general. It is hardy to Zone 6. I have no information on the hardiness of var. *australis*, but a young tree thrives for me in Zone 7.

Magnolia grandiflora, Bull-bay ("bull" being an allusion to its large size), Southern or Great-flowered Magnolia, or simply "Magnolia," is without a doubt the best known of the native species in this country, a massive evergreen tree native from North Carolina to Florida, west on the Coastal Plain to east Texas, and up the Mississippi valley as far as Arkansas. This is perhaps the finest flowering tree in the world, and it is grown extensively wherever it is hardy, in this country and abroad. Throughout our South it grows easily, of course, and will do well farther west as long as it is given humus-rich soil and plenty of moisture in summer. On the Pacific slope it grows to perfection. In the East it survives as far north as New York City, though only in sheltered sites. On the estates around Philadelphia it is seen fairly often, there being an enormous specimen in a garden at Moorestown, New Jersey, just across the river. There are several large trees of this species growing well in the protection of the Winterthur Museum, some of them espaliered against its wall (a good way to grow tender shrubs or trees in cold climates). I have several young trees in my garden, standing free, though protected by large conifers, and they are doing well. In southern Delaware they feel at home. There are two on a lawn near Ocean View, near the southern border of the state, which are as large and as impressive as any I have seen in the Carolinas. (The owner told me that these were planted thirty-five years ago.) It seems that some clones are hardier than others, so it is well to experiment if you live in border-line areas (that is, where the minimum winter temperature occasionally plunges to zero but seldom far below). This is one American plant which is commonly offered at garden centers and roadside nurseries (usually as seedlings in gallon cans), at least in my area. There is no difficulty in procuring it. Its lacquered, dark sage-green

MAGNOLIA GRANDIFLORA
perhaps finest flowering tree in world.

leaves, often a rich red-brown below, and its enormous creamy-white blossoms, produced from early June throughout the summer, recommend it to gardeners from Zone 7 south. I recently acquired a container-grown plant of the clone 'St. Mary's,' which blooms at an early age. It is less than three feet tall and is blooming in the container.

The rest of the native magnolias are rather different in aspect. Tallest, hardiest, and, unfortunately, least showy, is the Cucumber-tree, *M. acuminata*. This is a real tree, of oak or elm proportions, reaching nearly a hundred feet when mature. Apart from its massiveness, it hasn't much that is distinctive about it. The flowers, cup-shaped, two or three inches long, are hardly in proportion to the size of the tree, and are a plain greenish or yellow-green in color. I frankly cannot ever remember noticing one, though I have known the tree since I was a child. Cucumber-tree is native in and west of the Alleghenies as far north as Ontario and as far south as Arkansas. It is hardy in Zone 5. The common name refers to the fruiting cones or strobili, which before ripening somewhat resemble small cucumbers.

Native only in a small area of Georgia is a close relative, so rare that it has no common name. *M. cordata* is so close botanically to the preceding that it is often considered a mere variety. For horticultural purposes, however, it is quite different, for it is a shrub or small tree seldom exceeding twenty feet in height, with two-and-one-half-inch bright yellow flowers. Its leaves are about five inches long (half the size of *acuminata's*) and are rather broad and rounded in shape. *Cordata*, "heart-shaped" in Latin, presumably refers to the deciduous leaves, though they become heart-shaped only with considerable exercise of imagination. This magnolia is a showy little thing and should certainly be grown more than it is. Its flowers are early (for an American species), appearing in this latitude during the first and second weeks in May. In color they are that shade of warm bisque yellow that one finds in Mollis azaleas. Since it blooms at about the same time as these azaleas, it offers considerable opportunity for combination with them. I would like to try it some-

Cucumber-tree hardiest of the native magnolias.

day with another azalea, the southern native *Rhododendron aus-trinum,* which is quite similar in color—and perhaps grows with *Magnolia cordata* in the wild. According to all the books, this mag-nolia is a small tree. A specimen at Longwood Gardens, however, is ninety feet tall. It can be procured (I recently bought one) at nurseries which specialize in unusual plants. It is hardy in New York City and in eastern Massachusetts.

There is a curious similarity of events surrounding the discovery and cultivation of this plant and that of *Franklinia* (see pp. 146–7). Both were discovered in the wilds of eastern Georgia—*Franklinia* in 1765, *M. cordata* about thirty-five years later. Both were subse-quently "lost" in the wild, the only plants then known being those in cultivation. *Franklinia* has not been rediscovered to this day in spite of intensive searching. Our magnolia was rediscovered growing in the wild in 1913, over a century after its initial discovery! In both cases cultivated plants assured at least the survival of the species.

The remaining American magnolias have many things in common: they are all small or medium-sized trees with large white or cream flowers and enormous deciduous leaves which are clustered in whorls toward the ends of the branches, giving a lush, tropical effect (like banana trees). They are usually called "Umbrella Trees" because of this effect, an apt description but one which often confuses them with cultivars of both catalpa and Chinaberry, which is commonly called "Umbrella Tree" in the South.

A widespread species in *M. tripetala,* called usually Umbrella Tree or Elkwood. It is native in the Appalachian system from mid-Penn-sylvania and Ohio to Oklahoma and Alabama, a slender woodland tree to forty feet, with large, light green, thin leaves a foot and a half or more long, and creamy flowers which attain a width of about eight inches. It blooms in late May, with rather ill-scented flowers. This is one of the easiest magnolias to grow, but its rather narrow-petaled blossoms pale when compared to those of the next species.

For sheer spectacle, the prize must surely go to the Bigleaf Mag-nolia, *M. macrophylla.* A tree of fifty feet or so in height, native from

Combine: MAGNOLIA CORDATA *and Mollis azaleas.*

For sheer spectacle: the Big-leaf Magnolia.

the slopes of the Alleghenies in West Virginia and Kentucky west to Arkansas and south to Louisiana and western Florida, it is hardy to Massachusetts and middle New York in the East, and well worth growing wherever there is enough room for it. Everything about the tree is *big*. Its light green leaves, whitish beneath, grow often three feet in length. So tropical-looking are they that once my friend Dick Ryan used them at a Hawaiian *luau* in place of banana leaves, and no one knew the difference. Its flowers are sometimes a foot and a half across. In June 1970, I picked a bloom from a tree of a friend and jotted down this description: "fifteen-inch flower composed of six segments, the three outer about eight inches long and four inches wide, the three inner about six and one half by three. Color rich waxy cream-white, the three inner petals each with a purple crescent at base. Stigma ivory, dark dotted. Stamens numerous, yellow, soon falling. Flower turns soft brown as it ages. Shape: a great flat bowl with the tip of each segment dipping downward in a graceful curve. Absolutely spectacular—with its collar of giant green leaves, a bouquet three feet across!" I should have mentioned that it is fragrant, with that rich perfume that most magnolias have. It blooms the first week in June.

Bigleaf Magnolia is less well known than M. *tripetala*, though both are rather common in cultivation. Some gardeners confuse the two, but they are really quite different, *macrophylla* being bigger in all its parts and much showier as well as later in blossom. A sure guide to identification is the shape of the leaf-base. In *tripetala* this is wedge-shaped, tapering gradually until it meets the petiole, while in *macrophylla* there is an abrupt flare outward on each side, producing two distinct *auriculae*, literally "ear lobes," at the base of the leaf.

The remaining American magnolias are "Umbrella Trees" like the two preceding species and are quite rare. Since I have not grown any of them, I am reluctant to discuss them. All, from published descriptions, seem more or less like either of the two preceding. *Magnolia fraseri* of the southern Appalachians has smaller leaves and flowers than *macrophylla* and leaves with very long auricles.

This is another of the species that Bartram writes of in his *Travels* (he calls it *Magnolia auriculata*). The "very large rosaceous, perfectly white, double or polypetalous flower" he finds attractive, but he finds the leaves, which are more obviously auricled than those of *macrophylla*, most distinct. He takes pains to describe the "two long narrow ears or lappets, one on each side of the insertion of the petiole." *M. fraseri* is hardy at the Arnold Arboretum near Boston.

Finally we have *M. pyramidata* and *M. ashei*. Both, from what I can find on them, resemble *macrophylla* but are much smaller in all their parts. I can find no accurate accounts of cultivation of either. *M. pyramidata*, which may not be specifically distinct from *M. fraseri*, is native in the southern Appalachians of Georgia and Alabama and into Florida. *M. ashei*, which may be no more than a subspecies of *macrophylla*, is found only in Florida.

A word on the care and use of these plants. Magnolias have long, sparse, fleshy roots. It is difficult to get a compact root ball when transplanting them, and the damaged roots tend to rot when subjected to prolonged periods of cold and dampness. The best time to plant them, in my experience, is early spring. With the evergreen species spring planting is an absolute necessity (in the South, of course, these strictures may not apply). As usual with difficult materials, the best rule applying to size of plant is: the smaller the better. As much of the root system should be saved as possible, and as much as possible of the soil it grew in should come along with the plant. I have had good results with rather large Sweet-bays (six to eight feet tall, but leggy) dug from densely shaded woodland in early spring and watered profusely during the first year or two after transplanting. Leggy plants like the foregoing should be cut back severely, since they will break profusely from the base and trunk in good light anyway. Cutting them back forces this new growth and in addition balances the shock to the roots more adequately. The soil for magnolias in general should be similar to that used for azaleas, camellias, and hollies—rich in humus and more or less on the acid side. In the wild they will be found invariably in the rich litter beneath big trees, or along stream or pond edges.

Transplanting magnolias? The smaller the better.

Swamp dwellers like Sweet-bay will do well under the above conditions, though they will grow in poorly drained soil also.

Some other considerations: first, many magnolias do not begin blooming until they reach a large size, especially the tree species. Some which bloom when quite small, though, are *cordata, virginiana,* and to a lesser degree *tripetala* and *grandiflora.* The big-leaved species are overpowering in small gardens unless very carefully placed. *Cordata* or *virginiana* are good choices where space is at a premium. This is not to say that species such as *macrophylla* should be excluded from small gardens purely on principle. I have seen it used very effectively in a limited space. One should simply bear in mind that its exaggerated proportions may cause any space in which it is placed (or any structures nearby) to appear much smaller than it really is. The large-leaved species make magnificent specimen plants, at their best in a sweep of lawn or at the edge of a woodland. The same applies, I suppose, to all magnolias. Remember that leaf texture in the big-leaf species is quite thin. The plants suffer in windswept locations. A farmhouse near Rehoboth Beach has two trees of *macrophylla* in its dooryard which always look crouching and stunted, beleaguered by sea winds—in a word, unhappy.

VII

Early Summer

The first day of summer, the earth at summer solstice and days so long that night seems forever in coming. Hayfields cut, grainfields ripening, and along the roadsides a summer pall hot and dust-laden on the seeding grasses. The whistle of a bobwhite whips through my open window as I drive down a country road, the only sharp and penetrating sound in a landscape of dulled and softened outlines and noises.

Late June is a lull in flowering. The spring flowers which painted woodland and roadsides a few weeks before have finished blooming, are setting fruit. The flowers of late summer, the butterfly season, are not yet ready to open. The result is a landscape that is quiet. There are, of course, some flowers—no season save the dead of winter is entirely bloomless. An occasional *Viburnum pubescens* still shows its flat, creamy umbels, and along all the fencerows its much more weedy relative the common Elder (*Sambucus canadensis*) is covered with similar creamy heads. Still, compared to the floral display which only a few weeks previously graced the countryside, the landscape is now dull.

All the more spectacular then are the occasional instances of really showy plants which occur on my travels. When, for example, I pass a thicket or wood-edge where a catalpa is blooming, its great candelabrum trusses of white trumpets raised above the enormous pale green leaves, the almost tropical showiness of the tree is the more pronounced because of the season in which it blooms.

CATALPA

The genus *Catalpa* contains ten or so species, among the showiest flowering trees in the world, native to eastern North America and eastern Asia. Only two species are really common in cultivation, however, both American natives. Neither is native in the East, but at least one is so completely naturalized here that it is thought of as native by all but botanists. This species is *Catalpa bignonioides*, the Southern or Common Catalpa. The other species is the Western Catalpa, *C. speciosa*. They are closely similar to each other, though there are important differences between them that it behooves the gardener to know. Both are trees with very large, more or less heart-shaped leaves, tubular white flowers spotted purple and yellow which appear in late spring and early summer, and long, slender, cylindrical seed capsules (the "Indian beans" of many a country boy's childhood) which are conspicuous in winter.

The Common Catalpa is a spreading tree, broader than tall, which seldom exceeds fifty feet in height. Its flowers are a bit smaller than those of its western relative, but there are more in the cluster, so that in its effect it is definitely the showier of the two. It blooms in late June, which removes it from all competition with its relative, for it blooms as the western species is fading; there is little overlap, and the two plants combined give almost a month of superlative flowering.

For a month of superlative bloom: combine native catalpas.

I had seen these trees in bloom all my life, but had not really looked closely enough at the flowers until I had to describe them for this book. On close inspection I saw many very interesting details, some of which are the following: the panicles arise from the tips of the branches. On a big tree, with every branch tip a cluster of flowers seven inches long and five broad, the effect is stunning. The flowers are on branches of a central stalk or rachis some eight or nine inches long. Branches and branchlets of the panicle are in threes. A sample panicle had four whorls of main branches, three per whorl, plus two single flowers at the tip. Each branch divided into three branchlets, each of which ended in three flowers. The total number in the panicle was 110. Since the individual flower measures more than an inch long by almost two inches wide, one can see the sort of effect this gives. Each cluster of three branches arises from alternate sides of the main rachis, so that each tends to fill out the spike from different sides.

The flower is roughly trumpet-shaped, with five lobes, three above and two below, the margins very much frilled and crisped. The two stamens and single pistil, clustered together into a point, protrude slightly from the top of the mouth. On the floor of the mouth are two ridges which run back into the flower's throat. Along these ridges are spots of brilliant cadmium yellow, obviously nectar guides. The yellow spills out onto the lower lobes of the flower. The throat is finely stippled with royal purple, also, which gives it a dark effect. This spills out onto the three lower lobes around the cadmium blotches. These colors, against the very pure whiteness of the blossom, are very bright. The general effect is of a dense pyramid of flowers, all very white with dark interiors. The flowers are fragrant, but not heavily so. I noticed honeybees, wasps, fireflies, and bumblebees among the blossoms, the last predominating. The throat is just the right size for a bumblebee, his furry back rubbing against the pistil as he enters and dislodging the pollen from the stamens as he backs out.

Originally native only in the South, the species is hardy into southern New England, and is naturalized throughout the East. My childhood memories include those of many expeditions to "Indian Cigar" trees, to collect the pods for later smoking in secret. I am not sure now whether these trees were *bignonioides* or *speciosa*, since I was not looking for flowers at the time.

C. speciosa, a tree of the Mississippi Valley, is also widely planted and naturalized. In fact, I have recently found it more common in my area than the other species. Its most obvious difference from its relative is manner of growth: it is upright rather than spreading, and reaches almost twice the height. Even young trees have this distinctive habit. It blooms early in June, a good two weeks earlier than *C. bignonioides*, with slightly larger flowers that are less heavily marked with purple and yellow but otherwise similar. The total effect of its flowers is, as has been remarked already, less showy because the truss is more lax and open. The Common Catalpa is showier, and is perhaps more valuable because it flowers later, when fewer comparable trees and shrubs are in blossom. However, both are excellent flowering trees, and the Western species might be preferred where an upright form is wanted, or where a tree flowering from early to mid-June is required.

By far the most common form of catalpa seen in American gardens is the "Umbrella Tree," the so-called *Catalpa bungei* (of nurserymen, not the true species, which is a native of China), actually a dwarf form of the common species grafted on normal trunks at about shoulder height. Planted eternally in pairs, in front of houses and flanking front walks, these grafts are given haircuts each autumn, so that all winter long we see a thick trunk topped by a crown of bristling branches lopped off at two inches. In spring the plant commences, or rather recommences growth, and makes a comfortably expanding globe of light green foliage surmounting the thick trunk all summer long. Why these "Umbrella Trees" are so popular with the American public has long puzzled me. They do not bloom. There isn't the least thing graceful about their habit. They are absolutely hideous from the time they are lopped back in autumn until they are well in growth in late spring. I suspect that their appeal is partly prestige or faddishness and partly the fact that of all plant material they respond most easily to the pruning shears. Those gardeners who spend their waking hours trimming their privets, forsythias, flowering-quinces, arbor-vitaes, and spireas into perfect globes love the "Umbrella Tree," for with one pruning it makes a summer-long sphere.

The normal catalpas, of course, are not trees for the front walk, unless the front yard is quite large. They are trees on the grand scale, and their huge foliage especially gives a dwarfing effect to their surroundings. They make small yards look even smaller. Yet for all this, the almost tropical effect of their foliage, flowers, and fruit is impressive, and I have seen many a backyard dominated by a catalpa that was a most interesting place.

"Catalpa" is a variant of "Catawba," an Indian word—the name of a tribe and a word which Thomas Wolfe used in place of his native North Carolina in his books. Catalpas grow quickly and are easy to establish and transplant. They are quite indifferent to soil conditions, provided that the soil contains at least some nutrients. I have a thriving young plant of *speciosa* at present which I pulled out of pure white sand at the base of a pier along the salt estuary of the Indian River in southern Delaware. Its parent is growing with Loblolly Pines and Spanish Oaks in the acid sand a few feet back from the river. Periodic floods raise the salinity of the soil there to toxic levels, killing many of the larger oaks and pines, yet the Catalpa persists, not happy perhaps (its growth is stunted and its leaves are small), but still living and reproducing. One wise consideration in transplanting this species: its large leaves lose a great deal of moisture. Transplant in early spring if possible, before it breaks into leaf.

Catalpas: transplant easily, grow quickly.

A word might be inserted here about a tree which is often mistaken for Catalpa: the Empress or Princess Tree, *Paulownia tomentosa.* It blooms in early spring, before the leaves appear, with large clusters of foxglove-like flowers of clear, rich lavender. *Paulownia* belongs to a different family, has a different flower color and a different blooming date, yet when not in flower it is very similar to *Catalpa bignonioides*. I shall not soon forget the effect at Winterthur when half of a planting of newly purchased "Catalpas" (bought and planted, I might stress, for their flower color and especially their late blooming season) bloomed in mid-May with clear lavender flowers! They were, of course, Paulownias which some nurserymen had mistaken for Catalpas.

Actually, only the fact that they were young trees permitted the misidentification, for mature Princess Trees, even though they are closely similar to Catalpas in leaf and habit, have always either developing flower buds (clustered at branch tips and covered with rusty down) or seed capsules (oval, beaked capsules, very different from the long cylinders of *Catalpa*). *Paulownia* is actually a native of East Asia, but it is quite extensively naturalized in North America, especially around cities. It is a member of the *Scrophulariaceae*, a family which includes such herbaceous garden favorites as foxgloves and snapdragons but few trees.

Catalpa, on the other hand, belongs to the related but distinct family *Bignoniaceae*, a mainly tropical family which is represented by very few species in colder regions, and these mainly vines. A close relative is a very abundant and representative American plant, the Trumpet-vine, *Campsis radicans*.

ROADSIDE WEEDS

July first. The landscape is empty of any color save green. A few roadside weeds—Chicory, Queen Anne's Lace, white and yellow Melilot, daisies, Common Milkweed, Black-eyed Susan, Tawny Day-lily—are in bloom, but these seem to congregate right along the roadsides and do not count for much in the total landscape. The long view is now almost entirely a deep and restful green.

Spring is a time of color everywhere, including the air—the white and pink of dogwood and shad bush scattered through the forests, the pale pinks, beiges, chartreuses of oak catkins and unfolding leaves, the vivid pink of the wild crab, the magenta of the redbud. Late summer is, on the other hand, a time of horizontal sheets of color—whole fields golden with bur-marigolds and goldenrod, purple with Joe-pye, ironweed, asters, white with boneset. But early summer is a transition: color has left the forest and thickets, has not yet appeared in the fields and marshes. One has therefore to look a bit harder than usual for good plants in bloom in the wild during this period.

Needless to say, they are there. I am strongly tempted, always, by the so-called roadside weeds. On dewy early mornings there is, for example, no lovelier sight than Chicory and daylilies blooming together in blue and orange by the roadside. The Chicory unfortunately closes in the afternoon, but there is available in the wild no blue with quite the exquisite cerulean quality of this plant and it has the bonus of attracting goldfinches. The Tawny Daylily (*Hemerocallis fulva*), like Chicory not a true native but a naturalized immigrant, is superseded in the garden by the magnificent new cultivars of *Hemerocallis*, but it is still excellent in out-of-the-way spots and as a binder for eroded banks and hillsides. It is a vigorous plant, spreading rapidly by stolons, but it does not seed. 'Europa,' the form naturalized in this country, is a triploid whose genetic makeup prevents the setting of seed. Its origin is a total mystery. Many parts of the plant, by the way, are edible, and highly valued by Oriental cooks.

When I discussed this book with Charles van Ravenswaay, the director of the Winterthur Museum, he asked me half jokingly whether I was going to tell people how to get rid of such plants as Evening-primrose, once they'd succeeded in establishing them in their gardens. Well, I suppose the best thing to do is not establish the hayfield weeds such as Evening-primrose, or the rest of the plants I will mention in this section, in your *garden*. They are successful plants whose success most often depends on producing copious seeds, and they will seed themselves anywhere to the detriment of anything weaker. On the other hand, if you have a weed problem to begin with, I see no reason to prefer Lamb's-quarters and Crabgrass to them, so you might introduce them. The ideal place for them, however, is a field, mowed once a year, in spring, where they might be introduced and allowed to establish themselves. Such a planting might include the three plants just mentioned, as well as Wild Daisies, Black-eyed Susans, Milkweeds, St.-John's-wort, Starthistle (*Centaurea americana*), Viper's Bugloss (*Echium vulgare*), and others, and would be a medley of white, yellow, orange, blue, and mauve throughout much of the summer. One might even mow this field again in midsummer, after most of the plants have passed their peak of flowering, and expect a second crop of fall flowers

Confine roadside weeds to fields mowed once or twice a year.

from nearly all the species mentioned. To get such a planting started, simply collect seeds in abundance and scatter them where plants are desired. If the field already supports a heavy growth of grasses, it might be plowed and disked to great advantage, and the seeds of the plants scattered on the bare ground before or after disking (keep in mind that wild birds will eat many of the seeds that are broadcast on the bare ground if they are not raked or disked in).

Little remains to be said about these plants, since they are so familiar to all of us. A few things bear mention, though. *Daucus carota*, Wild Carrot or Queen Anne's Lace, is a pernicious weed with an exquisite flower. It is a wonderful addition to any cut bouquet and may be very effectively dyed other colors if one wishes to disguise it. I have seen really charming arrangements with flowers of this plant lightly tinted pastel pink and blue with floral spray-paint. This may be gilding the lily, I suppose. The wildflower really needs no disguising. Evening-primrose, *Oenothera biennis*, is the homeliest member of a large genus, some of which are excellent garden plants. It is also the most successful member, and its light tan candelabrum spikes of urn-shaped seed capsules may be seen in almost every weed patch in America. Its pale yellow flowers are pretty, but not quite in proportion to the robust plant. They also close in bright sunlight. I would, however, always have a patch of Evening-primroses if I could, because they are a staple of goldfinches, who rip open the capsules and feed on the small dark seeds all winter long.

Evening-primroses: staple of goldfinches.

Echium vulgare or Viper's Bugloss, a plant which sounds equally horrible in English or Latin, is really a very beautiful plant. I first saw it at sea, from the ferry which travels between Woods Hole, Massachusetts, and Martha's Vineyard. As we pulled into Vineyard Haven I noticed what seemed to be a whole corner of the island a magnificent blue in color. Later, in the borrowed car of a friend, I discovered what the plants were (and even, in my ignorance, collected seeds for my garden).

It is a borage, and like its relative *Mertensia* exhibits a curious combination of pinkish buds and pure blue open flowers. The leaves and stems are rough and almost spiny, so that eradicating unwanted plants is nearly as painful as eradicating thistles. It is a biennial, producing the first year a rosette of leaves and no more. These can take a great deal of abuse. I blush to admit that I have allowed it to seed in my lawn, survive a year's mowing, and bloom—much stunted, of course—between mowings the following year! It is attractive as a garden plant, but must be watched, as one of its colloquial names, "Blue-devils," implies. "Bugloss," incidentally, has nothing to do with losses or bugs, but is from the Greek *bous* and *glossa*, "ox" and "tongue," perhaps because the rough, tongue-shaped basal leaves suggest ox tongues.

So much for the showy weeds. Looking further afield, we come to a more delicate and less familiar selection of plants which bloom in early July. The most showy of this group, "Adam's Needle," is perhaps not quite meritorious of the term "delicate," since it reaches six or more feet in height. Yet with its cluster of basal swordlike leaves and its tall open panicle of white flowers it gives an airy effect that few other plants achieve. *Yucca filamentosa* is the species native on the East Coast as far north as Delaware and southern New Jersey. But there is considerable variation in the yuccas one sees, both in the field and under cultivation. Obviously there are other species (and perhaps hybrids) involved. The species *filamentosa* has rather broad leaves, abruptly pointed and rather stiff, and somewhat concave in cross section. Plants with very concave leaves may be var. *concava* (sometimes considered a separate species), and plants with narrow leaves which droop somewhat at the tip are probably Y. *smalliana*, introduced from farther south. There are several other yuccas in cultivation, all American, most from the western part of the country. The famous Joshua Tree of the Southwest is *Yucca brevifolia*. Little has been done with these yuccas outside their native range, and the majority would probably not stand the wet winters of the East. Y. *glauca*, which extends northward into South Dakota, is as hardy, however, as the eastern species (Zone 5), and is attractive with gray-green very narrow leaves. It grows well with me.

YUCCAS

Yucca for evergreen winter accent and summer flowers.

YUCCA
Yucca filamentosa

Although related to lilies and tulips, yuccas in the landscape function as shrubs rather than herbs because they are evergreen; they are thus doubly valuable. Nothing is perhaps quite so striking an accent as a crown of sharp-pointed yucca leaves in the winter, and that crown surmounted by a towering spike ("vast heavy ivory pyramid," V. Sackville-West calls it) of creamy flowers in summer. In cultivation also are clones with variegated leaves, which are useful for bizarre or striking effects. Yuccas spread by offsets, and may be propagated by division of the crowns. They will take a year to reestablish themselves after division or transplanting. Their only drawback is that the leaves of most species do have quite sharp points which could do an unwary and overly inquisitive child (or adult!) an injury.

In Delaware *Yucca filamentosa* is found often on the dunes behind the beaches and in the dry open pine woods of the lower part of the state. Farther north it occurs occasionally in sterile fields (it cannot compete with the thickets and tall tangles which grow up on rich, moist soil), roadsides, and the sites of old houses. These locations give a clue as to how to use it in the garden. As lawn specimen, accent in open shrub borders, very large rock garden subject or patio plant, or accent in any flat, open expanse, it is unique. I grow three species in a dry field of broom-sedge and short grasses.

The plant is much appreciated in Europe, even in humid England. Along the Mediterranean, in a climate that suits all the species of the genus perfectly, it is much used. During the last quarter of the nineteenth century and the first quarter of the twentieth a plant breeder by the name of Deleuil in Marseilles raised many hybrids, and the famous plantsman Carl Sprenger named over a hundred hybrids as the result of his breeding program in Naples. One would have to go to France or Italy to find these, I suppose. There are several variants of the species with striped white or yellow also, which are hard to find but would be interesting in select spots of the garden. These are usually called "Marginata," "Striata," or "Variegata." Yuccas may be propagated by division, seed, or by cuttings (two or three inches long) of the larger roots placed in warm sandy soil in winter or spring and given gentle heat.

The uplands of the East are the home of several interesting plants of the Ranunculus Family, such as Baneberry, various Anemones, Meadow-rues, Columbines, and Bugbanes. Most of these are spring bloomers, or, if summer bloomers like the Meadow-rues, are plants of wet glades and river banks, rather than plants of the shady woodlands. Bugbane, *Cimicifuga racemosa*, however, is that true rarity, a woodland plant which blooms in shady summer. It is a statuesque plant which, though lacking large, showy flowers, is showy in bloom and attractive all through the season. It becomes about six feet tall, nearly half of that flower stalks. Cleft, delphinium-like foliage makes a dense, handsome foliage plant. From this mound, in late June, sparsely leaved stems rise, bearing at their branching tips long, pointed racemes of small white flowers, each like a tiny powderpuff. The racemes are well over a foot long. Their pointed, elongated shape, like gothic steeples, is very elegant.

BUGBANE AND STAR-GRASS

Bugbane: excellent for shaded gardens.

Other names for this plant are Black Cohosh and Black Snakeroot. *Cimicifuga* (Latin *Cimex*, bug, and *fuga*, flees) means the same as Bugbane. I am not sure which came first. I *am* sure that this is an excellent plant for shaded gardens. It succeeds in any moderately humusy soil.

On my travels I often passed a stretch of scrubby, acid-soil field with what seemed to be the merest hint of a bog in its center. This stretch looked quite likely for rare plants but never attracted my attention enough to cause me to stop until one day, at the beginning of July, I noticed while speeding by that the field was dotted with silvery-white spires, so delicate that they had not intruded themselves on my senses until I was a half mile beyond. I knew I must go back, because they were something new. The only similar thing that I knew was *Cimicifuga racemosa*, and I was a long way from the Piedmont slopes where that plant blooms. So I went back and found my first Star-grass or Colic-root, *Aletris farinosa*, a plant which looks very much like a yucca in miniature, bearing a rosette of pointed evergreen leaves from which a straight scape of white bells rises two feet in late June. The whole plant is possessed of an infinite grace and delicacy.

I took one flowering plant for my acid-soil garden and it has done very well there, blooming the following year and increasing its rosettes and bloom stalks to three the next year. It is planted in drier soil than that from which it was taken. Encouraged, I collected another blooming plant and about six seedling rosettes the next year, and I have no regrets about that now, since I noticed the piece of property where they are growing advertised for sale the last time I traveled by it. Later I also found *Aletris* growing in the Pine Barrens of New Jersey and on the edge of a salt marsh in southern Delaware. It is an easy and pretty plant for the wild garden, with apparently only one requirement: an acid soil.

ROSES, MILKWORTS, AND TRUMPET-VINES

Other flowers well worthy of cultivation are the wild roses of the region, the Swamp Rose, *Rosa palustris,* and the Low or Pasture Rose, *R. carolina.* These two plants have become very much confused in the various manuals, the scientific name of one being applied to the other because Linnaeus somehow named them both *Rosa carolina,* one in 1753 and one in 1762. In the field they can never be confused, however.

Poor drainage? Try Swamp Roses.

Rosa palustris always grows in wet spots, often in standing water, and in winter there is no prettier sight than a stand of this rose with its claret stems and abundant scarlet hips bright above the frozen waters of a swamp-edge or roadside ditch. It is really worth massing in shrubberies for the effect of its winter bark and fruits alone. But its deep magenta-pink flowers, five-petaled, of course, with a mass of yellow stamens at the center, are very pretty. It is a tall rose, growing usually about five or six feet, sometimes higher. It cultivates easily, but will not tolerate extremely dry soils, though it does not need a swamp to grow in. I have always thought that it would be ideal for those people who have problem spots with poor drainage in their gardens. It also does well by the sea.

Rosa carolina is very different in habit, a slender, dwarf stoloniferous thing with paler, pinker flowers, worth growing for its simple grace alone. Occasionally one sees a white form of the species which is perhaps even more pretty. The Pasture Rose transplants with no difficulty as long as one gets a sufficient chunk of the creeping root. It will not remain in one spot in the garden, though, but will spread unless one grafts or buds it on such stock as Japanese *multiflora* which is not stoloniferous. This is not to say that the plant will become a pest. It is too delicate for that, I think. But it won't be tidily confined. It looks well in bays between and in front of evergreens, or at the edge of a naturalistic woods planting, in a situation where it can get some light. It begins blooming in mid-June, a few weeks earlier than *R. palustris.*

In open bogs, growing usually in full sunlight in sphagnum or occasionally in other mosses in the soft shade of pines, grows one of the most spectacular but, alas, uncultivated of all native plants: *Polygala lutea*, the Orange Milkwort or "Bachelor's Button." In open spots in the Austral Forest it literally dots the landscape with orange all summer long, sometimes coalescing into great glorious carpets of orange in some peaty meadow or bog-edge. It is a spreading, branching plant with smooth pale green stems and leaves and orange heads of flowers the size and shape of the heads of red clover. These remain in color for an astonishingly long time, since they continue to grow from the center but never appear elongated because the lower flowers drop off as they fade. I have succeeded with it in pots of pure sphagnum growing above an acid sand/peat mix (other bog plants—fringed orchids, Swamp-pink [*Helonias bullata*], Common Pitcher-plant, and Venus Fly-trap I have grown the same way), but even here it lives lustily for only a season and is loath to reseed itself. The plant is a biennial, which adds considerably to its difficulty. Mature plants transplant well as long as they are kept moist, even when in full bloom. Young rosettes also transplant well, but tend to die out over the winter. It is a pity that the plant is not easier, but the fact remains that it is almost impossible without a bog to grow it in.

Have a bog? Introduce Orange Milkwort.

A very easy July flower is the flamboyant Trumpet-vine *Campsis radicans.* Almost every old-field cedar in some areas of the Coastal Plain has its trumpet-vine twining through it and flashing deep burnt red-orange trumpets against the somber evergreen branches.

It is such a showy plant that it is often cultivated—given the same requirements as wisteria, which suit it very well. It is also, like wisteria, sometimes trained as a small lawn tree. In order to train it thus, it is necessary to give the plant some support until its trunk thickens sufficiently so that it can stand alone, and to keep trimming back the leaders into a compact round head. For the first few years this is time-consuming, for the vine will attempt to put all its effort into twining and vining, but after a few years the vine becomes reconciled to its status as a small tree, blooming heavily and showily for much of the summer. The way I prefer to grow it is naturally, in a Red-cedar (*Juniperus virginiana*), which fortunately I have growing on my grounds, or on a rail fence.

There is a variant, *flava*, which might also be grown for its butter-yellow flowers. This clone clambers up the south-wing wall of the Winterthur Museum, a gorgeous sight when alight with its yellow trumpets. It is in commerce and easily obtainable. Also in commerce is a beautiful hybrid, *C. x tagliabuana*, which is undeniably showy, but not quite so hardy. Also listed is variety *speciosa*, which is supposedly more a bush than a vine, but it unfortunately has smaller flowers than the type. The species stands in Zone 5.

BUNCHFLOWERS

Among the least known of our wildflowers are members of the bunchflower clan—rare denizens of swamps, bogs, barrens, and acid woodlands throughout the East. All are perennial plants which grow from roots which may be tuberous or even bulbous, their leaves in grasslike tufts, often evergreen, and their small flowers, usually of white, greenish, or pink, arranged at the apex of a leafless stalk in dense spikes or branched clusters. They are included by most botanists in the Lily Family, but usually considered "primitive"—close to the rushlike stock from which the *Liliaceae* developed. And indeed, there is something of the rush, even of the sedge, about them. They have a certain architectural quality lacking in many liliaceous plants but present in the tufted, hard-foliaged rushes, from which they are, of course, distinguished by showy, colored flowers.

Their closest relatives across the Atlantic are probably the asphodels, the "lilies of the dead" which grew in the Elysian Fields of Greek mythology, and around which cluster many folk stories connected with death. Our plants, of course, do not have many centuries of folklore connected with them; yet it is a curious fact that many of their common names refer to their alleged poisonous qualities. We find, for example, "Fly Poison" applied to two different plants, "Crow Poison" to another, and the grim epithet "Death Camass" to yet another. No doubt these names derive either from old-time pharmaceutical uses or from instances of livestock poisoning. The botanist Harold Moldenke claims that cattle are poisoned by at least one species, and that large quantities of another are gathered in the Appalachians each year for sale to a firm which makes an insecticide from the roots. Two of the plants discussed here, Swamp-pink and Blazing Star, bloom early in the year. The great majority of bunchflowers, though, are flowers of early summer.

My acquaintance with these plants goes back several years, to a summer morning when I investigated a local bog in which Turks-cap Lily grew and discovered a curious sedgy or grassy-looking plant about three feet tall crowned with dense, much-branched clusters of green flowers. I dug one of the several plants that I ultimately found, and it flourished for several years in rather dry clay behind my garden pool. It turned out to be *Melanthium virginicum*, the Common Bunchflower. When it bloomed the year after digging, I discovered that the flowers open cream and gradually age green, lasting a very long time on the stem. It may be found from New York west to Minnesota and south to Florida.

Closely related to the foregoing, but rather different in aspect, is *Veratrum viride*, the False-hellebore or "Indian Poke." This plant bears in late spring creamy, abundant flowers like those of the Common Bunchflower, but its leaves are lush and broad and strongly ribbed. The first colony I ever found I took to be Showy Ladyslipper until I looked more closely. False-hellebore inhabits wet woods and swamps from Canada south to Maryland and North Carolina. It is a magnificent foliage plant for the pool or bog garden.

Another attractive bunchflower occurs in upland woods from

Canada to Florida, *Chamaelirium luteum,* a plant which to be honest hardly lives up to some of the dramatic common names applied to it—Devil's Bit, Blazing Star, Fairy Wand, Rattlesnake Root. It is a slender plant with an attractive rosette of evergreen or partially evergreen spatulate leaves from the center of which arises in May a scape up to two feet long topped by a six- or eight-inch dense spike of small cream flowers. It hardly blazes, but it is pretty, and the plant itself is quite handsome. It grows happily with violets, trilliums, and other woodland flowers and is a welcome addition to any shaded garden. In the Serpentine Barrens north of Rising Sun, Maryland, it grows right out in full sun and becomes considerably taller and more robust, possibly because of the mineral balance of the soil.

Blazing Star for shaded gardens.

Blazing Star is dioecious—that is, male and female flowers are borne on different plants. The pistillate spike is longer and more tapering than the staminate, and is thus more showy. *Chamaelirium* means ground (*i.e.,* low or dwarf) lily; *luteum* means yellow, an obvious misnomer. The plant was named by Linnaeus, who apparently based his description on herbarium specimens, since the white flowers turn yellowish when dry.

The most beautiful of all bunchflowers, and indeed one of the most beautiful of American wildflowers, is *Helonias bullata,* the Swamp-pink or Swamp-hyacinth, a rare inhabitant of sphagnum bogs and shady swamps from Staten Island to Virginia and (upland) to Georgia. The smooth, spatulate evergreen leaves are arranged in a plantain-like rosette which closely resembles that of Blazing Star (in fact when I found my first Blazing Star, I thought it was a helonias that somehow had gone upland). In the center of this rosette a fat bud forms in autumn, elongating in April to an unbranched scape two or even three feet tall, topped by a dense six-inch spike of flowers. These are a beautiful deep pink with blue stamens, the combination appearing a shimmering lavender-pink at a distance.

Swamp-pink lifts its beautiful candlelike blooms very early in spring, in the same sort of wet woods where later Sweet-bay, Swamp Azalea, Sweet-pepper Bush, and Fringe Tree will blossom. It is a rare plant, daily growing more rare as its habitat is destroyed. To grow it successfully one, unfortunately, has to supply it with lots of moisture. I grew it as a pot plant in pure sphagnum moss, keeping it in a cold greenhouse over winter. I also succeeded in naturalizing it in the Primula Quarry in Winterthur and along a spring-fed stream in the garden of a friend in southeastern Pennsylvania. It does not need either sphagnum or extremely acid soil to thrive as long as it gets its feet wet. The plant is a gorgeous addition to any bog garden, and everyone who is able to grow it should do so. It combines well with Marsh-marigold and early bog primulas.

Combine: Swamp-pink with Marsh-marigold and early bog primulas.

As specialized in its own way as the Swamp-pink is the Turkey-beard, *Xerophyllum asphodeloides*, which grows only in acid pine barrens from New Jersey to Georgia. August in the New Jersey barrens is made more enjoyable by the conspicuous white minaretlike heads of this plant towering above the Sweet-fern, Bearberry, and Bracken among which it grows. The Latin names are descriptive: *xerophyllum*, "dry leaf," refers to the clusters of narrow, grassy, stiff and dry leaves, which somewhat recall those of a bromeliad: *asphodeloides* means "asphodel-like." "Turkey-beard" is also purely descriptive. The cluster of leaves and the bracted stem, turned upside down, resemble the beard adorning a tom turkey's breast. There is a larger western species, *Xerophyllum tenax*, which is called Elk-grass, so grasslike are its leaves. The eastern plant is, in my experience, none too easy to establish except in well-drained, acid soil in a fairly sunny location. It is very much worth experimenting with, having a distinctive personality as a plant.

An attractive bunchflower blooming in late June and early July is *Amianthium muscaetoxicum*, a denizen of open woods of the Piedmont. From a clump of channeled, light green, daylily-like leaves it sends up narrow scapes two or three feet tall surmounted by spikes of white flowers. On the plants I have seen these are some three inches long, though in illustrations they are sometimes longer. The spike is quite dense and showy, with abundant yellow-tipped stamens giving it a kind of golden halo. Its root stock is bulbous.

I first found this pretty plant growing along a creek winding through the fascinating Serpentine Barrens of Chester County, Pennsylvania. Though its bloom season was past, its leaves caught my attention. This spring my plant-loving friends, the Roots, brought me a clump almost ready to bloom, which it subsequently did, after being planted in the partial shade and acid soil beneath a Scrub Pine. With the plant are growing Teaberry, Sheep-laurel, and some sort of blueberry, all acid-soil plants. The only common name for this plant is "Fly Poison," which is not common at all, but literary, no more than a translation of *muscaetoxicum*. Whether it is (or was) used to poison flies, no one now seems to know. In any case, the plant is valuable in the garden, since it rivals Blazing Star for showiness. Its flowers do not fall, but turn green as seed sets. They last a long time, either on the plant or cut.

There are several other bunchflowers which I have not grown. Most are very attractive. All already are rare and local, and should be saved in our gardens. Many bunchflowers are poisonous to eat, at least to man, and should be used carefully if one has leaf-chewing children. This applies to many plants, though—among them yew, larkspur, buttercup, and many members of the tomato family. I think that poisonous plants, like poisonous snakes, are really made too much of by most people.

VIII

High Summer

August first, a cool morning, with a particular clarity in the high blue sky, bright but not hot sun, far clouds, mild breeze, and vivid green of fields and thickets. Miles and miles of roadside are blue and white and gold with the mingled blooms of Chicory, Wild Carrot, and Early Goldenrod (*Solidago juncea*). It seems for a moment that the oppressive summer heat is broken, though of course one knows that it will return. Families of white-breasted tree swallows congregate into flocks on the telephone wires lining the roads. So many times have I seen them flock like this on the first of August that my mind automatically supplies their liquid singing as they course the fields and swoop back to their wires, though in reality I cannot hear them, the roar of my engine and the rush of wind at my window drowning all other sounds as I speed toward my destination.

It is high summer—no winter's chill in the air, no turning leaves, yet the flocking birds in the long shadows of the afternoon herald the approach of autumn as clearly as the more obvious signs which will appear later. From today on, I will be ever conscious of shadows becoming longer and longer, the gold of the sun alloyed with silver, as it declines toward its winter solstice. There will be chill and much dew of mornings, silvery dew hoaring the grass in a foreshadowing of frost. The black roads of the back country will collect the sun's heat morning and evening, attracting insects from the surrounding woods and meadows and, with them, the familiar hordes of martins and side-slipping swallows, constantly swooping back and forth across these roads until one day they disappear, all at once gone, vanished, migrated to their winter homes.

But the year is really all of a piece, and anyone who would divide it into halves or quarters or seasons does so unrealistically. When winter's beginnings first appear, summer has barely slid over her zenith, though her effects are still so abundant that we hardly even notice the changes in light and atmosphere until autumn really sets in and leaves begin to turn in earnest. There are still flowers and greenery everywhere. As I drive into the long sun I smell this summer for the first time, the pungence of barnyard weeds—pigweed, goose-foot, sow-thistle, lamb's-quarters—all those coarse and familiar plants with the names of animals. Not one of them is pretty, nor do any of them really smell pleasant, yet there is about their very rankness something which epitomizes summer and conjures up sweeter memories and smells, and indeed "sets" the glorious, clear, dewy, fresh smell of a clear August day as, in perfumery, civet or ambergris sets the delicate scent of jasmine or rose.

Combine: Hardhack and Swamp Milkweed.

There are finer flowers to be seen, however. I drive along a road-side ditch, where blackberries tangle from a wooded edge down to the moist ground where the mower's sickle keeps them in check, and I see the dusky pink spires of *Spiraea tomentosa*, the Hardhack or Steeplebush, mingled with the flat or mounded heads of the Swamp Milkweed, *Asclepias incarnata*, a wonderful combination of flowers exactly the same in color but opposing and contrasting in form, and a combination that we would do well to imitate in the garden.

In every wet spot grows this milkweed, soon to be joined by its doubles, the various Joe-pye weeds and bonesets, to carpet swale and ditch with mound-flowers of white, pink, flesh, dusky rose, magenta. Already the big butterflies of late summer, orange monarchs and viceroys, blue-black swallowtails, russet-spangled fritillaries, sail back and forth over these wet spots, searching for the milkweed and eupatorium flowers that they love so well.

The flower of early August which is for me the most beautiful of all is very unlike these clustered pink and white flowers, though it grows often among them. It is a lily, with all the grace and presence of that inimitable genus, *the* lily over much of the East, the spotted red and yellow Turks-cap, *Lilium superbum*. I usually first notice it as a kind of wash of orange high in the distant landscape, for though the color of the flowers travels a great distance, the tall purplish stems and fine architecture of the inflorescence become apparent only on closer inspection—a great pyramid of blossoms, two, even three dozen of them, each borne on a long pedicel which twists sharply downward near the flower to give it a graceful nod. The six segments of each flower are green at base, then yellow, and then a deep cinnabar scarlet at the tips, each tightly recurved or rolled backward so that the nodding flowers seem red on top and yellow below. The yellow portion of the sepals and petals is heavily spotted mahogany, a color echoed by the pollen-laden anthers of the six long and gracefully exserted stamens. The whole effect combines extreme showiness with a great deal of grace.

This lily is by far the commonest of the three native lilies in my area. In fact, while the other two species have become nearly extinct, the Turks-cap still manages to appear almost miraculously in disturbed and cut-over swamps and woodlands. It must have a tremendous potential for survival. For years I found its seedlings growing in the densest of wooded areas, far too shady to permit the plants to mature, and thought that these little plants were some sort of woodland orchid before I realized that they were the result of the abundant, waferlike seeds produced by Turks-cap Lilies grow-

LILIUM

The Turks-cap: beautiful and easiest to grow.

ing far beyond the limits of the woodland. This strength carries over into the garden, where it is by far the easiest of the three eastern natives to grow. So common was it in my youth, and so easy is it to grow, that I (and perhaps other wildflower enthusiasts as well) have often taken it for granted. The alarming state of our environment will not permit this, however, much longer. We should be grateful that it remains with us in the abundance that it does.

Predictably, the English value it much more highly than we do. Patrick Synge, in his great book on bulbs, says that it is a "lily indeed worthy of its proud name." And one must remember that it was the great Linnaeus, who undoubtedly saw many beautiful lilies in his day, who named it "superb."

Its near relative, *L. canadense*, the Meadow Lily, is, if anything, even more superb. It is certainly the most graceful of all lilies, and

The Meadow Lily: still more superb.

it is also very much coveted by European gardeners. I first saw this plant growing on the edge of a bog in Dover, New Hampshire, during a summer jaunt to New England in my student years. It grew there in two stands, one of orange-red and the other of yellow, each spotted with black on the insides of the bell-shaped flowers. I was enthralled at the sight of the many strong stalks, six feet high and bearing a dozen or more buds and flowers above the rank herbage of the bog. When I later found the species growing in my home state, and when I tried it in my garden, I was to appreciate more fully the vigor of those New Hampshire stands. It is not easy to please this lily.

Still, it is worth every effort to grow it, for it is a unique plant. The flowers of *canadense* are neither "turks-cap" (nodding but with the six flower segments rolled back toward the base of the flowers, so that the stamens and pistil protrude strongly), nor trumpet-shaped, nor upright and saucer-shaped like those of some of its relatives. They are actually turks-cap flowers which allow their segments to reflex only slightly, so that the flowers are gracefully bell-shaped. The grace extends further, also, to the way each flower stalk extends sharply upward from its juncture with the main stem, to bend suddenly downward before culminating in bud or flower. A full inflorescence of this lily has the balance of a fine but delicate chandelier.

In the garden (and this advice applies to the previous species also) select a spot where it will have some sun during the day, but will be sheltered at its base by other plants (azaleas or rhododendrons make fine companions for it). It should have somewhat acid soil and must be watered abundantly during the growing season. The bulbs that I have dug in the wild are invariably in a heavy, wet clay loam, with not a great deal of humus content, but constantly moist because of the high water-table caused by nearby bogs or springs. Since such soil is difficult to duplicate in the garden, the next best thing is to attempt to hold moisture by other means— namely humus—and to supply an abundance of overhead water during the summer. Peat and leafmold—especially oak and conifer leafmold—also help to acidify the soil, and so serve a dual purpose here. The more such material incorporated in the soil the better. The best specimen I have ever seen in cultivation was in the garden, near Kennet Square, Pennsylvania, of my late friend Mabel Thatcher. But she was lucky enough to have a spring-fed stream, on the banks of which this lily, along with other difficult rarities, grew. *L. superbum* is easier to please, but really does best under these conditions. In dry soil it becomes stunted, while *canadense* usually refuses to grow at all.

Bulbs of *canadense* are small, white, compact, not very much like the bulbs of the commoner garden lilies. They proliferate by forming rhizomes, at the tip of which new bulbs grow, so if you dig your clump of *canadense* and find white runners extending into the adjacent soil, you may be sure your plant is happy. Bulbs should be planted three to four inches deep and not disturbed thereafter if possible— unless the clump becomes too overcrowded (which seldom happens, unfortunately). One thing about the species is worth knowing: it resents disturbance so much that it sometimes remains completely dormant the year following planting. Nothing at all shows above ground, and of course, a discouraged gardener believes that his lily has died. But chances are that it will emerge the following spring, and even bloom. This has happened in about half the cases that

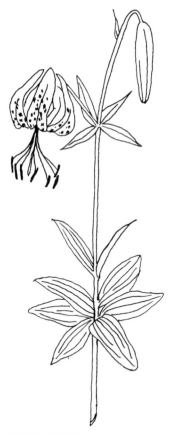

TURKS-CAP LILY
Lilium superbum

I've observed. There are two color phases of this species, one with reddish flowers, the other (prettier, to my mind) with yellow.

Time was when I would see the red-orange bells of the Meadow Lily nodding along the banks of the Brandywine in northern Delaware, but it is now decimated to the point of extinction there. Roads, housing developments, picnic grounds, public swimming areas, have gradually pushed it out. It was never common, as befits so elegant a plant, and it is now perhaps extinct in Delaware. Bulbs of this species may be purchased from dealers in wildflowers and from lily specialists as well. Don't dig plants from the wild unless you are absolutely certain that their habitat is about to be destroyed.

I should mention here that though my inclusion of both the Meadow Lily and the next species in this section is botanically sound, my order of discussion is chronologically artificial, since they both bloom in early July, well before the Turks-cap. The third of the commoner eastern lilies, the Wood Lily, *L. philadelphicum*, is by no means common in my area and probably never was. I must confess that although I have looked for it for several years, I have yet to find it in Delaware. The only places that I have seen it growing wild, in fact, are in the Berkshires of western Massachusetts and the Poconos of eastern Pennsylvania. As might be gathered from such information, the species is primarily a mountain plant. It differs markedly from the foregoing two species in that it is a denizen of dry, open woods, rather than stream banks, wet ditches, bogs, and swales. It is no easy plant to grow, needing strongly acid soil and apparently resenting disturbance a great deal.

The Wood Lily differs from the two foregoing species in aspect as well as habitat. It is low in stature, no more than two or three feet tall and carries far fewer—no more than half a dozen—orange-red flowers which are up-facing and chalice-shaped, totally different in effect from the Turks' turbans of *superbum* or the perfect bells of *canadense*. It is a pretty little lily, but should not be attempted unless one can give it something like the exacting conditions it requires.

Related to the Wood Lily is a species from the Southeast, *Lilium catesbaei*, the Southern Red or Pine Lily. It too has upright flowers, but each of the segments is elongated, frilled, and fluted. The flowers are solitary, and the leaves also are greatly elongated, almost grasslike. So unlike a true lily is it in appearance that several years ago, when sent a photograph of it by a friend from North Carolina, I thought it was a Blackberry-lily or some other iris-relative. It grows among sundews and fringed orchids in sphagnum bogs from the Carolinas to Louisiana, and is reputedly difficult to cultivate. Probably it would be tender in the North.

The rest of the eastern lilies are at least worth mentioning, though some are very rare and local, and most are quite similar to the species already discussed. *L. grayi* is the southern counterpart of *canadense*. It also has bell-shaped flowers, though the plant itself is always more delicate and is fewer-flowered. The flowers are reddish, and it is found in the wild in the Appalachians in the Carolinas, Virginia, and Tennessee.

L. michiganense is the midwestern counterpart of the Turks-cap and might be grown in its place where conditions require. In aspect it is roughly intermediate between *superbum* and *canadense*. Somewhat similar is *L. michauxii*, the Southern Turks-cap or Carolina Lily, which is found from lower Virginia to Florida and Louisiana. Finally, we come to what is probably our most recently discovered lily, *L. iridollae*, found in Florida and Alabama in the forties by Mary Henry. It is a turks-cap in bright golden yellow.

The center of the genus *Lilium* is Asia, but there is a secondary center in western North America. Here there are literally dozens of species in several different forms and colors. Many are native to the gritty and humusy slopes of the Cascades, Rockies, Sierras, and like many mountain dwellers are strongly specialized as to habitat requirements. These are connoisseur lilies, difficult to keep but very beautiful: *L. washingtonianum*, with trumpets of purple-spotted white which age to lilac; *L. parryi*, with turks-cap flowers of clear lemon-spotted mahogany; *L. bolanderi*, a low species with reddish bells which resemble the flowers of a fritillaria more than a lily, are three of the choicest. All of these are, unfortunately, touchy when removed from their mountainside homes, but with a bit of extra attention they can be grown in places as far removed from their native soil as Europe and eastern North America. They are, however, not everyone's flowers.

Sunset Lily easiest to grow of the western species.

Not all western lilies are finicky. One of the easiest of all to grow is the Sunset Lily, *L. harrisianum* (formerly *L. pardalinum giganticum*), a robust plant with red and yellow turks-caps resembling those of its eastern relatives. The plant does very well under garden conditions in the East. I have grown it in moderately acid soil which was quite dry during the summer, and it bloomed well and even increased. For many years a colony of these has also flourished at Winterthur among rhododendrons and azaleas, growing up through the tangled branches of these shrubs and blooming above them.

There is in the trade a group of hybrids of the western lilies called Bellingham Hybrids, with blood in them of the easily pleased *Lilium pardalinum* and the more fastidious species *ocellatum* and *parryi*. The best of these inherit all the best qualities of their parents. "Shuksan" (from *ocellatum* and *pardalinum*), a graceful and beautiful turks-cap in pure yellow with maroon spotting, is one of the few named clones left on the market. Much more common are straight-run hybrids offered simply as "Bellingham hybrids." These, in my experience, are risky because a good percentage are simply orange turks-caps no better than, and sometimes not as good as, the species. Some lily breeders, for obviously pecuniary reasons, offer such "strains" of seed-grown hybrids when they should not, since there are few instances in the plant kingdom where all or even a large percentage of a hybrid progeny is even as good as, much less superior to, its parents. All Bellinghams, in my experience, grow well in the garden. They also naturalize well in the same sort of conditions that suit the native eastern species (acid soil, plenty of moisture), and will do well in open woodland plantings. Their whorled leaves, so characteristic of American lilies, are attractive and strongly architectural in a woodland setting. The great plant breeder Luther Burbank, by the way, was one of the first to begin developing these plants, an early cross of *parryi x pardalinum* bearing the name *L. x burbanki* in his honor.

In midsummer no flower quite enlivens the landscape so much as the big and showy Rose-mallow, *Hibiscus palustris*. Every creek, river, and tidal gut is fringed with these plants, every open swamp, bog, slough, or salt marsh covered with them, their enormous white or pink cups expanding in the summer sun. So showy are they that they are noticeable even to those who hardly ever notice natural things. Time and again I have had people ask me what the big pink and white flowers growing in the marshes around Atlantic City (where they are particularly abundant) are, for example.

Since Rose-mallow occurs naturally wherever the soil is wet, it is a good subject for bog gardens, plantings around ponds, and the like. Unlike many semiaquatics, however, it does not need wet feet to survive; it is, in fact, an extremely adaptable plant. It grows very well in the perennial border or as a specimen in lawn or shrub plantation (where I grow mine) as long as the soil is moderately rich and it gets an occasional watering. In very dry and poor soils it will survive, but the plant is impoverished—stunted, yellow, and unattractive.

One might not suspect this adaptability from observation of it in the wild, for it is invariably connected with water. Only once have I seen it growing high and dry, the sight astonishing me because it made me realize how intimately the plant is tied to the lowlands. I was driving south along Interstate Highway 95 below Wilmington one August morning and noticed great plants of Rose-mallow covering a steep hill from foot to crown. It simply did not look right. Rose-mallow does not climb hills. I realized then that the "hill" was an enormous mound of earth, the result of dredging a new channel for the river which winds through tidal marshes in that spot. Obviously the seeds and roots of the hibiscus were transported along with the rich black muck and ultimately sprouted. The richness of the soil—tons on tons of topsoil from the uplands, laid down by centuries of tides, assures that the plants do well even atop the hill.

Hibiscus palustris is a stout herbaceous plant, with tough almost woody unbranched stems to six feet, set with large, rather rough leaves which are oval to triangular in shape, sometimes more or

HIBISCUS

Rose-mallow for bog gardens, pond-side, and perennial borders.

less lobed. In the axils of the upper leaves are borne the flowers, each six inches or more wide, on stems which are slightly longer than the petiole of their subtending leaves.

The flower is typical of the mallow family: a green, cup-shaped, five-lobed calyx, five large petals, and stamens united with pistils in a long column rising from the center of the saucer-shaped blossom. At the base of the calyx is a distinctive involucre of pointed bractlets, like a spiky collar around the bud. The color of the type is pink, varying from palest blush to deep purplish pink, with or without a crimson center. *Forma Peckii* is white, usually with a crimson eye. This latter form is by far the commonest in my area.

Hibiscus palustris may be found from Massachusetts, Michigan, and Ontario south to coastal North Carolina and Indiana. South of this, to Florida and the Gulf States, it is replaced by *H. moscheutos*, which differs mainly in its narrower leaves. The two are probably no more than variants of one species. Other closely related species are *H. lasiocarpos*, native in the Mississippi Basin north to Indiana, and differing from the preceding mainly in its soft-downy pubescence. Its Coastal Plain counterpart is *H. incanus*, with leaves covered by a gray wool, native from Florida and the Gulf States north to Maryland. Both of these are very similar to *palustris* and *moscheutos* in flower.

Native in the valleys of the Mississippi and Missouri as far north as Minnesota and as far south as the Gulf of Mexico is *H. militaris*, named for its arrow- or halberd-shaped leaves. It has pink flowers, and again is closely allied to all the plants mentioned so far.

The South has a number of fascinating and distinct plants in this genus. *H. aculeatus*, from North Carolina south, for instance, has crimson-eyed flowers of clear lemon-yellow. I have to my regret been unable to locate this species, but I have grown for several years a southern species which is beyond doubt the glory of the genus (at least insofar as the herbaceous species are concerned; "Hawaiian hibiscus" are another matter!). I refer to *Hibiscus coccineus*, found in coastal swamps from Florida to Alabama and Georgia.

This is a tall plant, growing to ten feet in moist soil, with reddish stems two inches or more thick at base, tapering to slender tips, and bearing large, finely divided leaves which are apple-green with red petioles. The elegant leaves look like those of a cutleaf maple. The eight-inch flowers are a clear, bright red, the color exactly of a ripe tomato. The spoon-shaped petals are ribbed at their broad apices but smooth as glass at their concave bases and a shining, glossy red as though lacquered. The petals do not overlap, as those of the other species do. The effect of this is quite striking, for one sees in the gaps between their bases the large, expanded calyx of apple-green in sharp contrast to the bright red of the corolla.

The Scarlet (for so *coccineus* translates) Rose-mallow is the most elegant member of the group. It makes the popular hybrids, with their huge and showy flowers, coarse and plebeian by comparison. Everyone who can grow it should do so. The plant's one drawback is its relative lack of hardiness. It is surprisingly hardy for a species with such a southern range, surviving most years in the latitude of Philadelphia. My plants tend to die out in cold winters, though, so I find it advisable to keep plenty of youngsters coming along. It is simplicity itself to grow from seed, as are all Rose-mallows, and it blooms the year following germination. In southern Delaware it lasts indefinitely. I am acquainted with plants that have stood in their present positions for ten years.

For southern gardens: the Scarlet Rose-mallow.

Hybridists have been working with the rose-mallows lately, producing what are called in the trade "mallow marvels" from crossing the species mentioned (and perhaps others). The result are handsome and adaptable perennials with more or less the habit of *H. palustris* and enormous flowers which vary from pure white to deep crimson-red. Some of the two-toned pinks are especially lovely. Critical selection has eliminated some of the faults (from a gardener's point of view) of the species—strap-shaped rather than rounded petals, and flowers which cup rather than open widely. Most hybrid rose-mallows have flowers the size and shape of a dinner plate. One red seedling I raised regularly bears fourteen-inch blooms. For sheer spectacle they cannot be surpassed, and since they bloom in tired, dusty August, they are doubly valuable for our gardens. The reds among the hybrids, incidentally, are always dark crimson, not true brassy scarlet like *H. coccineus*. Dick Ryan back-crossed a red "Avalon Hybrid" (*H. militaris x coccineus*) on *coccineus* and got a handsome hybrid much resembling *coccineus* except that it is much hardier.

A final note: Many individuals among the wild plants can be found which are just as beautiful and nearly as gaudy as the hybrids. Do not shy away from them just because horticultural propaganda convinces you that man-made plants are "superior" to the natural product. Some clones of the wild species open just as flat and are just as showy as the hybrids. Select the best when you collect. *H. palustris* (and no doubt others) is excellent, incidentally, for sea-shore gardens.

CLETHRA

A flowering shrub of the East which occurs consistently in swamp, bog-edge, damp acid woodland, the haunts of Swamp Azalea and Sweet-bay Magnolia, is *Clethra alnifolia*, the Sweet-pepper Bush. Like its two companions it is distinguished for its white flowers and its heavy fragrance. Unlike them, it blooms late in summer, and its floral display consists not of a few large flowers but dense clusters of many small ones. These, nodding bells, are raised in upright candles four to six inches long, at the tip of every branch in July and early August. They look like spikes of Lily-of-the-valley in miniature.

Like most white flowers they are fragrant, presumably to attract night-flying insects as pollinators. To me the fragrance is cloying at close range but pleasing at a distance (I have the same reaction to Swamp Azalea). Smell is one of the most individual of the senses, however. Seldom do two people sniff alike. For example, Herbert Durand, in one of the finest books on native plants ever published, said almost fifty years ago of Sweet-pepper Bush's scent:

> It is nature's most delightful and most tantalizing fragrance—nothing insipid or cloying about it—but a fragrance with a tang that makes the nostrils tingle and creates an insatiable desire for more.

I will defer to Mr. Durand, but still avoid thrusting my nose at the blossoms.

Since clethra comes into bloom as Swamp Azalea fades, it is desirable to plant them together for succession of bloom (and fragrance) as in nature. That the same situation suits both makes managing them a bit more practical also. The addition of Sweet-bay to the pair gives an even longer season, from mid-May when the first magnolia blossom opens to late August, when the last clethra blossom fades.

This trio should certainly be planted by anyone with wet or poorly drained problem spots on his land, though none absolutely requires a wet soil. I grow all three in well-drained ordinary soil with no more preparation than a few shovelsful of peat moss at planting time and a mulch of wood chips. I might add, though, that my soil is on the acid side, as most soil in the East is. Several years ago, when I was a struggling student, I transformed a bleak northern wall of my house with no expenditure other than work by using native shrubs dug from a nearby woodland (which, incidentally, has since been destroyed by development). Clethra, Sweet-bay, and Swamp Azalea were among the first shrubs planted, followed by Spice-bush, Strawberry-bush (*Euonymus americanus*), Pinxterbloom Azalea, Ironwood (*Carpinus caroliniana*), all underplanted with violets, wild ginger, columbines, and similar low herbs. The effect was very beautiful, long in blooming season, rich in fragrance, and extremely satisfying. The soil there was very light and well drained, drying out rapidly in summer. With an occasional watering, however, the shrubs all thrived.

Clethra alnifolia is a deciduous shrub to ten feet or so, upright and open in habit, with dark brown bark and deep green ovate leaves three or four inches long. Its foliage is handsome from spring to fall, remaining green and unmarred by pests until it turns clear yellow and orange in October. Its flowers are individually small but collectively showy, cream white and fragrant. The form *rosea* (called, if I remember correctly, 'Pink Spire' in the trade) has flowers of blush pink with stamens and pistils bright pink. It is worth growing. Another form or cultivar, called 'Paniculata,' has longer spikes which are somewhat compound, at least according to nursery manuals. It

For succession of bloom: combine Clethra and Swamp Azalea.

looks like ordinary *alnifolia* to me, though I admit that none of the plants I have seen of it is healthy or robust. The specific name of the species means "alder-leaved," and an alternate name for it is White-alder. To me it looks like anything but an alder, but perhaps Linnaeus, who named it, had alders other than our American species in mind.

Like its relatives the wild azaleas, this clethra tends to grow as a straggling, stoloniferous, colonial undershrub fringing wooded roadside and swamp edge, straining for light. Like them it also responds to cultivation by abandoning its straggling ways and becoming a noble specimen shrub.

It occurs from Florida west to eastern Texas and north to southern Maine. In Delmarva and southern New Jersey it is one of the commonest of woodland shrubs, yet time and again people have admired my plants under cultivation after passing through woodlands (by car of course) which fairly reek of it. It is hardy in Zone 4.

Clethra has a rather extraordinary range: with one exception it is typical of the Old (pre-glacial) Flora, with representatives in eastern North America and eastern Asia. One species occurs, however, on Madeira, in the eastern Atlantic. Proponents of the validity of the Atlantis legends, take note!

A closely related southern species (by many considered only a subspecies) is *C. tomentosa*, which differs mainly in being very downy, while *alnifolia* is quite smooth in all its parts. It is native from North Carolina to Florida and Alabama and is hardy in Zone 7.

Very distinct is a third American species, *C. acuminata*, Mountain Sweet-pepper or Cinnamon Clethra, native in the Appalachians from Virginia to Georgia to Alabama. It is larger in every way, becoming in the wild a tree to twenty feet. The plants I have observed in cultivation, though, have been spreading, rather than treelike, and not so tall. The leaves are twice the size of those of the common species, and the branches are heavier. More importantly, its flowers are much larger, really very showy. They come about two weeks earlier, and thus do not give the common Sweet-pepper much competition. A final feature to note is its rich cinnamon-orange bark, which contrasts beautifully with the deep green foliage in summer and shows up just as beautifully against the snows of winter. This is the bonus which makes *C. acuminata* a really choice shrub.

Another common but interesting native is *Cephalanthus occidentalis*, Button Bush, often a neat, globular bush with long, ovalish deep green leaves and perfectly spherical heads of fuzzy white flowers (which look much like the heads of the unrelated mimosa and albizzia). When very old it becomes a dark-trunked, gnarled, and usually extremely picturesque tree, at least in shade. In the wild it is always found in wet ground, sometimes growing right in shallow water, but it is one of those plants which will tolerate much drier soils in cultivation than they will in the wild.

BUTTON BUSH

It is one of the few woody members of the coffee family, *Rubiaceae*, hardy in temperate zones, and perhaps for that reason alone is worth experimenting with. But it is also a rather ornamental plant in its own right, its white blossoms being attractive as well as interesting. In addition it blooms through much of summer, a time when relatively few shrubs bloom. If it has any real fault it is that its flowers often turn a dingy brown before falling. I have observed this trait in some specimens but not in others. Whether it is genetic or environmental I am not yet sure; it might be, though, that careful selection will discover clones which do not have this fault.

Coming home one summer afternoon I saw a plant of Button Bush growing along a bog-edge with *Clethra alnifolia*, the two—one completely orbicular, the other steeple-like—of similar color but different shape, looking very well together.

The mainly American genus *Asclepias* (milkweeds, silkweeds, flossweeds, butterflyweeds) is much neglected by gardeners. Wildflower manuals generally illustrate two or three of the commonest species and gloss over the rest, as though they were too insignificant to bother about. Deprecations abound in horticultural literature. You will notice, for instance, that each of the common names listed above contains the epithet "weed." Except for the gorgeous Butterflyweed,

BUTTON BUSH
Cephalanthus occidentalis

MILKWEEDS

Don't dismiss milkweeds
and butterflyweeds.

A. tuberosa, garden writers are unanimous in calling milkweeds weedy and undesirable, or at best coarse.

"Desirable" and "undesirable" are, of course, value judgments. Fashions in gardening change, and so do individual tastes as one matures and gains experience. A plant may be too coarse in one setting but spectacular in another. At any rate, I believe that the people who condemn milkweeds too often have insufficient acquaintance with them.

To begin with, they are a highly advanced group, with intricately and fascinatingly designed flowers. These consist of a shallow tube which is divided into five down-turned segments ("petals") from the center of which rises a thickened, clublike column to which adhere the five stamens. The structure is analogous to that of another highly advanced (but totally unrelated) group, the orchids. Like orchids, milkweeds have heavy pollen which is aggregated in a waxy mass called a pollinium. Around the column are grouped five growths called "hoods," which protect the stamens and give the flower its strange shape. From each hood a horn protrudes over the flat end of the column. The reasons for this weird structure have to do with pollination. The hoods protect the pollinia from insects which are too small to pollinate the flowers. Only the strong, hairy legs of insects such as bees can force their way beneath the hoods and pull away the pollen masses.

But milkweeds are not interesting solely because of the design of their flowers. Before the late sixties, I might have been inclined to agree with plantsmen's judgment of them, since the word was synonymous for me with the Common Milkweed, *A. syriaca,* a tall, common, and admittedly coarse (though not ugly) plant with large leaves and axillary clusters of flesh-pink blossoms. Then, speeding through the pine forests of southern Delaware one morning in June of 1968, I glimpsed a bold clump of wavy deep green leaves topped by dark pinkish flower heads as I sped around a curve. It was totally unfamiliar to me, that I knew even from a quick glimpse, but what was it? I was fairly familiar even then with Coastal Plain plants. There was a milkweed look to it, but that swirling, undulate foliage belonged to no milkweed that I knew, and those flowers on long, naked stalks were very different in disposition from those of Common Milkweed.

On my return from school that night I watched for it. It proved to be a milkweed indeed—one look at its horned and hooded flowers showed that—and one of the easiest to identify: Blunt-leaved Milkweed, *A. amplexicaulis* (formerly *A. obtusifolia*). Blunt-leaved Milkweed. What an uninspired and nondescript name for this dramatic plant! It occurred to me then, as it has since, that by its common name you may judge how common and familiar to the general public a plant is. Fascinating names like Jack-in-the-pulpit, imaginative names like Skunk-cabbage, historical names like Celandine arise from usage, from the folk, from a real familiarity with and knowledge of nature. Names like Blunt-leaved Milkweed are the coinages of botanists and writers of manuals (blunt-leaved being a mere translation of the older specific name for this milkweed, *obtusifolia*). No botanist would ever be so descriptive or unscientific as to call the aroid *Symplocarpus foetidus* a cabbage. "Stinking Symplocarpus," perhaps, but never an arum a cabbage! Leave it to an unlettered farmer to call the plant Skunk-cabbage because it has big leaves, which smell precisely like skunk when they are bruised. Botanically unsound, perhaps, but it beats "Stinking Symplocarpus" any day, as far as I am concerned.

Better "Clasping-leaf Milkweed" (for so translates *amplexicaulis*) for our milkweed, or best of all perhaps "Wavy-leaved Milkweed," for the most distinct attribute of the plant is its leaves, or rather their shape and disposition. They are large—to six inches long—oblong in shape, deep green in color with prominent pink midrib and outer margins. They are disposed in pairs along the stems, and lack petioles; each pair is thus joined base to base so that it appears as if the stem grows through the center of one great single leaf. The leaves themselves are extremely undulate or wavy-edged. A three-foot plant in full swirling, writhing leaf seems to be in constant motion. Even out of flower it is architecturally effective, a distinction belonging more properly to woody plants than herbaceous.

Blunt-leaved Milkweed, one of our finest wildflowers.

Unlike most milkweeds, which bear their flowers in short-stalked umbels arising from the axils of the upper leaves, this species raises its blossoms on a leafless stem nearly a foot above the topmost leaves. The umbels are single, not compound as in many other species, nearly spherical in shape, and many-flowered, with individual blooms on stalks about an inch long. In the commonest phases these have greenish purple petals and flesh-pink hoods—pretty if somewhat pallid. Other forms may have purplish petals and deeper pink hoods, some approaching a true claret color. It seems a pity that the flower color is so muted and, often, so muddy. The plant would be an absolutely stunning garden flower if it had blooms of lemon-yellow, say, or crimson or even bright pink. Still, in its brighter forms it is an excellent plant, and the soft tones of its flowers echo the colors of its green leaves with rosy midribs and margins. The smooth stem adds to the plant's handsomeness, for it varies from reddish to bright maroon, or, in some dark-flowered specimens, deep purplish. The bright green undulate leaves with colorful midribs and margins and strongly contrasting transverse veins are more distinctive, however, than the flowers. The plant is as dramatic as a baroque painting. To me it is one of the finest of our wildflowers. It is native from Florida and Texas north to New England and west to the prairie states. In my area it is uncommon, nearly always found in sandy, acid soil in clearings, wood-edges, or, most often, along partially shaded roadsides.

In the same sort of places grows another, perhaps even showier milkweed. Dick Ryan, whose specialty is sighting botanical rarities from the window of a speeding automobile, discovered this one on an afternoon in late June as we drove toward the town of Millsboro in search not of wildflowers but of soft-shell crabs. "I saw what looks like a dwarf *Viburnum carlesii* back there," announced Dick as we emerged from a stretch of pines, and, since that viburnum neither grows wild in Delaware pinelands nor blooms in June, we turned back for a look. There in the sparse grass in the safe zone between mowed edge and trees bloomed an elegant and totally new milkweed—two feet tall with four pairs of large, very deep green leaves, and a terminal cluster of flowers of an exquisite ivory white, each marked deep in its center with a touch of purple. My manuals soon disclosed its name: White Milkweed, *Asclepias variegata,* a species whose range extends from Florida and the Gulf States north only to Connecticut and Missouri. Like several other milkweeds, it grows in the partial shade of pine woods but, unlike most of these, seldom if ever ventures out into fields or onto sunny roadsides. It appears to be a delicate plant. Aside from its beautiful flowers, its deep green leaves recommend it. These have a very distinctive, almost glittering surface—the poetic word "hyaline," "glassy-surfaced, like the sea," describes it accurately. White Milkweed grows as tall as three feet, but usually stays lower. The majority of plants encountered consist only of a single stalk from the crown, with only a cluster or two of flowers at the summit. Robust and happy old plants, however, may consist of several stems from the crown, each with five or six flower heads. This plant is extremely valuable because it is one of the few plants inhabiting shady areas which will bloom in summer.

White Milkweed for summer bloom in shade.

The following year Purple Milkweed, *A. purpurascens,* revealed itself to me. By this time my eyes had been opened, so to speak, to the beauties of the genus, though on the day I first found it I was not plant-hunting at all, but clipping along a country road at fifty mph on my way to what was bound to be a tiresome, taxing, and boring conference. Milkweeds were not on my mind, but I knew at once as I saw a flash of wine color along the roadside that I had found a milkweed, and a new one.

It was growing almost in the road, on the shoulder that surely must be scraped and sprayed and cut throughout the summer. Above it, atop an embankment and extending back into a weedy field, grew a dense stand of the Common Milkweed, at this time (late June) only in bud.

Purple Milkweed is an upright plant two feet in height (I have since found plants growing taller by a foot or so), with unbranched stems each bearing twelve or so pairs of bright but light green leaves, with prominent pale veins and conspicuous pink midribs (as in *amplexicaulis* and *variegata,* incidentally). The leaves are velvety in appearance and to the touch. The flowers occur in terminal umbels, with a few in the axils of the upper leaves. The habit, then, is intermediate between the bee-pollinated Common Milkweed, with usually single umbels in the axil of each leaf, and butterfly-pollinated Butterflyweed, with terminal and axillary umbels united into a compound, flat-topped cluster at the apex of the plant.

The individual flowers of Purple Milkweed are about half an inch long and each simple umbel is about two inches in diameter. The color is a vibrant claret, not really purple, with a sort of orange undertone; the column of fused stamens in the center of each blossom presents a sort of showy eye of straw yellow. Later plants of this species which I have found have been coarser, less pubescent, and not so bright in coloration. It seems to me that these plants may be contaminated by blood of the Common Milkweed, which they resemble in various degrees. Fortunately, I was able to propagate the first plant discovered—I say fortunately because the following year a sewerage line was installed for a new housing development in the area, and the plant was dug under tons of soil. It never reappeared.

Purple Milkweed occurs here along roadsides in sun or shade. Every area where I have found it growing has been dry in summer, though I find in my own garden that very dry soil stunts its growth. Unlike the preceding species, it seems to be a plant of upland more than Coastal Plain. I have found it thus far only in the northernmost county of Delaware and in adjoining Chester County, Pennsylvania (near Pottstown). Always it has been growing along roadsides, a factor which may be responsible for its rarity, since it ensures that the plant will be mowed down regularly (if not killed by poison sprays) and thus be prevented from setting seed. The same applies to A. variegata, and indeed to most milkweeds and to roadside plants in general. The present trend on the part of local state highway departments to use sprays as labor-saving devices in place of mowing is deplorable. Most roadside plants will survive an occasional mowing and every so often succeed in ripening a seed or two. Chemicals kill the plants outright, as well as rendering our roadsides hideous with brown and twisted foliage throughout the summer.

I turn now to the best known and best loved of the genus, the Butterflyweed, *A. tuberosa*. It is a variable plant in height, habit, and color, having numerous rather small and narrowish hairy leaves, disposed alternately on the stem, and heads of small flowers which may vary from pure yellow through all shades of orange to nearly true red. It is often found on roadsides, where it reaches a height of two or (infrequently) three feet and has upright to arching stems. In open woodlands it grows more delicately, as would be expected from its diminished supply of sunlight. In fields that are occasionally mowed it also survives, though it blooms later and usually remains only a foot or so tall.

Butterflyweed: best known and best loved.

Some phases grow with stems almost entirely decumbent—nearly parallel to the ground—and it is these (once segregated as a different species, *A. decumbens*) which usually survive in mowed grass. One assumes that they grow this way because of mowing, but such seems not to be the case. I have growing in my garden numerous individuals dug from an infrequently mowed field in Sussex County. These grow in open, cultivated soil now, but still arch close to the ground as though ducking the mower's blade. Such specimens are valuable, of course, for special situations, where low or decumbent plants are desired. A further characteristic of the decumbent phase is that its leaves clasp the stem at their bases. The upright form of the species has ordinary ovalish or elliptic unclasping leaves on upright stems.

The plant's glory lies in the color and abundance of its flowers, these typically a glowing orange with coral undertone, one of the brightest hues of summer, but varying from true canary-yellow to nearly scarlet. Some give a bicolored effect, their petals of yellow and hoods of orange or petals of pale and hoods of deeper orange. The deeper forms have stems of maroon, while those of yellow and very pale orange have stems of bright green. The more deeply colored specimens, then, can be distinguished even out of flower.

A plant of Butterflyweed in full bloom is a flat-topped mass of color, a brilliant landing-field for butterflies. Not the least of its attractions resides in its irresistibility to these beautiful creatures.

Once, while riding through a pine woods near the sea with a citified friend, we passed a stand of Butterflyweed and he exclaimed, "Look at that!" The roadside was swarming with white cabbage butterflies, pale sulfurs, silver-spotted fritillaries, orange monarchs, yellow and blue swallowtails, all dancing attendance on the *Asclepias* blossoms. It was the only time I'd ever heard my friend comment on natural things.

Butterflyweed one of easiest wildflowers to move.

Butterflyweed, unlike many milkweeds, lacks milky juice. It is a good cut flower if plunged in cold water immediately after cutting. Huge bunches of it can be seen in the flower markets of Philadelphia. A florist friend uses it extensively in his work. He tells me that people usually exclaim over it but never know what it is. The plant grows from an enormous, thickened root that does indeed look tuberous, as its scientific name suggests. All the books say that it is difficult to transplant because of this root, but this statement is pure nonsense; in fact, it is one of the easiest of wildflowers to move. It is quite cosmopolitan as to its habitat, being found from Florida west to Arizona and north to eastern Canada, the Great Lakes region, and the Great Plains. In my area it may be found everywhere, but is most abundant in the sandy soils of the Coastal Plain. Wherever I see it, I am reminded of summer by the ocean, of sand and burning blacktop roads. It occurs on sunbaked roadsides and dune hollows and also in the semi-shade of pine woods.

Saltmarsh Milkweed most unusual and beautiful of all.

The only other native milkweed with orange flowers (except for *A. currasavica*, a Mexican species naturalized in the Southeast but tender this far north) is in many ways the most unusual and beautiful of all. This is *A. lanceolata*, the Saltmarsh Milkweed, another austral plant which reaches its extreme northern limit in Delaware and southern New Jersey. Its one-inch flowers, largest of any of the milkweeds, are produced in relatively few-flowered compound umbels which are so elongated as to give the effect of short spikes. They are borne well above the greatly elongated and narrowed, sparse, almost grasslike leaves. The whole plant gives the effect of one of the Orange Fringed Orchids (*Habenaria ciliaris*), so much so that I am often still fooled when I see a stand of the plant while driving.

The reason for such mimicry is as yet undiscovered by me, however, though no doubt it has to do with pollinators.

The species begins blooming in early July. It is found mainly on the edges of salt marshes, though I have also found it flourishing on the edges of roadside bogs a mile or so from the shore, and in boggy hollows between dunes at the ocean. I once found a fine stand of it in a sphagnum-covered dune hollow in southern Delaware where it made a veritable wild garden with the magenta Swamp Rose (*Rosa palustris*) and Grass-pink Orchid (*Calopogon tuberosus*), the white Ladies Tresses (another orchid), and blue-black huckleberries in abundant fruit. Finally, one time only I discovered an excellent specimen blooming in dry soil among Loblolly Pines several hundred feet from a bog. A Butterflyweed bloomed nearby. The vast majority of plants of Saltmarsh Milkweed are, however, found only in the narrow zone where salt marsh meets upland, whether this be field or pine woods. It is probably the most specialized species in the family, and undoubtedly the most endangered, since its limited habitat is being more rapidly destroyed than any other in the country.

Because of its rarity, I have always been loath to collect specimens for cultivation. In August, 1970, I dug one plant, cut it back, and potted it in a mixture of sand and peat until November, when I planted it in a sunny part of my wild garden where I had succeeded with a few pine-barren plants. The milkweed resprouted in the pot, grew slowly, and was alive when planted, but failed to appear the following year. In the early autumn of 1973, my friend Dick Ryan tried a different approach: he dug a plant with a root ball of about a foot in diameter and equal to the length of a spade in depth, and planted it a day or so later on the shore of my pond. The plant remained green and in fact matured the single seedpod that it bore. The following spring it sprouted and in July bloomed magnificently. It would seem that it does not require salt to thrive but must have some moisture.

Saltmarsh Milkweed, like Butterflyweed, produces flowers which range from near-yellow to deep orange. Those that are bicolored are quite striking, since the individual flowers are so large. It is a very showy summer-flowering plant, one which would amply reward the labors of any gardener who experiments with bog or water gardening.

Nearly as specialized as Saltmarsh Milkweed is another entirely different species, the tiny Whorled Milkweed, *A. verticillata*. The manuals say that this species occurs in dry, open, or sterile soil from Mexico to Canada. In my area it is certainly rare except in the Serpentine Barrens of Chester County, Pennsylvania, a few miles north of the town of Newark, Delaware. Here it is abundant, covering the dry, shaley hills with its white flowers in early August. I have not found it growing anywhere else, in spite of diligent search.

Those who characterize *Asclepias* as a genus of coarse plants have overlooked this species. Under certain conditions it may reach three feet; nearly always it grows less than two. Its leaves are narrow, with inrolled margins like the leaves of the herb Rosemary, and are verticillate (arranged in whorls, or circles, around the unbranched stem). The whole plant resembles that of Rosemary.

Its flowers, white or greenish white, occur in the axils of the leaves. A flowering stem may look like a fluffy white foxtail, punctuated by the spiky gray-green leaves which protrude beyond the flower clusters. This is not a showy species, but it is a pretty little plant for specific situations—the rock garden, for instance. It is adaptable and easily transplanted. My plants grow with native heaths and Birdsfoot Violets in the sterile soil beneath a big Scrub Pine. Here they seed themselves. They get plenty of sun, though none from directly overhead.

Whorled Milkweed for rock gardens.

A last species, one of the most common in terms of number of individuals, but probably seldom noticed as a milkweed: *Asclepias incarnata*, the Swamp Milkweed. This species grows abundantly in every ditch, swale, swamp, marsh, bog, and wet meadow in the East, its range extending from Nova Scotia to Florida, west to New Mexico, Wyoming, and Manitoba. It grows in exactly the same habitat as Joe-pye Weed, and bears an astonishing gross similarity to this totally unrelated plant. One usually sees them growing in large stands together, and can hardly tell where one leaves off and the other begins. Beyond doubt they are adapted to the same pollinators.

Swamp Milkweed bears small flowers of mauve, pink, or white which are gathered in many compound terminal umbels to form a large, flat or slightly convex cluster at the summit of the plant. The color is most commonly that called "dusky rose," the exact hue of the old-fashioned 'Anthony Waterer' spirea. They are very useful, as is 'Anthony Waterer,' in bouquets. Like Butterflyweed, Swamp Milkweed has little milky juice and cuts well. It blooms in late July and presents no difficulties in transplanting or growing in ordinary garden soil, in spite of the fact that it is a wet-soil plant in the wild.

Swamp Milkweed for bouquets.

Like Butterflyweed, *A. incarnata* is a variable plant. In every stand may be found plants with flowers so pale as to be nearly white and so deep as to approach raspberry pink. Individuals with variegated leaves often turn up also. There are two main geographical variants: *incarnata* proper and a more pubescent form called *pulchra*. The latter is the common plant in Delmarva. It is densely fuzzy-hairy, which gives its leaves a grayish cast. *Incarnata*, by contrast, is smooth, and its willowlike leaves are deep green, not gray. The clusters of *incarnata* are often larger than those of *pulchra*, and of a color more closely approaching crimson—the poetic "incarnadine," as the Latin name suggests. Among the millions of plants of this species that I have observed in the East, I have only once found true *incarnata*—along Route 72 in the Pine Barrens of New Jersey. Generally speaking, this form is common only away from the coast.

The list is not exhausted, though for present purposes it is. I have yet to find three species listed for Delaware—the rare *A. rubra*, a bog species with reddish flowers; *A. quadrifolia*, a small woodland species with dainty pink blossoms; and *A. exaltata (phytolaccoides)*, Tall or Poke Milkweed, a coarse upland species which I wonder how I've missed so far. Then there are other areas. I recall driving through the Santa Cruz Mountains in California in 1971 and looking with longing at a handsome, big milkweed with silvery leaves growing there. The South has a number of interesting species, including several delicate types native in pine barrens or coastal dunes.

Transplanting milkweed?
Follow rules.

Information on the cultivation of *Asclepias* is likely to be as inaccurate, or at least as debatable, as information on the aspect of the plants. Most manuals, for example, state that Butterflyweed is difficult to transplant, which is simply not so. It is deep-rooted but can be moved at any time of the year if certain rules are followed: first, dig as much root as you possibly can; second, place the dug plant as soon as possible in a plastic bag or container which prevents its drying out; third, and most important, cut back all stems to an inch or two. At the base of each stem you will see one or two tiny buds. These will form new stalks, and often bloom again that season, after replanting. The cutting back applies only, of course, to plants gathered during the growing season. Collected plants should be replanted at the approximate depth at which they were growing and kept well watered for several weeks after planting.

A couple of years ago Dick Ryan transplanted an enormous plant of this species. It had more than seventy stems, each with a head of flowers, and an enormous woody taproot. About two thirds of the root was collected with the plant, the rest being accidentally cut away and left in the ground. The plant was cut back and set in a flowerbed. It promptly resprouted and threw several stems which rebloomed that year. The following year it made a fine heavy plant, full of bloom. The piece of root left at the site sprouted and made a new plant which bloomed the following year also! I have collected dozens of color variants of this species, in bloom, and treated them as described. I have lost none.

Not all the species in the genus, however, are so easy. Those with which I have had contact fall into two categories: those with deep, heavy, nearly tuberous roots, like Butterflyweed, and those with cordlike roots which radiate from a shallow crown. In the first category belong:

tuberosa
lanceolata
amplexicaulis
purpurascens
syriacus
variegata

In the second category belong:

    incarnata (including var. *pulchra*)

    verticillata

Those with shallow cordlike roots in the second category transplant easily, and do not need cutting back as long as ample earth is moved with them and they are well watered after planting. I have transplanted many of the two species listed and find them still thriving in my garden.

Those in the first category offer more difficulty; some seem more difficult than others. Besides *tuberosa*, described in detail above, I have transplanted all the species listed. *A. variegata* was bare-rooted and cut back as described. The following year it made a small plant. Three years later it bloomed. Later collections were transplanted in spring, young plants being chosen and moved with a large shovelful of earth, and not cut back. One of these bloomed the following year. This species is none too vigorous under most conditions and should be well watered when transplanted. It appears also to favor some shade, and definitely does best in light, sandy soil.

Of the other deep-rooted species listed, the most difficult to move appears to be *amplexicaulis*, mainly because its roots are so very deep, and because the juncture between stem and root is extremely brittle and easily broken in moving. I have succeeded with only about half of the plants I have moved, and these have suffered severe setbacks. None has yet bloomed for me. I would recommend root cuttings (see below) here.

The shallow-rooted species may be increased through seed or through division of the crowns in spring. The deep-rooted species may be propagated also by root cuttings: the heavy roots are cut into pieces of an inch or two and placed vertically in sandy or sandy-peaty soil and kept well watered. Most books recommend spring as the best time for this, but I have succeeded in late summer also. The cuttings may lie several months without producing growth, then shoot up and grow strongly thereafter. Root cuttings of Blunt-leaved Milkweed have produced plants for me which are as robust as those transplanted with roots intact at the same time.

The Purple Milkweed (and probably other deep-rooted species)

Shallow-rooted species easy to transplant.

may also be propagated in the following manner: carefully pull up a few selected stalks from the clump. Trim these back to the bottommost pair of leaves and place them in a mixture of sand or perlite and peat, treating them thereafter like stem cuttings. You will find that a tiny piece of root has come away with the stem, and from this will grow new shoots and new roots in a short time. When new roots are several inches long, the plants should be placed in pots and established before being placed out of doors in their permanent positions.

Collect seeds before pods open completely.

Seed is produced in abundance from all milkweeds, their long pods, with flat, brown, floss-tipped seeds being quite ornamental. Sow the seeds as soon as ripe (be sure that you get them before the pods open completely, or the wind will carry the seeds into the next county). I simply scrape the surface of the ground, sprinkle seeds on it with or without their silky parachutes (which rot quickly), and cover with a half inch or so of soil. The following spring the seedlings appear. These will take about three years, in most species, to bloom. It is well to mention that the leaves of certain species in the seedling stage may not resemble those of mature plants at all. For example, leaves of my seedling *amplexicaulis* the first year were pointed, flat and very narrow, not at all blunt and wavy. The second year they began looking like their parents.

All milkweeds have a very long blooming season in midsummer. This can be prolonged if the flowers are prevented from going to seed. Butterflyweed, for example, can be had in bloom for two months of the summer if the first flowers are cut as they begin to fade and the plant cut back to six inches or so. Within a few weeks new shoots appear with a second crop of flowers.

IX

Salt Marsh, Sand Dune, and Seashore

On my trip I smelled the sea forty miles before I reached it, in the saline reek of salt marshes and meadows below Dover. These are the northernmost of the peninsula—great treeless expanses of black salt mud and green cordgrass, intersected by tidal guts of brackish water and haunted by herons, ducks, redwings, and boat-tailed grackles nearly the size of crows—the uppermost fingers of the sea, where the salt tide is reduced to a mere brackish flow but is still sufficiently strong to give a decidedly marine cast to both vegetation and animal life. All along the Coastal Plain one encounters them, from just behind the beach to the head of salt tide, sometimes many miles inland. Chemical reaction between salt ions and nitrogenous matter in the muck creates the odoriferous gas which characterizes the salt marsh. It is perhaps too strong an odor for the average person, but smells sweet to him who knows and loves the ocean.

Salt marshes and meadows offer neither boating, walking, swimming, nor sunbathing to the vacationer; therefore to the "development mentality" they are worthless, and no shore terrain has been so ruthlessly destroyed by ditching, filling, and bulldozing as salt marshes. Recently, however, conservationists have alerted officials and members of the public to the fact that salt marshes are anything but useless. On the contrary, they are the kitchens of the ocean, as it were, the breeding grounds of billions of organisms of countless kinds, initiating and supplying the food chain which culminates in the large fishes (and other animals, including man) of the sea. Destroy them and the fish leave our shores.

Even this public vindication of salt marshes seems insufficient to me, however, for it concedes only their necessity. Granted, the salt marsh is not beautiful as, say, the redwood forests of California or the mixed woodlands of the Appalachians are beautiful. Nor is it hospitable to man as these are: the sun beats fiercely by day, and there is little vegetation tall enough to give shade; the muck is too liquid for walking but too solid for boating, and the dense tussocks of cordgrass and reedgrass demand persistence and considerable acrobatic skill in traversing.

But in this overpopulated land of ours, the environments so hostile to man that they have thus far resisted his altering them (as opposed to his totally destroying them, of course) are the only environments in which a real abundance and diversity of wild creatures remain. Nowhere else that I know of can such a variety of living things be observed. As I walk along the edge of the salt marsh my toes touch venus clams in the mud. Silvery schools of mullet and killifish skitter up shallow channels at my approach. Enormous blue crabs mate among the submerged culms of the reedgrass, and hideous, though perfectly harmless, horseshoe crabs lurch through the shallows. Big, dark seaside sparrows buzz from tussock to tussock, run across the mud, wade in waterfowl fashion after marine prey. Turkey vultures and ospreys soar above; marsh hawks course close to grasstops. Fiddler crabs swarm out of holes at the falling of the tide. A clapper rail steps from the grass and minces across the flats with tail in the air, cackling like a cartoon chicken. Other noises—terns fly screaming back and forth between their nest sites on the dunes to the east and the fish-filled bays inland, often with silvery fish glinting in their beaks. Their rasping "kee-aaaagh!" fills the sky. Territorial-minded willets—gray, overgrown sandpipers—fly at one's head shrieking hysterically "pill-will-willet, will it? will IT???" Then, an explosion: two black ducks flush from the tidal gut, their underwings flashing white satin against dusky flanks as long wings pull them splendidly and quickly into the sky and away.

Where the marsh meets the bay and fingers of silt extend into the water rest hundreds of waterbirds. Sandpipers and plovers in incredible variety, big herring and black-backed gulls, smaller laughing and ringbilled gulls, many kinds of terns, including the stately royal and Caspian terns. Herons, great blue, American egret, tiny snowy egret. Brant geese. Once, on the 4th of July in 1968, I even saw to my everlasting astonishment a flamingo fly up with sunburst wings at my approach and land in the shallows a hundred feet away. For three vacation days I watched this gaudy coral-pink creature feeding in the muddy shallows. No one knows how it got there or where it went, but if not an escaped zoo bird it was the northernmost natural appearance on the East Coast of this species.

And the flora of the salt marsh? Not as dramatic as the animal life of course. Plants never are. But just as rich. Dominating the wettest areas are the Reedgrasses and Cordgrasses (*Spartina*), tall, green, handsome plants. Slightly back from the water Black Rush (*Juncus gerardii*) and Salt-meadow Grass (*Spartina patens*) form a flat, low expanse of grayish green, their slender leaves harsh and biting to the touch. On the edges of the salt meadow stand thickets of Bayberry, Groundsel Bush, and Inkberry Holly, all three marching out into the meadow wherever a slight rise occurs. The general effect is green, green, green, but a green that on close inspection is starred with many other hues. Out in the meadow among the rough Black Rush and Cordgrass blooms the soft blue Sea-lavender (*Limonium carolinianum*) in company with starry Sea-pinks (*Sabatia stellaris* and *S. campanulata*) the color of pink nougat. I shall never forget seeing a stand of these—two-inch, yellow-centered stars of pink

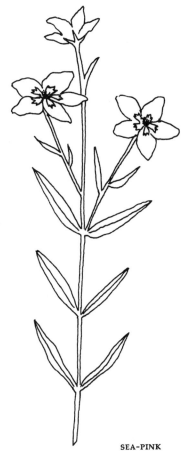

SEA-PINK

and white among the grass surrounding a solitary bayberry in which a male redwinged blackbird bowed and teetered excitedly, his scarlet shoulders leaping flame as he balanced with spread wings of velvety black.

Only Sea-pink and Sea-lavender brave the wetter part of marsh and meadow, but the drier sections are populated by several species of white thoroughwort (*Eupatorium*), the very beautiful Saltmarsh Sun-flower, *Helianthus angustifolius*, exotic-looking Deer-grasses (*Rhexia*) in mauve and vibrant purple-pink, and golden Sundrops. Here also, as in wet spots throughout the Coastal Plain, grows the adaptable Rose-mallow in great tropical splashes of pink and white.

And here and there grow the endemics, the true gems of the salt marsh and meadow, which are found nowhere else: *Pluchea purpurascens* with flowers of fuzzy mauve, reminiscent of ageratum; *Kosteletzkya*, a pink hibiscus in miniature; and, just at the point where marsh meets upland, the flaming orange *Asclepias lanceolata*, Saltmarsh Milkweed, whose upright spikes of bright flowers and elongated leaves cause those (I among them) who search in vain for the Orange-fringed Orchis considerable consternation at each encounter, so great is the resemblance.

In lower Delmarva and most of the coast south of New England, the geography of bay and ocean is thus: one travels south on a road cut through the dunes a few hundred feet from the shore. On the left is the pounding ocean, hidden most of the time by tall barrier dunes. On the right at varying distances from the road are usually enormous, shallow expanses of salt bay. Marshes occupy areas between dunes and between road and bay. Sometimes the dunes are covered with thickets of Bayberry and Inkberry from which miniature forests of Black-jack Oak and Pitch Pine rise. In other places they are covered by little more than Dune Grass and Beach-heather. In wet depressions, "dune hollows," between the shifting dunes miniature salt marshes occur, where grow milkweed, mallow, and other salt marsh plants. Here other bog plants may also grow—beautiful rarities like Grass-pink (*Calopogon tuberosus*), an orchid fully as gorgeous as any grown under glass, true Cranberry, Pipeworts

(*Eriocaulon*) more descriptively called "White Buttons," and various species of the tiny insect-catching sundews.

The dunes themselves are another ecological microcosm. As life in the salt marsh revolves around one great factor—an excess of salinity, all living things therein being able in some way to withstand this excess—so life in the dunes revolves around another great factor: desiccation, from porous soil which holds little moisture and from constant drying winds. It is a harsh and unstable environment, and its plants are characterized by their urge, their absolute need, to stabilize themselves by means of their long, searching, binding roots. The root area of dune plants is enormous, hundreds of times the area of their above-ground parts. This fact is of practical importance to the seashore gardener in two ways: first, it makes the transplanting of dune vegetation a science unto itself, and, secondly, it makes gardening by the seashore not a pastime but a survival activity, since it is vegetation which holds the barriers between the sea and you.

Many people bemoan the fact that they cannot grow roses, say, or geraniums near the ocean because of salt spray or winds. It is indeed true that gardening by the sea has its own special problems; the constant, desiccating winds, the high salt content of the soil, salt spray, and occasional inundations during storms or spring tides, are the major of these. And, since Coastal Plain shoreline is pure sand, an added problem is that the surface soil dries out immediately after rain or watering. Plants which will grow here, then, are those that will withstand high salt content in air, soil, and water, drying winds, and extremely porous soil. Typical seashore plants have adapted themselves to these rigors in a variety of ways. Some, like the dune grasses, possess narrow leaves which offer little resistance to wind and have hard, smooth surfaces which keep air out and water in. Others, like Sea-blite and Seaside Goldenrod, have developed more or less fleshy, water-storing leaves sealed by a smooth, plastic-like integument. Others, like *Hudsonia*, are brittle, woody, and covered by a gray, resistant coating. All have deep, questing roots.

In spite of the fact that nature poses such deterrents to gardening by the sea, it still can be rewarding. In fact, I believe that seaside gardening is the most positive sort on earth. A hundred minor and annoying difficulties besetting the inland gardener are here cleared away. We needn't worry about crab grass in the lawn, couch grass in the perennials, black spot on the roses; about soil tests, cut worms, white grubs, ragweed, lamb's-quarter, witch grass, or stinging nettles. There are no weeds by the sea, simply because plant life is at such a premium that we are happy to see anything grow. Unless your garden is formal (and chances are it won't be at a beach cottage), a stray rosette of witch grass is not out of place on the dunes, and its roots contribute to holding the dunes in place. Since a shore house is very literally built on sand, dune-binding vegetation is extremely valuable. All plant life is useful here. The object is more vegetation.

What about the more aesthetic aspects of gardening—color combinations and so forth? Petunias and gaillardias may grow cheek by jowl with dune grass and broom-sedge; Japanese Black Pine with Beach Goldenrod and Bayberry; climbing roses with thicket-forming wild grapes and Beach Plum. I have seen many strange combinations at the shore, and, to be perfectly honest, none has ever seemed displeasing to me. The environment itself is so emphatic—sun, wind, waves, white sand—that it produces its own context. Anything that will grow is welcome in this immensity of blowing, glaring sand, near this vastness of roaring, seething water.

On New Jersey's Long Beach Island I have seen dune-top thickets of Poison-ivy a beautiful olive green through summer and glorious crimson in fall, and I have had to remind myself of what a pernicious thing it is, or can be, to those allergic to it. At Barnegat I saw a large beach house surrounded by billowing thickets of Bayberry and Inkberry Holly, nothing else, just deep green on all sides which seemed to echo the cool ocean across the dune, and I thought what a marvelous effect it created, and what a trouble-free planting!

Seaside gardening is perhaps the most conservative, in the original sense of the word, sort of gardening. Its aim is maintenance, or, if change, then change through accretion rather than alteration. Survival is as much a result as is beautification. Since it is dune vegetation which maintains the dunes, which in turn prevent the ocean from biting chunks out of the land during every storm or flood tide, the wise gardener conserves and encourages new plants in order to preserve the very land on which his house is built. The cardinal rule here, then, is "Don't pull it up; plant it." There may, of course, be circumstances under which you break this rule. Thickets of Poison-ivy at the back porch may be a mixed blessing, for example. Or you may live sufficiently far back to experiment: the farther your house is from the ocean, the less danger there is of its overtaking you, and the more easily plants establish themselves and grow. But, generally speaking, gardening at the seashore involves covering every square inch of bare ground with deep-rooted vegetation. The way, then, to begin a seaside garden is to start work with the plants already there. The second step is to introduce plants which will survive the rigors of the seaside environment.

Step 1: Work with existing plants.
Step 2: Introduce plants which are adapted to the environment.

If I were landscaping a shore cottage, how would I do it? What would I use? I asked myself this question while sitting at cocktail time on the verandah of a rented place at Barnegat a few years ago, and it was answered for me, in some detail at least, by three neighboring cottages.

WHAT PLANTS TO USE?

A few doors toward the beach stood a small house set in a rectangle of sand and gravel. Cars parked everywhere, right up to the front door. The only ornament, if it can be called such, was a round bed with a piece of driftwood, some whelk shells, a few Dusty Millers, and six very salt-sick geraniums. This was no doubt a maintenance-free garden, but I would not want to be in that cottage the next time the sea comes sweeping over the barrier dunes as it did in the early sixties.

Next door to me was a two-story cedar shingle house of pleasing lines and proportions which provided the very antithesis of the first cottage. Instead of a bare expanse of gravel, raked and compressed, sand lay soft and white from the front door to the street, dotted with dark green goldenrods and clumps of various wispy grasses. Trees and shrubs grew everywhere. There was no parking lot—cars parked along the street—and there was no path to the front and back doors. A wooden platform walk extended from the street to the front door and around the house to the back. Doubtless this was built for a practical reason: to prevent the feet of returning bathers from becoming clogged with sand. But it also prevented walkers from disturbing the plants which grew in the sand beneath it, and all manner of creeping, knotting, binding things grew right up to its edges.

Only two exotics grew on this property, both of which, the owner informed me, had been obtained from state conservation agencies a few years before. These were Japanese Black Pine (*Pinus thunbergi*) and the broadleaved evergreen *Euonymus japonicus*. These stood tall and dark green beside the brown house. Among the natives were Seaside Goldenrod (*Solidago sempervirens*) in great bushy clumps of emerald green which erupt into heads of bright yellow in autumn; Dune Broom-grass (*Andropogon littoralis*) in tussocks of needly leaves of unusual color—blue-green with mauve and lavender lights; running, rose-flowered Beach Pea (*Lathyrus maritimus*); shrubby Bayberry and Inkberry Holly, both mounds of olive green. "Weeds" were literally all over the place. Witch Grass (*Panicum capillare*), that scrubby little grass with large panicles of flowers that break away after frost and become tumbleweeds, dotted the white sand and was very pretty, its wine-colored flower heads making airy masses above its green leaves. Even crab-grass and knotweed, those two banes of the inland lawnmaker, made pleasing geometrical patterns as they crept over the sand, and seemed somehow right where they were.

This place seemed to me to illustrate conservation through total retention of natural vegetation and near-total lack of interference with it. The owner never pulled a weed, and almost never planted an exotic plant. Its total effect was relaxed and natural, yet quite pleasing aesthetically.

Across the street stood a low white stucco house of faintly Spanish appearance set in the middle of an elaborate and beautiful garden.

Combine: Seaside Goldenrod, Dune Broom-grass, Beach Pea, Bayberry, and Inkberry Holly.

It seemed that the owners of this place had adopted a policy of retention of native plants also, but to this had added the introduction of as many suitable and attractive exotics as they could find. Near the white house stood a tall, dark *Pinus thunbergi*. Around the pine, extending from the house to the driveway, was planted a ground cover of *Artemisia stelleriana*, a Dusty Miller or Beach Wormwood commonly naturalized on the Atlantic Coast. Through this cover grew random seedlings, obviously self-sown, of the old-fashioned *Petunia grandiflora*, its flowers of mauve, purple, pink, and white very pleasing among the silvery gray leaves of the artemisia. In the forward part of this area rose a single clump of Seaside Goldenrod, vase-shaped and statuesque, a substantial green like a small echo of the pine above the mass of gray leaves and purplish flowers. One imagined that in bloom it would be even more effective with its bright yellow flowers.

Combine: Dusty Miller, petunias, junipers, bayberries, Rose-mallows, golden coreopsis, orange gaillardia.

Across the driveway were more petunias and artemisias, though this time the ratio was reversed: the petunias were massed, and the artemisias were used as random accents. Trimmed native junipers and bayberries stood in the background, while here and there Rose-mallows (*Hibiscus palustris*) lifted their huge, red-eyed white blossoms on five-foot stems. This combination, along with random groupings of golden coreopsis and orange gaillardia, extended around the whole house, giving way finally to informal billows of sage-green Bayberry and Inkberry Holly interplanted with pink *Rosa virginiana* through which clambered the rose-colored Beach Pea.

This was an extremely effective garden, illustrating a conservation as valid as the first. Though it used more exotics than the other, for example, it used only those that were suitable—the artemisia, to cite one case, which is so well adapted to conditions on our coasts that it has become naturalized. Moreover, the garden seemed to reflect a compliance with nature that was admirable. The average gardener, for instance, might rip out the Seaside Goldenrod as a weed instead of allowing it to remain as these gardeners did, or they might attempt to "improve" on the self-sowing old-fashioned petunia by adding some of the mammoth and brilliant hybrids available today. These people apparently realized that not only would these new hybrids be of poorer constitution than the old plants but that their brighter colors might detract from the garden's color scheme. It will be noticed that this scheme was rather limited: all the reds were on the purplish side, the only other colors being a minimum of yellow and orange in the scattered tickseeds and blanket-flowers, the gray of the wormwood, the white of mallows, and the many variations of green in the shrubbery. All these against the pale sand and beneath the brilliant, burning skies of the seashore were restful and lovely.

If I were planting a house on the beach I would first investigate other seaside gardens carefully. Every shore community has a number of houses which are practically, effectively, and beautifully planted; and there is always something to learn from such places and their creators. Then I would turn to nature, learn to recognize the local flowers, study the plant communities of the shore. One quickly sees that certain plants recur in certain situations. For example, in pure sand just above the line of high tide grow the most salt-resistant of seaside plants, the halophytes or salt lovers. These are all low plants of rubbery texture with succulent, thick leaves or stems: Sea-blite (*Dondia* or *Suaeda*), Glasswort (*Salicornia*), Saltwort (*Salsola*), Sea Purslane (*Sesuvium*), Orach (*Atriplex*), and a few others. None is exceptionally ornamental, but all are very valuable as sand-binders. They are the pioneers of shore plants, extending closer to the sea itself, sometimes right to the wrack line, than any other plants.

Just behind them grows the backbone of the shore, the dune grasses whose masses of subterranean roots bind the dunes and withstand incredible pressure from wind and water. These, unlike the halophytes, are all aesthetically pleasing plants. The most common (and probably the most effective as dune-binder) is Marram or Beach Grass, *Ammophila brevilinguata*, whose tough, cordlike leaves rise in graceful green tufts from the white sand. Its dense foxtail spikes of whitish seeds are quite ornamental.

Other beach binders are Panic Grasses, members of the huge genus *Panicum*. *P. amarulum* forms conspicuous clumps of tall glaucous leaves and airy seedheads in late summer. It is very handsome. Less clumpy but more attractive is *P. amarum* (beware the confusing similarity of names here). It is very distinct by reason of its beautiful glaucous leaves and stem and its really colorful flowers. These appear in August as open, feathery flower heads with nodding branches. In color they are silvery blue like the rest of the plant, each spikelet (the tiny oval which later becomes the grain) tinted rose on its sheath and projecting tiny flowerets of deep mauve and pollen-laden orange. The total effect is muted and lovely. The plant reaches three or four feet and is rather slender and delicate in appearance. It blooms at the same time as *Eupatorium hyssopifolium* and makes a fine companion plant for it (see p. 258). Neither *Panicum* has a common name other than "Beach Grass."

From coastal Massachusetts northward grows the Sea Lyme Grass or Strand Wheat, a handsome and hardy beach grass whose large seeds are a source of flour. In the South grows a very beautiful beach grass, *Uniola latifolia*, popularly called Sea-oats because of the appearance of its nodding flower heads, which are very often used as indoor decorations. At least two of the large genus of grasses known as broom-sedges grow on dunes—*Andropogon virginicus* and *A. littoralis*. In these the flower heads are inconspicuous, but the plants themselves, densely tufted in growth and a bluish, sometimes mauve-tinted green in color, turning rich russet in the autumn, are very beautiful.

The dune grasses are the most important plants in the seaside garden, for they form the absolutely necessary barrier between the hostile sea, close to which nothing but halophytes will grow, and you. The more effective that barrier, the more you will be able to grow behind it. There are many native plants, besides grasses, which are almost as resistant to salt, drought, and heat as the dune grasses. Some of these, in fact, like Seaside Goldenrod and Beach Plum, are in places as effective as the grasses as dune-binders. These should be tried if for no other reason than to add variety to your planting.

Perhaps the most adaptable, certainly one of the most beautiful

For especially attractive beach grass try PANICUM AMARUM. *Combine it with* EUPATORIUM HYSSOPIFOLIUM.

Most adaptable: Seaside Goldenrod.

SEASIDE GOLDENROD
Solidago sempervirens

of all shore plants, is the Seaside Goldenrod, *Solidago sempervirens*. Plants of it appear everywhere along the coast, from the crests of the dunes down into the soaked salt marshes. They grow as though artificially sheared and shaped in the wide, flat expanses of cordgrass meadows, rising as high as six feet, like shrubs rather than the herbaceous plants they are. Male redwings whose territory includes the meadows use them as lookout perches, launching themselves, all black and scarlet iridescence, into the air to hover above us as we approach and to settle back into the branches of the goldenrod as we pass by.

This is perhaps the best of all the native seashore plants. It transplants with no trouble. It multiplies quickly by division of clump or by seed. Its gracefully vaselike habit and smooth, bright foliage are attractive throughout the season. It will grow anywhere—atop dry dunes, the water-logged interior of the salt marsh, open pine woods, the perennial border inland.

Finally, its great sheaves of yellow flowers are spectacular, being larger, individually, than those of other goldenrods—quite noticeably tiny yellow daisies in large compound clusters. If it has a fault it is that it doesn't bloom until the beach season is nearly over: mid-September into October and November. Its foot-and-a-half panicles tightly packed with tiny yellow daisies have brightened many an autumn day for late-comers to the shore, though.

Like many abundant plants, it is somewhat variable as to height, blooming season foliage value, and blooming season. I write this sitting at the base of a sand dune that is dotted with plants of this species. The date is September 12th. Some plants near me are six feet tall, great globular shrubby masses, while others only a few feet away are half that height. Some of the plants have very deep green leaves, others have foliage of a succulent pale green. One plant is in full bloom; another plant will not be in bloom for perhaps another month: the buds which will become the enormous compound clusters of flowers are now nearly microscopic disks nestled in the axils of the upper leaves. Between these two extremes lie the rest of the plants. Some have the branches of the panicles just beginning to develop, while in others the flowers are beginning to color in various intensities of golden green. One wonders whether all these variations are environmental or genetic. It would seem that they are inherited, since the plants exhibiting them inhabit the same environment. But environmental factors are sometimes very complex and subtle. Though I can see no pattern in the variation of the plants around me, there may yet be reasons for it, reasons hidden beneath the soil surface, behind the winds and rains, deep in the beginnings of the summer. Such questions, however, needn't plague gardeners. From a pragmatic point of view it means that through careful selection and experimentation we can have Seaside Goldenrod in bloom throughout the whole autumn.

With Seaside Goldenrod on the dry dunes are two very different little plants—mat-formers rather than tall perennials. The first of these grows well out onto the outer dunes and is well worth any trouble incurred in locating it. It is called Seabeach Sandwort or Sea Chickweed, *Arenaria* (or *Ammodenia*) *peploides*. An inhabitant of northern shores around the globe, the species forms a dense dark mat of small, succulent leaves starred with tiny white flowers in late spring. Essentially a northern plant, it has never been common in the Middle States, and development of our seashores bids well to eradicate it in our area.

Encourage Seabeach Sandwort and Beach-heather.

Another mat-former dots the white dunes behind the head of the beach—*Hudsonia tomentosa*, called Beach-heather though not a true heather at all. As attractive in its steel-blue, needled foliage and prostrate growth as any cultivated creeping juniper, and possessing the added virtue of being covered in spring with hundreds of sulfury flowers like tiny yellow single roses, this is perhaps the prize of all beach plants. Unfortunately it is as difficult to establish as it is beautiful. Even the usually noncommittal botanist Alfred Rehder says in his *Manual* that hudsonias are "rarely cultivated, difficult to grow, and short-lived."

It is almost impossible to transplant (though I once succeeded with a young plant in sandy soil under tall, sparse pines). Fine, wiry roots penetrate deeply into the dunes, making the plant impossible to dig with an intact root system, the resulting shock causing death almost immediately.

My success occurred with a plant growing not on the dunes but on a barren of Black-jack Oak and Pitch Pine where the soil had some humus content. In early spring I selected the smallest plant I could find, about three inches tall and hardly more in extent. Then I dug a circle three feet or so around the plant and, digging as deeply as I possibly could, worked the roots out of the soil. It was impossible to make any sort of ball around it, so I immediately coiled the roots and placed the plant in a large plastic bag with moist moss and a quantity of the soil from the hole. On replanting it I took care not to cramp or crowd the roots, and I placed around them the sandy soil in which I had packed them. With immediate watering and regular doses thereafter the plant survived for over a year, though it never seemed robust to me. A group of heavy-footed electrical repairmen caused its death the following year. Someday I plan to attempt transplanting *Hudsonia* in the winter, chopping a ball of frozen sand with pick and axe. The only way to get a stand of it seems to be by seed.

Highly recommended: Dusty Miller.

Another dune plant is very much worth growing—the well-known Dusty Miller. It is botanically a star-thistle, *Centaurea cineraria*, as its rose or mauve thistle flower heads attest. These go often unnoticed, though, for the plant's chief attraction is its leaves, cut into many angular lobes and covered with a fine, white, cobwebby pubescence which enables them more efficiently to withstand the salt, heat, and drought of the shore. Dusty Miller grows almost anywhere—straggling up and down the barrier dunes, even going out onto the beach as far as the wrack line, or springing up in the bone-hard, broiling parking areas behind the dunes and in front of cottages. Its white foliage is handsome in combination with the dark green of yucca, cactus, coreopsis, or bayberry. It roots easily from cuttings and is a valuable addition to any seaside garden, but will not thrive where soils are rich and moist. Not a native at all, the type hails from Italy, and as may be expected is none too hardy. It grows naturalized all over the beaches of New Jersey, however, and from there south is hardy. Farther north it may be replaced by another, similar plant also called Dusty Miller, but perhaps more properly Beach Wormwood, *Artemisia stelleriana*. This is taller, with leaves more finely cut and with insignificant flowers. It is hardy into Canada. There are several other exotic beach dwellers called Dusty Miller. I have grown a beautiful one known botanically as *Chrysanthemum* (or *Pyrethrum*) *ptarmicaefolium*, but it will not winter with me. Any of these which will grow in one's garden are eminently suitable for seaside landscaping and are to be highly recommended. *Centaurea cineraria* is originally native to the Mediterranean, *A. stelleriana* to northeast Asia (which explains its hardiness), and *Chrysanthemum ptarmicaefolium* to the Canary Islands.

Besides the halophytes, mat-forming plants, and dune grasses, there are certain other plants which will grow on the dunes. Probably no pine is as resistant to salt spray as the introduced Japanese Black Pine (*Pinus thunbergi*), but eastern beaches abound with Scrub Pine (*P. virginiana*), Pitch Pine (*P. rigida*), and (from Delaware south) *P. taeda*, Loblolly Pine. All of these become low and contorted along the dunes and, though they suffer occasional burn from wind and spray, make effective windbreaks.

For resistance to salt and wind, try these trees.

Other trees which withstand much wind and salt and which might be attempted on the barrier dunes, are American Holly, Wild Cherry, many oaks, especially Post, Black-jack, and Spanish Oak, Red-cedar and perhaps other junipers, and Persimmon. The closer these grow to the ocean, the more stunted and shrubby they will be, of course.

Certain shrubs also are adapted for life along the dunes, and it is of course these which should be selected to form the dominant plants of our planting.

At least two roses will grow along the dunes: the naturalized "Sea Tomato," *Rosa rugosa*, with rich green foliage and white or vibrant magenta flowers followed by enormous edible hips, and *Rosa virginiana*, with large flowers of soft pink, perhaps the prettiest of the native roses of the East. Finally, the Inkberry Holly, *Ilex glabra*, should not be overlooked. This valuable evergreen makes a low dense cover close to the water, but further inland becomes a small

Beach roses? ROSA RUGOSA *and* ROSA VIRGINIANA.

tree. It grows natively from Nova Scotia (along the coast) to Florida.

Bayberry (*Myrica pensylvanica*) and Wax-myrtle (*M. cerifera*) are denizens of the seashore and of acid plains, pine barrens, and pine woods as well, the first native from Newfoundland to North Carolina, near the coast or on sterile soils locally as far west as Ohio, the second native from southern New Jersey and Delaware west to Arkansas and south to Florida and Texas. Both have narrow, delicate olive-green leaves two or three inches long, inconspicuous flowers, and fruits like light gray buckshot clustered thickly on their stems. These berries have a coating of whitish wax from which fragrant bayberry candles are made. They are exceedingly valuable as bird food, also; tree swallows caught by premature freezes will survive by feeding on them in the fall, and those that overwinter provide food for early returning bluebirds, catbirds, orioles, and similar migrants. In addition, their pale color against the dark foliage gives a pleasant ornamental effect during winter.

For beach shrubs: Bayberry and Wax-myrtle.

The two species (which hybridize where they occur together) differ mainly in size, Bayberry seldom exceeding ten feet in height, much shorter in exposed sites, and Wax-myrtle growing to thirty feet in certain situations. Bayberry is at least semi-evergreen in the southern part of its range; Wax-myrtle fully so. In harsh, windy, very cold situations either tends to lose a portion of its leaves, those remaining becoming a pleasing purplish bronze. An important difference between them, from a gardener's point of view, lies in hardiness. Bayberry is hardy to Zone 2, while Wax-myrtle will not survive beyond Zone 7.

In my part of the country both occur, the hardier species upland, on barrens and sterile hillsides, along coastal dunes, and in salt marshes, and *cerifera* in pine woods and magnolia swamps in the lower part of the state only. I have transplanted both with complete success and know of no difficulties connected with their use in gardens except that (I assume) they need acid soils in order to do well. Both are exceedingly handsome shrubs which, though they lack bright flowers, are perennially pleasing to look at. My preference is, of course, for the Wax-myrtle, mainly because it is more dependably evergreen and I am able to grow it. Its soft olive or sage-green foliage is redolent of pine savannahs and the South to me. Both species, like hollies, have sexes on separate plants, only female plants producing berries. Since they fruit at an early age, this is little deterrent if you can collect plants. If you live far from their natural haunts, though, you may find that you need a male plant to set fruits on your females. The Bayberry is, incidentally, often split into several species by botanists, according to height and persistence of leaves. This needn't concern the collector unduly, of course.

Very much a feature of the dunes is *Prunus maritima,* a true plum which is one of the most valuable dune-binders of all. In nature it usually occurs in low thickets, no more than a few feet tall, completely covering the dunes. Often these are no more than the exposed tops of much taller plants, though. In spring the plants are covered with myriad creamy white blossoms, which in August ripen to blue fruits like small Damsons, sweet and juicy out of hand or cooked. To me most Beach Plum fruits have a shade too much flavor of bitter almonds (Prussic acid?) to be really delicious. Most people, however, do classify them so. Beach Plum pie and preserves are discussed in tones of religious reverence by every transplanted New Englander I know.

Whatever the merits of the fruit, it is a plant of great value and aesthetic appeal that should be in every seaside garden. *Don't* try to transplant it from the wild because it is very difficult, even if you do find a small plant. Scatter seed of those you and your friends eat, or plant them in pots, and contact agents of both the U.S. Department of Agriculture and state agencies along the coast, many of whom specialize in this plant. A yellow-fruited variety is listed in the books, as is also one with double flowers (this one does not set fruit, however). Beach Plum typically makes a mound four to six feet tall and twice as broad, though inland it becomes a small tree. In bloom it is a beautiful thing.

A must: Beach Plums. But don't transplant.

Various men connected with the USDA and also with Agricultural Experiment Stations in the states of Massachusetts and New Jersey have in the last thirty or so years worked with clones of the species selected for large fruit and great productivity. George Graves, formerly of the Massachusetts Horticultural Society, lists nearly a dozen named or numbered cultivars in an essay on Beach Plums in Donald Wyman's *The Arnold Arboretum Garden Book* (1954). Any gardener with shore property would be wise, I think, to locate plants of these cultivars.

*Groundsel Bush an
excellent seashore shrub.*

Another excellent seashore shrub, one of the commonest yet most distinct, is *Baccharis halimifolia*, Groundsel Bush. This is the gaunt shrub or small tree with grayish leaves and angled branches that grows in impossible places—far out in salt meadows, perched above deep tidal guts, on the shores of salt lagoons—where few others thrive, is so common along the shore from New England to Texas, and is hardly noticed until its insignificant flowers mature in autumn, when it becomes a mass of white.

One of the very few woody members of the Daisy Family, *Compositae, Baccharis* is closely related to *Aster*. One would hardly guess this, though, because the two genera are visually very distinct. *Baccharis* is a spreading shrub reaching ten or twelve feet, with deciduous leaves and angled, greenish branchlets. The leaves are ovalish in outline, the upper being obversely wedge-shaped, one or two inches in length. The general effect is similar to that of the Bayberry and Inkberry Holly, with which this species often clumps. Color of the foliage is a curious matt gray-green, neither dull nor glossy, and grayish without being glaucous. The texture is thick and succulent.

The flowers of Groundsel Bush lack colorful rays. However, the pappus, which in most *Compositae* consists of minute scales or bristles, is elongated and plumose in this species, becoming stark white and quite showy en masse as the flowers age. Each half-inch flower looks exactly like a tiny shaving brush with white bristles.

Groundsel Bush is an interesting, salt-resistant shrub well worth growing anywhere for its late color. (It does well in sterile soils upland, but perhaps will prove more difficult in rich mineral soils far from the coast.) The genus is wholly American, an evergreen species from Patagonia being the most popular in cultivation (tender, of course, in the East). A few years ago, while walking through the chapparal at Point Lobos in northern California, I realized that the brush around me was composed largely of what looked like Groundsel Bush, though the dry, rocky habitat hardly suggested a salt marsh. Later I found that I was looking at Coyote-brush, *B. pilularis*, the Pacific counterpart of Groundsel Bush.

Groundsel Bush transplants easily, at least when young. Like hollies and bayberries, it is dioecious—that is, sexes are borne on different plants. Since only the female flowers have the showy plumes, it is well to select female plants to move. The common name alludes, I suppose, to its relationship, Groundsel being the name of another composite, *Senecio*. Two other names listed by Gray are "Sea-myrtle" (an allusion to its resemblance to Bayberry?) and "Consumption Weed." Whatever it is called locally, it is one of the really important seaside plants of the East.

Although this species occurs on dry, windswept dunes, it is more often found in moist depressions between dunes or along the edges of salt marshes and tidal estuaries. Several other plants share its ability to endure quantities of salt-laden moisture at the root. Seaside Goldenrod is, of course, one of these. There are others less adaptable but perhaps more beautiful. These should be attempted in the moister areas of your seaside garden.

One such, a beautiful plant, is the Narrow-leaved Sunflower, *Helianthus angustifolius*, which helps to yellow dune hollows and salt meadows in September and October. It has the deepest flowers, almost orange, of all the eastern perennial sunflowers, and by far the narrowest leaves. These are as narrow as grass blades, succulent in texture but harsh to the touch with a scabrous pubescence, deep dark green. The stem is rich maroon-black, and also rough to the touch. Even out of bloom the plant is distinct and pleasing to look at.

Its very showy three-inch flower has a deep purple-brown disk. The plant is usually smothered in flowers from summit to base. It grows to about six feet, but is often seen much lower than that. This sunflower has a typical Coastal Plain range: from coastal New York south to Florida and Texas, and up the Mississippi Valley

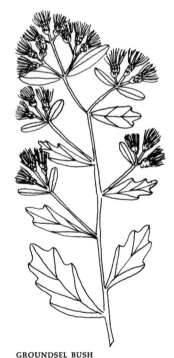

GROUNDSEL BUSH
Baccharis halimifolia

to southern Indiana. In the East it is seldom found far from salt water (though I have seen it growing on the edge of pine-holly woods in peaty soil twenty miles from the sea).

Excellent in combination with Seaside Goldenrod, which blooms at the same time, has flowers of about the same color, and often grows naturally with it, the Narrow-leaved Sunflower is easily transplanted and will grow in much drier situations than those in which it occurs in the wild. I grew it, though not well, in a wild meadow a hundred miles from the coast. Since in nature its woody root is often drowned through much of the growing season, it should probably prove less adaptable than its companion goldenrod. I would try it at the base of a dune rather than at the summit.

Combine: Narrow-leaved Sunflower and Seaside Goldenrod.

Another of the real beauties of the seashore is *Kosteletzkya virginica*, the Saltmarsh or Seashore Mallow, or Fen-rose. It is a close relative of *Hibiscus* and is often seen growing with Rose-mallow, but is altogether a more slender, smaller, more delicate plant. One might hope that it would be as adaptable as hibiscus, but as to this I have no knowledge. In my experience it is often seen growing with the latter in salt marshes or salt meadows but not in freshwater ditches or swamps, an observation which may indicate that it is not so easy away from its saline haunts.

There is no question, though, that it is potentially a very valuable addition to a shore garden. It has the same general flower form as hibiscus—five petals forming a saucerlike corolla from the center of which projects a long, golden column of fused stamens and pistils. The column of *Hibiscus* projects straight outward, however, while that of the Fen-rose shows a definite curve downward. The color of this plant is also not so variable as its relative. All specimens that I have ever seen have been a soft but deep pink, a very good color. Combining well with this is the foliage—more or less triangular leaves of ashy gray-green.

Unlike Rose-mallow, which forms a many-stemmed but usually unbranched plant from a single crown, *Kosteletzkya* is often single- or few-stemmed and much branched from the base, forming a great pyramidal head of pink flowers and grayish leaves which is quite showy. It reminds one somewhat of a hollyhock. The flowers are two or three inches wide, and a robust plant will reach five feet in height. *Kosteletzkya* occurs from Long Island to Florida and Texas, near the coast. It is named for a Czech botanist, B. F. Kosteletzky. Manuals say that it flowers from spring to fall in some parts of its range. Plants in the Middle States begin in the middle of August and flower throughout the autumn.

In addition to the true seashore plants like *Solidago sempervirens, Kosteletzkya, Baccharis,* and Saltmarsh Milkweed, there are many which grow elsewhere but adapt themselves to the shore environment with relative ease. Such are Butterflyweed, Flat-top Goldenrod, *Heterotheca* (an annual yellow daisy closely allied to and resembling Golden-aster), Coreopsis, Gaillardia, Yucca, *Opuntia humifusa* (the hardiest cactus in the East), Yarrow, Trumpetvine, False-indigo (*Baptisia*), and Shining Sumac (very handsome at the shore). All of these and more might be tried.

I stated earlier that change in the seashore garden is arrived at by means of accretion. To illustrate: establish a sizable pine among the dune grasses, surrounding it with deep-rooted Yucca and adaptable Coreopsis (these should be planted in baskets of earth, perhaps). In a short time a relatively stable microenvironment is formed in the vicinity of the tree. Its fallen needles, held by the plants nearby, begin to form a layer of humus which permits quicker increase of both existing plants and new plants which wouldn't have been able to start themselves in the bare sand. Birds, sheltering in the tree branches, drop seeds of Beach Plum, Bayberry, and Sumac. Wind-borne seeds of pines, composites, and grasses eddy into the shelter of the pine and germinate. In time the thicket spreads, its center becoming more protected and humus-rich, thereby allowing a greater variety of plants to establish themselves. Slowly a miniature forest builds itself, its roots binding the sand, its tops deflecting the sweeping winds. Such thickets are of incalculable value during the winter storms which push the sea across the barrier dunes and sweep whole resorts away every twenty years or so.

Achieve change by accretion.

HOW TO PLANT

So much for the enumeration of suitable native plants. In practical terms, how does one go about planting? Well, first he must locate the material, and there are, of course, two sources for this: the wild and cultivation. I mentioned earlier that the fact that beach vegetation is deep-rooted was important from a gardening point of view. Specifically, it makes dune plants very difficult to transplant successfully. The lovely little *Hudsonia*, for example, is impossible to ball and burlap because it grows in pure sand, and has such long roots that one simply cannot get more than a small portion of them. Other dune plants turn out, on digging, to be not "plants" at all but the tips of submerged trees. A friend of mine followed a two-foot persimmon seedling more than two feet below the sand and found no trace of root, and I have seen dunes upon which appeared to grow a thicket of small beach plums which, upon destruction, turned out to be built around a single twenty-foot tree, the tips of which flowered and fruited above the sand. Such plants are, of course, physically impossible to move. Moreover, most coastal states have laws which protect dune vegetation against the individual digger (though not, alas, against corporations and the Corps of Army Engineers!), so what is physically difficult is often illegal as well. The best way to start with dune plants from the wild is with seeds (or at least seedlings) and cuttings.

Use seeds, seedlings, and cuttings.

As far as sources in cultivation are concerned, there are only about two—commercial nurseries and state institutions. Most resort areas have nurseries which specialize in salt-resistant plants, and though these often stock exotics, many also offer such useful natives as Bayberry and Inkberry. Many states also have facilities in which dune plants are grown for restocking. Such plants as dune grasses, Bayberry, and various pines are often obtainable from these at no cost or, at most, for a nominal sum. State universities or agricultural services will help you locate such agencies.

The great advantages of starting plants from seed lie in the relative ease of the process. One can gather quantities of Beach Plum, Wild Rose, Sandwort, *Hudsonia*, or Dune Grass seed with very little effort and broadcast it where it is to grow. Much more seed is required than plants wanted, simply because, as in nature, a relatively small percentage of seed will germinate and live to maturity. The one great disadvantage of this method is that such a long wait is required (at least as far as woody plants are concerned) for mature plants. In contrast, cultivated material establishes and grows quickly, but most nurseries and agencies lack variety.

Whatever the method or source, there are certain rather strict requirements in establishing plants at the shore. First, because of the extreme porosity of sand, newly set plants will need far more frequent waterings than plants set out in ordinary garden soil. If watering facilities are not available, then it is advisable to put plants out only in early spring or in fall. This rule applies doubly to plants brought in from the wild, for while nursery stock has frequently absorbed much of the initial shock of moving, wild plants have not, and take longer to get new roots down into the sand.

Further, sand is often too light and open to support newly set plants of any size. They topple in the first breeze. For this reason, plants which have a ballast of clinging soil around their roots will establish more quickly than others. This soil also absorbs and holds moisture naturally, so serves a double purpose. Container-grown stock is probably the safest to use, for there is almost no transplanting shock, and the plants come equipped with an anchor of nutrient-rich and moisture-retentive soil which contributes greatly to their survival.

In fact, I would recommend establishing wild transplants in containers of suitable soil before placing them out in the dunes. One could, for example, put them in containers in a sheltered spot in spring, water them faithfully through the summer, and place them in permanent positions either the following fall or spring. Any sort of container could be used: the newer sorts of compressed paper, peat, or sawdust, which decompose beneath the soil, are perhaps best because they can be planted with the plant itself.

Plant seedlings in containers.

A further variation of this method: for really difficult situations, say dune crests or slopes on which almost nothing will grow, put your plant in a really large box, crate, or basket of good, rich soil. This should not be waterproof; a bushel basket is perfect, for example. A plant in such a container is virtually assured survival, and all that heavy soil makes an excellent stable base around which the blowing sand will collect.

Finally, don't be afraid to experiment in seaside gardening. An observant eye sees all sorts of strange things near the shore. Who would think that, for instance, White Poplar or Wild Cherry would survive with all but branch-tips buried by sand, or that a massive piedmont tree like the Post Oak would survive, albeit as a prostrate shrub, within a hundred feet of the ocean's waves, yet I have seen dunes held by White Poplar or Wild Cherry, and one of the most statuesque natural bonsai I have ever encountered is an ancient Post Oak growing on the dunes south of Rehoboth Beach in Delaware.

And don't overlook some of the commoner plants for difficult situations. The Giant Reed, *Phragmites communis,* for example, an ineradicable weed in the estuarine marshes of the East (as, for example, the Hackensack marshes across the Hudson from Manhattan Island), makes an excellent dune-binder, growing in restrained manner in the hostile environment of the shore, whereas inland it grows quickly into tall canebrakes which crowd other vegetation out. Another grass, the annual Seaside Cockspur Grass (*Echinochloa walteri*), is well worth establishing, in spite of the fact that it is closely allied to and resembles the weedy Barnyard Grass of ditches and waste ground farther inland. It is a vigorous plant, preferring plenty of moisture, saline or otherwise, growing to about five feet in height with apple-green leaves and stout green stems surmounted by huge reddish flowering heads all a-bristle with mahogany spikelets. The large milletlike seeds are much relished by birds, from the introduced California house finches, which winter on the dunes, to the native song sparrows, horned larks, and snow buntings, which are driven down the coasts by winter storms. If you are like many contemporary people and visit the shore during the off-season—Thanksgiving or New Year's Day—a planting of grasses such as these to attract winter birds will amply reward you.

X

Yellow Daisies

After I had spent a full year traveling my route, I became aware of a curious phenomenon: almost throughout the season I had seen some form of "daisy" growing by the way, all of which were yellow, the most common color among composite flowers. In May, ditch borders and swales came alive with flowers of the Golden Ragwort, *Senecio aureus*. A little later bloomed one of the tickseeds, *Coreopsis lanceolata*, originally native south and west of here but long ago escaped from gardens and common especially near the coast. In mid-June and early July appeared the first dark-centered daisies of the *Rudbeckias*—Black- and Brown-eyed Susans, and the vigorous orange-yellow Ox-eye, *Heliopsis helianthoides*. Soon the roadsides south were covered with a low, gray-leaved annual daisy, *Heterotheca subaxillaris*, an immigrant from the south which is slowly pushing northward. As summer moved toward fall, many different yellow composites began to bloom: other *Rudbeckias*; *Helianthus*, the many perennial sunflowers; *Helenium*, the sneezeweeds; *Bidens*, the tickseed-sunflowers and bur-marigolds; and finally, in September, the golden-asters, *Chrysopsis*.

Yellow daisies become a dominant motif in the landscape of late summer. In August the countryside seems to erupt with them; they are everywhere: blooming above fences and struggling through hedge-rows, leaning sunward from the borders of woods, covering whole acres of field, swale, weed-lot, dusty roadside, or tract of disturbed land. They belong to several genera, though most are known simply as "daisy" to the layman, and it is a tribute to their extreme showiness in mass that they are noticed by so many people who ordinarily do not see wildflowers.

In all this splendor, we may be sure that there are some desirable garden plants, and indeed there are. In fact, a good many have become thoroughly domesticated and have produced even showier variants through hybridization and in-breeding—mainly, as seems usually the case, in Europe. Today there are many cultivars of sunflower, helenium, heliopsis, rudbeckia, with flowers often doubled in size or in number of petals, with colors deeper, or paler, or altogether different in color—red or orange or mahogany, or combinations of these with yellow. Probably best known of all these cultivars in America are the "Gloriosa Daisies," Black-eyed Susans with doubled chromosomes, growing larger than wild plants and with flowers twice the size, as well as much more highly colored with orange and mahogany zones and stripes. There are cultivars of other species less known, many of them very much worth growing. Many of these I will mention in passing.

One of the first (if not the very first) of all composites to bloom is a creeping yellow daisy called "Goldenstar," *Chrysogonum virginianum*. Very rare and perhaps exterminated in my region, it becomes commoner southward and westward. It is unusual for a composite in that it is a woodland, not a field flower, which explains its early blooming season. Its ray-flowers are usually reduced to five, so that one has to look twice to see its affinities. Given a rich woodsy soil in partial shade, it is a valuable groundcover, blooming very prettily in May and early June.

If *Chrysogonum* is the most atypical of the plants discussed in this section, the tickseed-sunflowers, *Bidens*, are by far the most numerous in terms of individuals. These are the yellow composites that literally blanket, to the exclusion of almost all other vegetation, the wet, sedgy hollows and fields along the superhighways of the Middle Atlantic States in late summer and early fall. They comprise about three closely similar species—*Bidens coronata* and *B. artistosa*, both native, and *B. polylepis*, now the commonest, an immigrant from the Midwest. "Tickseed-sunflower" is a coined term which attempts to show the affinities of these plants to their very close relatives *Coreopsis* ('Tickseed') and their somewhat less close relatives the sunflowers. Another coined name is "Bur-marigold," alluding to the fact that some have seeds which actually stick to the coats of animals or clothing of men, the seed head then being a "burr." Neither term is entirely successful. *Bidens* (pronounced "By-dens") is shorter, as euphonious, and certainly as descriptive, for it means "two teeth," features which all of them have on their seeds. Spanish Needles (*B. bipinnata*) is a plain relative whose two long teeth are barbed, making its seeds an adhesive nuisance to anyone unlucky enough to blunder into a patch of it.

If one examines a stand of *Bidens* closely, he will see that the plants grow very thickly, in many cases only a few inches apart. Those close together are slender and little-branched, while those with more room are stout and wide-branching; thus each plant fills as much space as is allotted to it, and when each plant is crowned with clusters of yellow flowers, little else is visible except bur-marigolds.

They are annuals, springing anew from self-sown seeds each year so thickly that by early summer those sedgy fields in which they grow are covered by a dense stand of ferny growth of *Bidens* leaves and little else save an occasional straggling rush or sedge. The flowers, broad-rayed and a bit cupped, are most attractive, either individually or en masse. There is a bit of a nod to the way each flower is carried on its stem. This, combined with the slight cup or bell shape ("campanulate" is the descriptive botanical term), renders them more grace-

BIDENS

ful than most daisy-types. They close up entirely at night, also. A friend once asked me if they were Evening-primroses, I suppose because he thought Evening-primroses closed at evening.

But there is nothing of twilight about these flowers. The sun itself is in their color; their rich, polleny smell is the essence of noontime and high summer. Bur-marigolds grew in a field (now a drive-in theater) near my boyhood home. By June the plants were high enough to hide us from each other, and our summers were spent in a golden daze as we broke trails through a jungle of yellow flowers.

Normally found in moist ground, scattered individuals can be found in the driest and most sterile situations imaginable. Here they are often stunted (in the language of botany, much more expressive than most people think, such plants are called "depauperate"), blooming at a foot in height rather than five or six. Most healthy individuals bloom at from three to six feet, and an individual which has ample room to spread (plus sufficient moisture and nutrition) will make a globular, bushy plant as wide as it is tall, covered from top to ground with golden flowers.

Yet bur-marigolds are almost never cultivated. Even I, who have just sung their praises, have only grown them once or twice in my garden, and there only in a dryish and wild corner of the shrub border where they bloomed (somewhat "depauperate") with blue Mist flower (*Eupatorium coelestinum*). The reason we neglect *Bidens* is, I suppose, that like so many so-called weeds they are simply all around us. Why move them a few feet into our gardens? Yet I think that many of the species, *B. polylepis* especially, would more than repay real coddling in our gardens.

The genus is so close to *Cosmos* that botanists have trouble finding technical features that will serve to separate the two. Since *Bidens* grow in precisely the same way as the common *Cosmos bipinnatus*, reach about the same heights, and occur in yellow, a color not found in this species of *Cosmos*, they make excellent companion plants. Both should be sown where they are to grow (or the cosmos may be planted out from pots—no point in starting the *Bidens* early, since it will bloom late anyhow) and ruthlessly thinned after the seedlings

Try BIDENS POLYLEPIS *in your garden. Combine it with* COSMOS.

are a few inches high. A foot and a half between plants is not too much on good soil. With a rich soil the cosmos will bolt, so it is not advisable to use manure or fertilizer if your soil is moderately good. The trick is to provide sufficient moisture and nutrients so that the cosmos will make strong growth and begin to bloom in August, but not so much that they devote their time to making plant growth (I have seen them reach ten feet) and forget to flower before frost. The *Bidens*, since it is native rather than Mexican, will do its best in any sort of soil and bloom on schedule in August.

Seed is abundantly produced by these plants. All one has to do to get plenty for his garden is walk through a field around the time of the first frost and harvest the burry heads. If one forgets or neglects to do this, as he is likely to do, young plants may be transplanted in spring. (These are unmistakable; they look like smoother, more delicate, more pointed-leaved ragweed seedlings with reddish stems.) They have a tendency to wilt badly—as do the flowers when cut—but they can be revived with plenty of water. Transplanted specimens never seem to develop as well as those which bloom where they have germinated. Any bur-marigold will produce plenty of seed, so transplanted plants will yield many robust seedlings for the following season.

I have also pinched plants throughout the growing season—till mid-July or thereabouts, much as one does chrysanthemums and hardy asters, and have obtained extremely bushy and floriferous plants two feet tall. Like all annuals and biennials these plants will attempt to bloom and set seed in order to propagate themselves no matter what the odds. I have seen them blooming at six inches in hayfields at Thanksgiving during a mild autumn, where they have been mowed repeatedly all summer long, growing a little less vigorously each time cut back, and setting flowers a little less quickly until they are literally reduced to flower, in one last attempt before the end of the season, at a few inches in height.

All in all, these are fine plants for bright color and bold effects in the garden. The flowers are also beautiful as cut blooms, especially in "Williamsburg arrangements" of mixed summer flowers. They will wilt, however, unless plunged in deep water immediately after being cut.

Another, rather different *Bidens* is common in my area. One can hardly recommend it as a garden plant, for reasons which will immediately become apparent, but still it is beautiful, unique, and would be worth cultivating if one had the sorts of conditions to suit it. I am speaking of *Bidens laevis*, rather lamely called "Smooth Bur-marigold" in the manuals. It grows about three feet tall and has showy yellow flowers like its relatives, but undivided leaves. The chief difference between it and them lies, however, in habitat preference. *B. laevis* is an aquatic, growing right in the estuarine marshes of the Delaware River and its tributaries, ramping across black mud flats at low tide and standing in deep water at high. With its constant companion, Wild-rice (*Zizania aquatica*), it brightens the foully polluted marshes around the great cities of the East, coming into glorious golden bloom very late in the year, just when the Wild-rice is dropping its grains and beginning to lose its fresh green color. The seeds of both are eagerly sought after by waterfowl. Anyone lucky enough to have a stream or pond margin to plant should attempt both of these plants. If local seed cannot be gathered, suppliers of wild-fowl foods may be able to supply it. (Most of the latter certainly offer Wild-rice.)

For stream or pond margins: BIDENS LAEVIS *and Wild-rice.*

A common plant which, like *Bidens polylepis*, is both an immigrant from farther west and a welcome brightener of wasteland and littered roadsides is the Common Sunflower, *Helianthus annuus*. The manuals tell us that this native of the Great Plains was long ago carried throughout the country by Indians, who used its seeds for food and oil and its stems for cloth-producing fiber. The enormous cultivated sunflowers have been derived from this species, but the smaller-flowered, true wild original has little in common with these. It is a big plant—coarse, even—but its black-centered golden disks give it a great deal of grace to balance out its coarseness. The flowers are five or six inches across, blooming on plants perhaps six feet tall. These, unlike the cultivated sorts which often consist of one mam-

COMMON SUNFLOWER

moth flower supported by a straight unbranched stem twice the thickness of a broomstick, are very much branched, each branch and branchlet bearing a flower. The effect is very pleasing. Unlike the giant cultivars, too, which are all disk, the wild form has a pleasingly formed flower, the rays equaling or exceeding the diameter of the disk.

In my area it is most often seen in one locality: the industrial wasteland that lies between Philadelphia's International Airport and the city of Chester, Pennsylvania. Here in late August it absolutely transforms the landscape from hideous to beautiful. One's attention is diverted from the smog, soot, exhaust fumes, roar of jet and combustion engine, slag heaps and cinder piles by the myriad dark-centered golden flowers turning as the sun turns—in Blake's words "counting the steps of the sun."

I have not been alone in noticing them. Several years ago an acquaintance, a German exchange student, was so moved by seeing them after flying into Philadelphia from Germany that he wrote a poem about them—in English, and quite a good poem, too. Earlier than this, another very dear friend of mine painted them—in fact I first saw the airport sunflowers hanging on her living room wall. The painting hangs on my wall now. And just this year another friend, not a plant buff at all, asked me what the big yellow daisies near the Philadelphia airport were. Finally, in his *Stalking the Wild Asparagus*, Euell Gibbons mentions gathering seed for culinary purposes from this very stand.

The airport sunflowers grow with another immigrant, the weedy but spectacular *Lythrum salicaria*, Purple Loosestrife, and the two together make a barbaric but gorgeous combination of gold and magenta. If one decides that this sunflower, by the way, is too coarse for the garden, then by all means try it in an out-of-the-way corner for cutting. Its flowers are really superb in arrangements.

Helianthus annuus is, as the scientific name states, an annual. So used are we to thinking of this as *the* sunflower that we forget, if we ever learn, that most of the species of the genus are good, long-lived perennials. Most of these don't look much like our common con-

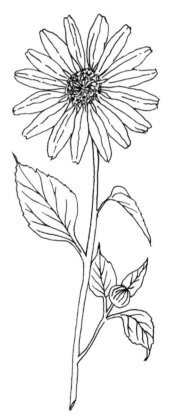

COMMON SUNFLOWER
Helianthus annuus

PERENNIAL
SUNFLOWERS

ception of sunflowers—few have dark disks, and most have flowers with very long rays and disks that are quite small. Moreover, the heads of most of them average about three inches in breadth, no size at all for a sunflower. However, the flowers of these perennial sunflowers are in proportion to the size of leaves and plant, and many of them make very fine garden subjects. In fact, several named cultivars of the various species have been produced—mainly, of course, in Europe. All of these bloom in August and September.

A plant which is economically valuable like its annual cousin and which was also cultivated by the Indians is *Helianthus tuberosus*, the "Jerusalem Artichoke." As most gardeners sooner or later learn from the botanists, this plant is neither an artichoke nor from Jerusalem. It is an American native grown for its potato-like tubers. Taken to Europe, it was cultivated extensively in Italy, where the name for sunflower is *girasole*—roughly translated, "turning with the sun." This *girasole*, returning with Italian immigrants to this country, became corrupted to "Jerusalem." The term "artichoke" apparently arose through confusion as to the origin of the edible part of the plant (since true artichokes are not tubers but flower heads).

Helianthus tuberosus is ornamental as well as edible. If you don't grow a stand of it for its nutritious tubers, try a stand along a fence, in the corner of a building, between big shrubs, or in similar places. The rough grayish green leaves and abundant yellow flowers are very showy in late summer and fall.

Try sunflowers along a fence, in corner of a building, or between big shrubs.

The rest of the perennial sunflowers are more or less similar to *H. tuberosus*. I have seen most of them in their haunts but have not tried all of them in the garden. Noteworthy, however, are a few rather distinct species. *H. mollis* I first saw growing along a mountain road in New England, where it apparently was introduced. It is native of the Midwest, a plant of medium size with large and showy clear yellow flowers which are beautifully set off by the white-wooly pubescence of the leaves. It is very much worth obtaining.

Noteworthy species:
H. TUBEROSUS, H. MOLLIS,
H. MAXIMILIANI,
H. SALICIFOLIUS,
H. ANGUSTIFOLIUS.

Another midwestern native is *H. maximiliani*, named for a German prince. It is much cultivated and like the preceding species has escaped in the East. A tall plant, with usually unbranched stems and narrow, drooping leaves the size and shape of peach leaves but rough to the touch, it has bright yellow flowers of medium size. But what is really distinct about the plant is the way the flowers are arranged— in long, curved, slender spikes or racemes at the apex of the stems. It reminds one of a gigantic goldenrod. *H. salicifolius* from the South-west has even narrower leaves. It grows well in the East.

With narrow leaves but flowers not really arranged in spikes is the bright-flowered *H. angustifolius*, the Narrow-leaved Sunflower of the coastal dunes and marshes. It has been discussed more fully in the section on beach planting. I have it growing in an acid field with other species. The final species is perhaps my favorite. It is known as *H. giganteus*, or Tall Sunflower, but I have always thought that its names are more or less inappropriate. Tall it certainly can be (but so can the rest of the species), gigantic it certainly isn't. In fact, it is a delicate-looking plant for one so large. It reaches twelve feet in height, as do several other species. Its stems are reddish or purplish, its leaves long and narrow, and its small flowers, two to two-and-a-half inches wide, are borne on slender branches along the upper half of the stem. These flowers are a clear sulfur-yellow, paler than any other wild sunflower of my area, with tiny green disks. For all its height, it is a willowy, graceful plant, and its pale flowers are quite distinct in color. It is the commonest wild sunflower in my immediate area, and each summer I look forward to seeing its flowers raised above the fencerows in the local fields, situations where it commonly grows and which suit it very well in cultivation also.

Mention should be made of some of the horticultural variants of these perennial sunflowers. Two species, *H. decapetalus* and *H. rigidus* (*H. scaberrimus*), both more or less midwestern in range, have been extensively cultivated in Europe and have given rise to several hybrids or cultivars, some with attractive double flowers. A good double form of *decapetalus* is sparingly available in that trade as "multiflorus flore-pleno." It is rather accurately described in one catalogue as having flowers like "miniature dahlias," although I would say large chrysanthemums (of the Intermediate Decorative class) rather than dahlias. Other cultivars of this species are 'Loddon Gold' and 'Soleil d'Or,' both double. Variants of *H. rigidus* are 'Daniel Dewar,' deep orange-yellow, 'Semi-plenus,' semi-double orange, and 'Latest of All,' a very large, very late semi-double orange-yellow. Another cultivar listed is a variant of *H. atrorubens*, a dark-centered perennial native to the South. This is usually sold as *Helianthus sparsifolius* 'Monarch.' It has large golden flowers each with a purple-brown eye.

Everyone should grow Indian-cup.

There are two wildlings which for all intents and purposes might be called sunflowers, though botanical technicalities place them in separate but related genera. One of these is the showy Cup-plant or Indian-cup, *Silphium perfoliatum,* one of yellow composites which inhabit the plains from the Mississippi Valley west but have become escapees from gardens eastward. Everyone should grow this plant. In moist, rich soil it becomes eight feet tall, with a thick, square stem and large, opposite heart-shaped leaves whose stemless bases grow together to form a cup which actually holds water. In late summer it raises its light yellow three-inch flowers in great abundance above the large leaves. Indian-cup has a relative which I have not grown beyond the seedling stage so perhaps should not recommend, but it sounds like such an interesting plant that I want at least to mention it here. Its botanical name is *Silphium laciniatum;* its colloquial, Compass-plant or Pilot-weed. It differs from the preceding species in having somewhat larger flowers and ferny, finely divided leaves. Its common names derive from its manner of growth—on its native prairies, at any rate: its stem leaves grow vertically (not horizontally, like those of most plants), with their edges pointing rigidly north and south. A stand of these plants must be quite a sight on the prairie, and a planting of them would be interesting if only as a conversation piece. Its yellow flowers are also showy.

The other plants which I want to discuss along with the wild sunflowers are members of the genus *Heliopsis*, Ox-eyes or False-sunflowers. There is one species in my area, *H. helianthoides*, Smooth Ox-eye, a robust sunflower-like plant which grows about five feet high and bears daisylike flowers about two-and-a-half inches wide. Two obvious differences between it and the sunflowers: it flowers in early July, and its flowers are deeper in color than those of most

23. Saltmarsh Milkweed *(Asclepias lanceolata),*
the rarest, most difficult, and possibly most
beautiful of all milkweeds.

24. White Milkweed (*Asclepias variegata*) growing in the pine forests of southern Delaware. An excellent wild-garden subject for both foliage and flowers.

25. Purple Milkweed (*Asclepias purpurascens*). A showy, sun-loving species that is rapidly disappearing from its native haunts.

26. Butterflyweed (*Asclepias tuberosa*) growing with Scotch Heather at Winterthur. This is the best-known milkweed and an excellent garden flower.

27. White Snakeroot, *Eupatorium rugosum*, a common woodland plant which makes a good autumn-flowering garden plant and cutflower.

28. *(left)* Hickory, Black Gum, Burning Bush, and White Snakeroot in the Quarry at Winterthur during the third week in October.

29. *(below)* *Helenium* 'Chippersfield.' A cultivated form of Sneezeweed which blooms for a long period in late summer and autumn.

30. The flower of the Franklin Tree, or Lost Camellia, *Franklinia alatamaha*. One of the best late-blooming shrubs.

31. Fruits of Jack-in-the-pulpit (*Arisaema triphyllum*) show more brilliantly than flowers in the autumn wild garden.

32. Red Chokeberry, *Aronia arbutifolia*, in early autumn, with bright berries and foliage beginning to turn color. This is the form known in the trade as 'Brilliantissima.'

33. White Wood Aster (*A. divaricatus*), a fine autumn-blooming wildflower for the woods garden.

34. Smooth Withe-rod, or Shining Viburnum
(*V. nudum*), in autumn.

sunflowers, almost a true orange. It forms secondary buds in the axils of the stem leaves and will often bloom nearly to frost if the flowers are trimmed off as they fade to keep them from going to seed. It is very easy in the garden. I had a clump growing among shrubbery in soil that was kept at Sahara dryness by a greedy maple nearby, and it performed beautifully, only tending to be a little poor-looking in leaf. With adequate moisture in the soil its foliage is excellent. There is a very similar, somewhat more northern species (or variety), the Rough Ox-eye, *H. scabra*, which is as good if not better in the garden. Its color and heavy flowering have long endeared it to Europeans, who have sent back to its native country several named cultivars (hybrids?) which are really excellent perennials. 'Gold Greenheart' is a butter-yellow double variety with a greenish center. It looks very much like a full double zinnia. 'Golden Plume' is a deeper yellow double. Single varieties with somewhat larger and fuller flowers than the type are 'Light of Loddon' and 'Summer Sun,' both deep yellow, and 'Orange King,' almost orange.

Early in this discussion I brought up the fact that the Gloriosa Daisies so popular at the moment are nothing more than tetraploid Black-eyed Susans. The diploid wild plant is a beauty in its own right, though in some places a bad weed. It begins here in mid-June, before the summer solstice. I have *Rudbeckia serotina* growing all over my property, and so pretty is it that I often wait until it blooms before pulling it out, cutting the flowers for the house. It is variable; reddish variants have been found, and one summer I found a form with very pale yellow rays, which unfortunately did not seed itself. The main problem with keeping such variants is that being biennials or at best short-lived perennials, they must seed themselves or eventually die out. One summer I found a whole patch of this species on my grounds with centers ("cones") not of deep blackish brown that one usually sees but bright chartreuse. A large seed company has since introduced a Gloriosa Daisy called 'Irish Eyes' which is similar. I pulled all the normal plants in the area in hopes that the plants would fertilize themselves. Several green-eyed plants have occurred in subsequent years.

BLACK-EYED SUSANS

Encourage variant Black-eyed Susans to seed themselves.

A very informative article entitled "Horticultural Opportunities in Rudbeckia," by Robert E. Perdue, Jr., appeared in *The American Horticultural Magazine* (the organ of the American Horticultural Society) for Summer, 1969. Dr. Perdue points out that of the fifteen or so species in the genus, only the Black-eyed Susan has been subjected to any sort of intensive breeding work by plant breeders, and that the other members of the genus provide ample new material for potential garden plants. There are some fascinating rudbeckias in the South and West, but unfortunately I have had little experience with them, so will discuss only the two other species besides *serotina* that I know.

One summer day as I was hurtling through the pine woods of southern Delaware I glimpsed in the partial gloom of the forest what appeared to be a rounded bush of dark-centered yellow flowers. I made a mental note to investigate the spot when I passed again. I did, and found to my surprise a plant which was obviously a *Rudbeckia,* but of a species unknown to me. Its flowers were smaller than those of the common Black-eyed Susan, being about two inches across, but they were a deep orange-yellow and literally covered the plant, which stood some two-and-a-half feet high and nearly as broad. The presence of three-lobed lower leaves indicated that this was *Rudbeckia triloba,* and further investigation verified the guess. It is a bushy, attractive plant, larger but much more restrained in effect than *R. serotina.* It is very ornamental. Dr. Perdue, incidentally, feels that variants of this species have the greatest ornamental potential in the genus. Two other plants grew near my discovery in the pine woods, and as so often happens after one makes a new discovery, a week later I saw a fourth plant growing in a windbreak of Scotch Pine nearly a hundred miles to the north, just across the Delaware line in Pennsylvania! It is introduced or an extremely rare native in Delmarva.

The last *Rudbeckia* that I will discuss here is *R. laciniata,* the Tall Coneflower of swamps, wet thickets, river banks, from Canada to Florida, west to the Dakotas and Oklahoma, and sporadically farther west. We had in our garden when I was a child a tall plant with double yellow flowers which my mother called "coreopsis." It was, I discovered when I grew older, not coreopsis at all, but "Golden Glow," the doubled form of *R. laciniata* and a common old-fashioned garden flower. Our Golden Glow grew sulkily for years, tending to lose half its leaves by late summer, although it flowered regularly. The reason for its difficulties lay in the fact that it was planted in packed, bone-dry soil beneath a tree, precisely the wrong location for a lover of alluvial richness like that of the plant's native haunts.

But the wild type itself is well worth growing—a tall background sort of plant with large, cut leaves and soft yellow flowers from late July into September. These flowers, unlike those of the two preceding rudbeckias, have centers or cones of pale green, rather than maroon or brown. The effect is totally different from that of the Black-eyed Susans. Some individuals have better flowers with much longer and more numerous rays than others, so it is advisable to select plants in bloom. There is in the trade a cultivar called 'Herbstsonne,' which is supposed to be a selection of the related *R. nitida*. It looks much like an exceptionally fine clone of *R. laciniata*.

According to Dr. Perdue, the tall, slender-stemmed populations of the East are ornamentally inferior to other populations, mainly western, with short, stout stems. While I do not feel that a tall plant is necessarily an inferior plant (even small gardens need accents and background plants), it is true that a shorter Golden Glow would be much more adaptable in the garden. A fairly recent German development approaches a better Golden Glow. Called 'Goldquelle,' it has double flowers like those of the old-fashioned plant but grows only three feet high.

This makes a good plant for the border, but my preference is still for the wild plant. It is really fine in damp places in sun or half-shade. The first Meadow Lilies I found in Delaware were growing with this species on the damp banks of the Brandywine Creek, and I have associated the two in my mind ever since. The two don't bloom together, but make a good pair nevertheless, the highly ornamental foliage of the rudbeckia providing just the right background

TALL CONEFLOWERS

Tall Coneflower for background flowers.

for the thin-stemmed and delicate-blossomed lilies, and its flowers giving color after the elegant lilies have faded.

SNEEZEWEEDS

As a boy, roaming the broad fields and tidal marshes of the great Delaware's tributaries, I used to visit each summer a place where a tall thicket of willows and viburnums pushed out into a marsh to be met by a stand of Wild-rice nearly as tall. Black-crowned night herons roosted there, reason enough to brave the dense tangle, and better still, we once found a blacksnake there which was longer than any of us was tall. One day in late August, I pushed completely through the thicket and stood in the ooze of the marsh. The Wild-rice and willows never really met; there was a zone, just a few feet wide, too dry for the tall grass but too wet for the shrubs. All manner of coarse marsh plants grew there: it was a zone of mixed vegetation. But that day I was enthralled by four plants in particular, all in bloom, a belt of color around the willow thicket. There was Turtle-head, *Chelone glabra,* with its ghost-white, puffed, closed-mouthed blooms like aborted snapdragons. There was Monkeyflower (*Mimulus ringens*), its mauve flowers also betraying its snapdragon affinities. There was Cardinalflower of vivid, deep, soul-satisfying red. And

For personality and color: Sneezeweed.

there were the clear yellow daisylike flowers of Sneezeweed, *Helenium autumnale.* Twenty years and more have passed and I can still see the medley of bright colors, smell the marsh gases that my tread released from the muck; feel again the pure delight I felt on finding a kind of wildflower garden in such an unlikely spot.

Afterward, I returned each year at about the same time to see them, such was the effect of the first sight of them. I would also gather a large bunch of them for my mother—no danger of over-picking, since one had to wade through nearly impenetrable vegetation or soupy mud whichever way he approached them. I really believe now that I was one of very few people ever to see this stand of plants. No one of my acquaintance knew of it except my brothers and one or two friends (who were far more interested in snakes than in flowers, in any case).

I often see the marsh from the highway as I drive to the city. Are the flowers still there? I hope so, but I really don't know for sure. More years have passed than I like to think of since I have been back there to see them. I grew up and lost my wonder at the beauty of the simple world around me. I found cardinalflower, turtlehead, monkeyflower, sneezeweed elsewhere; found them, in fact, to be rather common in Delaware marshes. More than that, I traveled, saw jungles of orchids and amaryllids, palm trees on the shores of tropical islands. How could a tangle of flowers in a few yards of stinking marsh compete with these? Nevertheless, today I wish that I could plant a garden to give me half the delight given by that belt of marsh flowers many years ago.

Helenium is one of the latest of the yellow composites to bloom in the East. The common species here, *autumnale*, blooms from late August sometimes into October, an upright branching plant to five feet with narrow leaves and many small, green-centered yellow "daisies." The disk of the flower is large and spherical. The rays tend to be somewhat sparse and to droop downward. These are spatulate and notched at the tip, giving a somewhat ragged look to the flower. The "buds" of the plant consist of the naked center, at first disklike, slowly becoming globular and developing fully before the rays expand. The effect, then, is concentrated on the centers —disks or globes, according to their stage of development—rather than on the rays. Since the centers of *H. autumnale* are greenish yellow, they do not contrast greatly with the ray-flowers, although the brighter green developing disks do provide considerably greater contrast. There are other species of *Helenium,* as well as several cultivated forms, which have dark centers, and in these the developing flower is as attractive as that in full bloom.

Much later in my life I encountered the only other species that I have found in Delaware: *H. nudiflorum,* Purple-headed Sneezeweed. It was growing along a dry roadside, a plant two feet tall with dark-centered yellow flowers like miniature Black-eyed Susans. So unusual was the site for a sneezeweed, so short the plant and dark-centered the flowers, that I was at first sure that I had a new species of *Rudbeckia.* Only on second and closer glance did its affinities to the

Common Sneezeweed—drooping, notched rays, winged and angled stem, leaves with short, winged petioles—become apparent. I found a few more plants and transferred one to my garden, where it bloomed but did not spread. Gray's *Manual of Botany*, Eighth Edition, describes it as spreading northward as a "weed." I would quarrel with the definition. Spread northward it has (since it is originally native from North Carolina and Georgia west to Missouri and Texas), but it is by no means either weedy or common around here. It is a very refined weed, in any case, its low stature making it considerably more delicate in appearance than its larger relative. Variants of this species may have rays partially or entirely chestnut or maroon instead of yellow.

Helenium is another genus which has interested hybridizers abroad, and some spectacular garden plants have been produced by them. Even these, though they are offered by several nurseries, are seldom seen except in the gardens of really dedicated gardeners. Like *Rudbeckia*, *Helenium* possesses genes for colors other than yellow, and cultivated clones or hybrids now appear in shades ranging from light yellow to deep crimson-maroon. In addition, the rays of most of the cultivated clones do not droop so much as those of the wild species, and they are longer and more numerous. The result is a showier flower, though one somewhat lacking in the personality of the wild sneezeweeds. Worth mention are 'Butterpat,' a bright yellow with yellow centers, much like *autumnale* but shorter and showier, with larger flowers; 'Wyndley,' with large, dark-centered yellow flowers, the dark developing disks nicely contrasting with the open blooms; 'Chippersfield Orange,' rather tall light orange-copper; 'Coppelia,' deeper and somewhat shorter orange-copper; 'Moerheim Beauty,' deep bronzy red with a velvety maroon disk; 'Peregrina,' very dark mahogany; and 'Bruno,' deep mahogany-crimson. Most of these grow about three feet in height. There is a dwarf yellow variety (*pumilum*) of *H. autumnale* which grows twelve to eighteen inches tall. This is usually known in the trade as 'Pumilum magnificum.' Incidentally, the rather unpleasant common name Sneezeweed (which nurserymen avoid, using "Helen's Flower" instead) is supposedly a reference to the fact that the dried leaves of the plants may be used as a substitute for snuff.

The last of the yellow daisies to bloom is a plant rather smaller in stature and finer in flower than those discussed so far. It is the Maryland Golden-aster, *Chrysopsis* (or *Heterotheca*) *mariana*, a plant with the habit and appearance of an aster but the color of a goldenrod, one of the prettiest denizens of pine woods and barrens in our region and one of the best native plants for the garden.

MARYLAND GOLDEN-ASTER

From an over-wintering rosette of long-oval leaves, dark green covered with peculiar, long whitish hairs, spring one to several sparsely foliaged stems which grow from one to two-and-a-half feet tall, each with the strange cobwebby pubescence (arachnoid, "of spiders" is the descriptive botanical term) that distinguishes many of the species in this genus. From September well into October these stems bear corymbs of golden inch-wide daisies at their summits. The rays are rather numerous and narrow, like those of aster or fleabane. They are of a clear, rather pale yellow, rather than gold.

Maryland Golden-aster excellent garden plant.

If it weren't for its color, the plant could very easily be taken for an aster, so close is the resemblance. I grow it with purple *Aster spectabilis*, so similar in every way save color. Though the blooming season of each overlaps rather than coincides, the aster beginning a week or two before the golden-aster shows color, little effect is lost. There are, of course, other asters which coincide more closely with its blooming season. It is always worth growing these along with golden-aster for the response they elicit from visitors to the garden, who invariably notice these two similar plants in complimentary colors.

Combine it with purple ASTER SPECTABILIS.

Chrysopsis mariana seldom makes the roadside splash that its relatives the true asters do. I have never seen it growing except on roadside or railroad banks in pine woods or sterile-acid fields and barrens. It cannot compete with the dense vegetation growing on richer soil. In my garden it grows in acid, but not particularly strongly acid, soil in the very light shade of a Pitch Pine, with Birdsfoot Violet, *Aster spectabilis*, *Liriope*, *Phlox pilosa*, and *Rhododendron mucronulatum* for company. It transplants with no difficulty, even when in bud or in full bloom. Plants moved in hot weather must, of course, be watered copiously until they establish themselves. The species is rare and beautiful enough to be considered a prize by most wildflower gardeners. It is a great piece of luck that it is as easy and amenable to cultivation as it is attractive.

There are several more species in the genus, many of them with the distinctive pubescence, and some of them with unusual grasslike leaves. Nearly all the species are native to the South or to the prairie region. Indeed, *C. mariana's* distribution is essentially southern—from Florida to New York along the coast. This seems appropriate, for whenever I think of these flowers I see the pine and oak barren and scrub of the southern Coastal Plain. Here they bloom both in the blistering heat of the sand flats or in the shade of the larger trees. They also are found scattered through the true pine forests, and it is here, perhaps, that they look their best, their canary flowers glowing like pale fire in the green shade of the pines.

XI

Autumn Color

Like the other seasons, autumn makes itself felt long before it arrives officially, sending advance scouts into the enemy territory of summer. It is present, for instance, on those mornings in late July when chicory is blue on roadsides, thistles lavender in fields, coneflowers gold in swales, and broods of young tree swallows cluster on electric wires between weak sallies across the fields. It makes itself felt in the first goldenrod of July and the first aster of August. It colors early the berries of thorn and dogwood, viburnum and honeysuckle.

Toward September the signs become more evident—a few freak scarlet branches among the green on Black Gums, Dogwoods and Persimmons slowly turning from green to bronzy, the swallow families collecting in huge swooping flocks, Sassafras leaves paling to yellow-green. With each passing week they increase. The fields are gold and white with goldenrod and frostweed, richly punctuated by clumps of purple New England Aster. Trim brown cedar waxwings sweep out of the north to raid my ripening crab-apples and firethorn fruits. A hemlock forest in the mountains a few miles north foreshadows winter with a storm of whirring chaff-colored seeds discharged from its cones. A great Honey-locust on my lawn casts its myriad tiny leaves all at once; they cover the grass like yellow snowflakes.

As the year slides beyond the autumn equinox, changes take place more rapidly and dramatically. One morning the flocks of swallows swoop no more; they have gone overnight, their absence almost tangible, an omission in the landscape. In my azaleas I see the gray and white flash of a junco, the bird which for me symbolizes winter, and in the woods at Winterthur I hear the melancholy ramble of a white-throated sparrow, another arrival from colder climes. More striking than winter birds, though, are the trees, for now the great leaf fall has begun in earnest. One by one, the leaves abciss—the life-giving ducts closed off, the cords which bound them to their branches severed—and drift, cast-off, dead or dying, down on the autumn winds. As I move through their swirling, rustling companies I am reminded of how much more vividly descriptive of the season is the word "fall" than the more elegant "autumn."

One year autumn arrived with a great storm which swept all the trees clean in a few minutes. It was October 15th, a gray, drizzly day turned to wet, slippery night as I drove into the hills of northern Delaware. The autumn, after a very wet summer, had been dry and hot. Few trees had even begun to color; all had leaves of a vitiated green, as if sapped of color by heat and drought. Only the Black Gums were scarlet, with an occasional Hickory or Tulip-poplar yellowing and an Ash or two turning that combination of pink, bronze, and yellow peculiar to ashes. This strange year the autumn seemed still remote almost a month after the equinox.

I rounded a hilltop corner and came down into a little valley where the road passed beneath a giant spreading White Ash. The black, glistening road with yellow centerline shone brightly in the beam of my headlights. Nothing but that yellow line marred the black expanse. But suddenly, as I neared the great Ash, a gust of wind took it and a thousand heavy, wet, yellowed leaves plummeted down, littering the road and pelting my automobile as I passed beneath.

After that one cold gust the wind continued. Deluge after deluge of leaves fell from elm, ash, cherry, maple, sycamore. By the time I reached home the roads were littered; the trees on my lawn were bare. Autumn moved like a giant presence across the countryside, engulfing me in grief and despair as momentarily profound as any that I have ever felt over the loss of another human being. I saw the death of the year as a metaphor for human mortality, precisely as the myth-makers of ancient times must have seen it.

But autumn is, like spring, a changeable season. Despair cannot long survive the dawning of one of those high, brisk days of late October or early November, when leaves swirl and drift like a golden snowstorm and flocking birds move endlessly south. Nor can it endure when one observes how bravely summer fights to retain its hold. There are still bees and butterflies, and nature provides abundant flowers for them. With one last great flush of bloom the flowers of autumn color the fields.

Only a few of these are really new. August with its goldenrods and thoroughworts has prepared us for a later display of more goldenrods and thoroughworts, as well as asters, liatrises, sneeze-weed, bur-marigolds, golden-asters, gentians. But all of them seem to come on at once, making field and roadside a carpet of white, gold, and lavender.

Much of the gold in the landscape of autumn comes from the goldenrods, *Solidago*. They are everywhere, as weeds on the outskirts of towns and in suburban lots, or as denizens of the remotest pine *GOLDENRODS* barrens, woodland glades, salt marshes, seaside dunes. There are so many species as to bewilder the casual observer (about seventy-five in the Northeast), and except for color (all save one species are yellow) they are astonishingly diverse, varying in height from a few inches to eight feet, and in many details of habit.

Some species (such as *S. erecta* and *stricta*) have slender, wandlike inflorescences more reminiscent of a liatris than a goldenrod. At the other extreme are the big flat plates of *S. graminifolia* and *tenuifolia*, the Flat-top Goldenrods. In between are such as that of the Wreath Goldenrod, *S. caesia*, a multitude of small, round buttons disposed along a wiry stem, each button flower tended by a leaf, the whole looking as though it really were a garland made by a girl; or the elegantly curling one-sided inflorescence of the Seaside Goldenrod (*S. sempervirens*), and the Old-field Goldenrod (*S. nemoralis*); or the pyramidal heads, composed of tier on tier of horizontal spikes, of species such as Bog Goldenrod (*S. uliginosa*), Early Goldenrod (*S. juncea*), or the three common tall weedy species, *S. canadensis, ulmifolia,* and *gigantea.*

In such diversity there are sure to be plants worthy of cultivation. And indeed there are many. Most of the species with flowers in more or less cylindrical heads are delicate rather dwarf plants occurring in woodlands or pine barrens. All of these are handsome additions to the wild garden. Some likely garden plants from this group are *S. bicolor,* "Silver-rod," unique because of its white flowers, a plant less than two feet tall (in my garden at least) which takes considerable shade; *S. puberula,* much like the last but with very large individual flowers of deep golden, and *S. erecta,* quite similar. *C. caesia* is a species of woodlands and damp barrens whose charms have already been enumerated. It is very pretty in woodlands in late August and later. A species which really does resemble a liatris in gold is *S. stricta,* narrow-leaved and bearing a tall, cylindrical spike of very showy flowers, it raises its golden wands in sandy woods from Florida north only as far as New Jersey.

Recommended garden species: S. BICOLOR, S. PUBERULA, S. ERECTA, S. CAESIA.

The species which have more or less pyramidal inflorescences are often more coarse than the foregoing, but not always. One of the most delicate and pretty is also one of the commonest: *S. nemoralis,* called Old-field Goldenrod because it is often found growing in barren or worked-out land. A colony of this plant grows in a patch of sterile sandy soil on my property, the plants seldom exceeding two feet in height and attractive even out of flower with their scabrous blue-gray foliage. When in bloom they are really attractive, their large flower heads of a more lemon- or primrose-yellow than most goldenrods, which contrasts nicely with their gray foliage.

The list of suitable goldenrods could be made much longer. Unfortunately, their very abundance prohibits us from cultivating them.

Like their close relatives the asters they have long been enjoyed in Europe, in England and Germany especially, where few perennial borders would be without them. One large American nursery currently lists four goldenrods (under the name "Solidago," of course!) developed in Europe: 'Cloth of Gold,' 'Golden Mosa,' 'Golden Shower,' and 'Peter Pan.' These are attractive plants, but hardly more so than the wild species. Like asters, wild goldenrods respond to care and are even more attractive in a well-groomed border than in the wild.

One attribute of goldenrods I have never seen in print: their fragrance. It is perfectly expressive of late summer to me—a touch of weedy pungency to it, yet overpoweringly sweet and sunny. It is sun, green leaves, grass, bees, bright flowers, pollen, ripeness, all combined. Many yellow composites blooming at this time have similar fragrance—tickseed-sunflowers, true sunflowers, oxeyes, cup-plants. Is it the smell of pollen rather than that produced by nectaries? There is a certain nose-tickling sensation associated with it which might be produced by pollen. Whatever the source, it is a marvelous fragrance.

Goldenrods, incidentally, are often blamed for the scourge of summer known as hay fever. In point of fact they do *not* cause it. Goldenrods have brightly colored flowers because they have evolved to attract color-sensitive pollinators. Their pollen grains are relatively large, heavier than air, because they are designed to be carried off by flies, bees, butterflies, even ants or birds, but not by the wind. Wind-pollinated plants usually have unshowy flowers (the wind has no eyes) and very light pollen in extreme abundance (bees take pollen from flower to flower; the wind scatters it over the whole countryside so that much more is necessary to ensure seed set). It is the pollinees of the wind—sedges, ragweeds, wormwoods, oaks, pines, and many other large trees, and, most guilty of all, the grasses—which cause hay fever. If wind removed the pollen of goldenrods before their yellow-loving pollinators got to it, the bright colors of the flowers would be useless, and, since nothing useless exists long in nature, it would quickly disappear.

Goldenrod not the cause of hay fever.

NEW ENGLAND AND
NEW YORK ASTERS

It would be difficult to overpraise the beauty and value of the wild asters. This thought comes to me whenever I am driving during the dull period in late September, after the last of the big floral displays of yellow and purple field-flowers but before the foliage is really brightly colored, and spy the purple dazzle of New England Asters in hedgerows. It is truly royal color, the purple of *Aster novae-angliae*, a deep color which seizes the eye and draws it into its smoky, smoldering depths. And it is all the more welcome because so many other colors have gone with the summer.

Until I took a trip by auto to Toledo, Ohio, in late September, I thought I lived in New England Aster country, but on the coast I had never seen the species in the abundance with which it grows from Pittsburgh west. Meadows, banks, roadsides wet and dry along the Pennsylvania and Ohio turnpikes, were bright, whole fields as purple and gold as Byron's Assyrian hosts with this aster and various goldenrods. One such brilliant field was being systematically cut (for hay?) by a stolid farmer as I sped past.

New England Aster the best of the natives.

This is by far the best of the native asters. Some others approach it, but none can surpass it or even equal it. It is beautiful, adaptable, and ease itself to grow. In all its forms, and it is a variable plant, the New England Aster is excellent for either wild garden or perennial border. It also rivals any of the named cultivated asters which have been produced in such abundance in this country and in Europe, especially in England.

The typical form is a stout, almost shrubby plant growing four to six feet tall in swales, meadows, and along fencerows, with grayish green leaves and great panicles of purple flowers. From mid-September to late October it opens its inch-wide daisies, rich deep violet with a gold center, sometimes varying to shades of rose and pink, all attractive. A white form is also reported, but this I have never seen. For several years I had in my garden a clone of deep rose with flowers twice the normal size. I lost it, alas, in a move from the old house. This fall a friend led me to a wild plant of clear strawberry-pink, clearer and brighter than any form—or hybrid—that I have yet seen.

Some of the many "Michaelmas Daisies" on the market are forms of this species. 'Barr's Pink' and 'Harrington's Pink' are two which are rose-pink in color and quite showy. A deep rose-red is 'September Ruby,' an effective color. If one does not live in New England Aster country, then I recommend these clones. If one does, then with a little patient searching he can find wild forms of *Aster novae-angliae* which will very likely equal them (after all, these named varieties are usually no more than selected clones of the species).

Recommended Michaelmas Daisies: 'Barr's Pink,' 'Harrington's Pink,' 'September Ruby.'

In nature the plant grows often, but not always, in wet spots. In the garden it thrives in rich, moist soil—precisely the conditions that most perennials prefer. It will grow in poor dry soil, but will be stunted in growth. If kept very dry, it is likely to lose the lower stem leaves. I used to grow mine as I grew chrysanthemums—divide and propagate the clumps in spring, set in enriched soil, water well, and cut back to a foot or so two or three times during late spring and early summer, so that the plants will be compact and bushy rather than leggy. This treatment produces a good border plant.

The species tends not to branch unless it is pinched or cut back. In the cutting garden at Winterthur, where they were very appropriately grown as cut flowers to decorate the rooms of period American furniture, they were allowed to grow tall, and each clump was severely staked. When they bloomed, they looked like enormous bouquets, each six feet tall. Recently I saw a mammoth old plant on the lawn of a friend's house. It had been allowed to grow as it wished, and it really had become an excellent lawn specimen—like a dense shrub over four feet tall and nearly as broad, starred from crown to base with purple flowers, a truly impressive sight.

My observations have convinced me that it is so responsive a plant that with a little judicious pruning, an ingenious gardener could achieve almost any height or shape with it. For example, several ruthless shearings (even with the lawn mower), right back to a few inches, during June and July will result in a "dwarf" and very dense plant a foot or two tall which flowers abundantly and, since the flowers are of normal size, quite showily. I well remember finding, during my freshman year in college, a field adjacent to the university where what I excitedly thought was a dwarf form of *Aster novae-angliae* grew in both purple and pink forms. My botany teacher was not impressed by my information, and I later learned why. In order to keep it from becoming a tangle of weeds, the field was mowed—or rather, cut—sporadically during the summer, not often enough to kill the plants but enough to make them low and bushy. That field is now, unfortunately, a parking lot, and dwarf New England Asters do not grow on university property any more.

One could almost stop talking about asters after discussing *A. novae-angliae,* so attractive it is, but there are many others. There are asters which are naturally low and spreading, not bushy like dwarf cultivated forms, but gracefully rising on short slender stems from a basal rosette of leaves. There are tall, rank species with enormous panicles of hundreds of flowers. There are bushy asters with tiny needle-like leaves and small white flowers, which look as much like moorland heaths as composites. All are interesting and pleasing in their own various ways, and all worth a place (the right place) in the wild garden or border. It is well to stress the fact here that all wild asters respond to cultivation by increasing in vigor and floriferousness.

Aster novi-belgii, the New York Aster, is usually discussed in conjunction with its relative *novae-angliae.* It is of course no more restricted to New York than the latter is to New England. Both are native to most of the eastern half of the country. Their colloquial names are simply translations of their Latin specific names (*novi-belgii,* meaning "of New Belgium," an early name for New York). *Novi-belgii* has even more cultivated forms than its relative. The myriad Michaelmas Daisies produced in England are mainly derived from it.

I must confess that I have not had too much experience with this plant except in its cultivated forms. It has always seemed to lack character to me; its light violet-blue flowers are pretty but not outstandingly so. Last fall I found a few plants on the edge of a ditch draining a salt meadow, just a few hundred feet back from the ocean, which were larger-flowered, a clearer blue color, and much more showy. This would seem to be var. *litoreus.* What information I can find on cultivation of the New York Aster indicates that it tends to be short-lived. This may be so, but it must surely be prolific enough to balance out, in the long run, this evanescence, else it certainly could not have produced the plethora of named cultivars which we see in gardens today. In the wild it produces flowers of white and rose-pink, as well as blue, and, as might be expected, these colors appear in abundance in the garden forms. There are also, in the cultivars, some very pretty forms with semi-double flowers ('Marie Ballard' is an example). Some recommended cultivars are: 'Winston Churchill' (deepest pink, almost red), 'Blue Gem' (semi-double deep lavender-blue), 'Lady Lloyd' (pink), 'Ernest Ballard' (deep rose), 'Snowsprite' (dwarf white).

Somewhat similar in flower to *A. novi-belgii* is the Red-stemmed Aster, *A. puniceus.* This is a robust, almost rank grower which is seen along fencerows and the edges of wet fields. Its small pale lavender flowers are borne in tremendous abundance, giving the effect of a blue haze from a distance. It is by no means a plant for either the small garden or the small perennial border, but it may have its uses. It may, like all tall asters, be kept shorter by summer pruning.

OTHER ASTERS

There are two of the many species of aster native to the East which are especially useful in both small wild gardens and in the perennial border. These are *Aster concolor,* the Silvery Aster, and *A. spectabilis,* the Seaside Aster. Both are very abundant along the sandy edges of the lonely roads through the New Jersey Pine Barrens, where they grow with sand-myrtle and bearberry, and make a lovely roadside strip of lavender from August into September. Neither grows more than a foot-and-a-half or two feet tall, and the habit of each is rather different from that of the bushy plants just described, for the flowers are borne on almost leafless scapelike stems which spring from a cluster or rosette of basal leaves. *A. concolor* is the smaller and earlier of the two, beginning to open its abundant lavender flowers in August. Its common name alludes to the silvery fuzz on its leaves. *A. spectabilis* (Latin for "showy") is appropri-

Silvery and Seaside Asters useful in wild gardens and perennial borders.

ately named, for showy in the extreme are its inch-and-a-half violet, yellow-centered flowers. Much less appropriate is its common name, for I have never seen it growing at the seaside. Both these plants transplant with ease. In the wild they inhabit sandy, acid soils in full or nearly full sun. I am fortunate in having acid soil in my garden, and most plants of pinewoods and barrens do well in it, but it may be that these two asters require acid soil to do well; *A. spectabilis*, at least, is cultivated overseas.

FROSTWEEDS

In late September and October the fields and waysides of eastern North America turn white with the flowers of a group of some six species of asters which are called in many old wildflower manuals "frostweeds." That common name (if common it is, and not some poeticism worked by a writer on wildflowers) strikes me as particularly apt, for the flowers are precisely the silvery-gray-white of hoarfrost, and they come at frost time—being among the latest in the genus to appear.

Botanically, the frostweeds fall into these species: *A. ericoides* (Heath Aster), *A. lateriflorus* (Starved or Calico Aster), *A. simplex*, (Panicled Aster), *A. pilosus*, *A. vimineus* (Small White Aster), and *A. ptarmicoides* (Upland White Aster). All are common on banks, roadsides, old fields—in fact anywhere the soil has been recently disturbed. All are bushy plants with usually small leaves and small white flowers borne in great abundance. Perhaps the most attractive of the six species is *A. ericoides*, whose names in both English and Latin refer to its tiny heathlike leaves. (Another common name, Wreath Aster, refers to its flowering habit—its flowers, borne in curved, usually one-sided clusters, literally wreathe the plant.) However, all of the frostweeds have much to offer. Further, they are often extremely difficult to distinguish since all are variable, often grow together, and apparently hybridize with each other. The sensible way to deal with them is, then, to select from them the showiest individuals one can find, and leave classification of them to the experts.

Unfortunately the frostweed asters are so common that they are taken for granted by Americans (though not by visiting foreigners: true to pattern they are grown in Europe and are used there in hybridizing new cultivars). To us they are weeds, and if weediness is measured by vigor and abundance, I suppose they qualify. All would, I think, be much more appreciated if they were rarer.

These white asters are to me the epitome of autumn, the very last of summer's yield, for they bloom over a long period in late fall, and a few plants of them bear flowers up until the first frost. The smell of a field of these asters is something special—a spicy, polleny smell, not a real "fragrance," I suppose, because it has too much of the weed about it, but a good, wild smell that is redolent of October sun and sharp nights. It evokes for me summer, its joys and its passing, and a feeling that like the smell itself is a mixture of the sharp and the sweet.

Many of us associate specific plants with certain events in our lives. *Aster ericoides* recalls for me one of those moments which are colloquially called magic, and which Jung named "numinous"—divine in the sense that during them we are brought a deeper awareness of ourselves and our universe, and because of this new awareness, the moments and the stimuli which provoke them remain imprinted in our memories permanently. It occurred some fifteen years ago, in late October. Nearly all the autumn flowers were gone; indeed, the leaves were falling from the trees, but the fields were still frosted with Heath Asters. The afternoon sun was warm, but thin and waning, seeming to me to prophesy the coming of winter cold. I walked through the tangled flowers, thinking a young man's thoughts on life and death and beauty, enjoying the moment, living it, *feeling* it as only the young really do. Then I noticed, among the myriad white heads, what appeared to be a brown twig dangling oddly from one full, drooping truss of flowers, and as I bent over to examine it more closely, the aroma of the flowers rising around me in waves, the "twig" suddenly expanded—exploded, almost—into dazzling scarlet, black, and white. It was a late butterfly, a red admiral, with wings closed above its back and first seen in silhouette, which obligingly lowered them to display the gorgeous upper sides when I bent my head to look at it. There it hung, only mildly alarmed, opening and closing its wings slowly, the magnificence disappearing each time the wings met above the back and materializing again as

Frostweeds for fall field color.

HEATH ASTER
Aster ericoides

they reopened. The last butterfly on the latest flowers of summer. The whole of that season was suddenly concentrated into the warmth of the sun on my cheeks, the smell of the flowers, and the glorious colors of the animal. Whenever I smell Heath Asters that moment is re-created for me.

And for all this I am ashamed to say that I have never attempted to grow this species in my garden. My reasons are two, I think: first, one doesn't need to cultivate it; it grows everywhere anyhow, and I frankly am loath (as I am with the Common Milkweed, with Chicory, with Evening-primrose) to plant it in my borders because it is so *obviously* an outsider. The second reason is perhaps more subtle but related to the first: I would much rather see and smell the plant in a natural setting.

A relative of the Heath Aster, but much rarer in my area, is *Aster depauperatus*, a plant which more truly merits the name "starved" than the rank *A. lateriflorus*. It is not common, being mainly restricted to the Serpentine Barrens of Maryland and southern Pennsylvania and similar areas of sterile soil. Here it grows into a tiny-leaved bush one or two feet tall, dotted in September and October (occasionally earlier) with hundreds of almost microscopic white flowers. The plant itself resembles a baby's-breath rather than an aster, and is quite valuable in special places in the garden because of its very distinct appearance. Tiny and delicate as it naturally is, it tends to become a floppy monster if it is given rich soil. I grow my plants in partial shade on the sterile soil beneath two Scrub Pines (*Pinus virginiana*). Here they are shaded during the morning, but receive the full blast of the afternoon sun all summer long. Their companions are acid-soil or pine-barren plants—Sand-myrtle, various heaths and heathers, Teaberry, dwarf rhododendrons, Rattlesnake-plantain, Wintergreen, Sheep-laurel, Shortia, Galax, Whorled Milkweed (which grows on the serpentine barren with it), and White Milkweed. Two or three times during the summer I clip it back to an inch or two of the ground. It blooms in the fall as a delicate foot-high plant with minute white flowers.

The wild asters which I have thus far discussed have been plants of open ground, whether wet or dry. There is a group of these plants which are adapted to woodland conditions, and, though none is as showy as the showiest of the open-ground species, some are quite valuable for autumn color in shady gardens. In rocky upland woods from Ontario to Georgia grows the commonest of these species, the White Wood Aster, *A. divaricatus*, in a basal tuft of heart-shaped leaves from which in September rise to about two feet flowering stems topped by many small flowers, off-white with a brown center. The flowers are not individually showy, though some large specimens of the plant can be veritable foaming masses of blossoms. The main value of the species is that it grows, blooms, even thrives in deep, dry shade, including that of beeches, the most death-dealing of forest trees. *Aster divaricatus* inhabits the same areas where grow White Snakeroot and Fringed Campion, and the three are excellent grown together because they provide interest for a long period when little else blooms in shady gardens.

For a shady garden: White Wood, Large-leaved, and Heart-leaved Asters.

Two somewhat similar asters with blue flowers and heart-shaped basal leaves are the Large-leaved Aster, *A. macrophyllus*, and the Heart-leaved Aster, *A. cordifolius*. Both are native in woodlands throughout the whole of the East, and both are valuable for the same reasons as outlined under *A. divaricatus*. *A. cordifolius* is doubly so, for it is one of the very last of native wildflowers to bloom, showing color well into November during some years. I have seen it growing in thickets of native Witch-hazel, its masses of delicate lavender flowers in pretty contrast to the pale yellow flowers of the shrubs above them. Another striking natural combination occurs when *A. cordifolius* grows in proximity to Jack-in-the-pulpit and False Solomonseal, both of which show bright scarlet fruits when the aster is in flower.

Combine: Heart-leaved Asters with native Witch-hazel.

The list of good native asters is hardly ended, for there are many more interesting and beautiful, as well as useful, garden plants in the genus. I am still discovering them, and the reader is encouraged to visit field and woodland during autumn to search the best ones out.

Late summer and early fall belong to the Bonesets, Joe-pyes, and Hempweeds (*Eupatorium*) more than to perhaps any other groups save the asters and goldenrods. From August until frost every swale,

*BONESETS, JOE-PYES,
AND HEMPWEED*

swamp, ditch, woodland, sand dune, pond, stream side, or thicket shows one or another species in white, pink, mauve, or lavender. That they are such noticeable components of the landscape is the more remarkable when one considers that no eupatorium (except possibly the Mistflower, *E. coelestinum*) is truly a *showy* plant, as, say, Butterflyweed or Cardinalflower is showy. Their flowers are individually tiny, wispy things, though aggregated into large clusters. Their colors, mainly grayed mauves or whites, are not bright. But they are excellent as fillers (both in the landscape and in flower arrangements), and many species have a charm that goes beyond mere showiness of flower and endears them to discerning gardeners.

They are also easy to cultivate, all having cordlike roots radiating from a shallow crown and transplanting easily. In nature they occupy nearly every habitat niche available, some indeed being quite cosmopolitan—appearing with frequence in all sorts of situations. One of the latter is *E. hyssopifolium*, a striking plant which is common in dry fields and wood-edges upland as well as on pine barrens and sand dunes near the shore. It has off-white flowers in large, platelike clusters, but its charm is architectural rather than floral. Several unbranched stems grow two feet or so tall from the crown, each topped by the compound flower cluster and each set at regular intervals with a tier of narrow, grayish leaves. But for the flowers the plant resembles some Mediterranean shrub—a lavender or rosemary, perhaps, or, as its scientific name implies, a hyssop. Very few plants give the regular, whorled effect created by the leaf arrangement of this plant (*Asclepias verticillata* is one); thus the Hyssop-leaved Eupatorium is very valuable as an accent plant in the garden. Even though its flowers (which, incidentally, are fine for cutting) are not brightly colored, the plant is always noticeable in the wild because of both growth habit and size of flower cluster. One of the most pleasant recollections of my trips into the southern part of Delmarva is that of a fine clump of *Eupatorium hyssopifolium* near Cape Charles, Virginia, one sunny day in early September, standing bright by the roadside with its flowers aswarm with tiny orange and lemon butterflies, glinting like solid bits of sunlight as they swarmed

*Hyssop-leaved Eupatorium
for an accent plant.*

around the plant. What more remains to be said about this desirable plant? Perhaps only that its varied habitats in nature indicate an adaptability which augers well for performance in gardens.

As different from the preceding as it is possible for related species to be is White Snakewort, *E. rugosum*. This plant is largely confined to dry, rocky upland woods, where it is a conspicuous component of the undergrowth in September and October. It bears oval, toothed leaves of a rather bright green, and pure white flowers (it looks rather like a giant white ageratum). It is a good cut flower. It combines well in gardens (and indoors) with chrysanthemums and hardy asters, and is valuable as well because it is one of the few plants which grow in shady situations which bloom late in the season. The species is one of the few eupatoriums available from wildflower nurseries (often under the names *urticaefolium* or *ageratioides*). Like the preceding species it is an easy, adaptable plant which thrives in gardens. It may, in fact, spread too rapidly in gardens where it is happy!

Combine: White Snakewort with chrysanthemums and hardy asters.

There are several other white-flowered eupatoriums which differ mainly in leaf shape and size. None is quite so elegant as the preceding species, but many are pretty, valuable late-flowering plants. The true Boneset, *E. perfoliatum*, is a tall (to about five feet), comparatively coarse plant which is useful in special situations. Its long, felted gray-green leaves, arranged in pairs with bases joined so that it appears that the stem is "perfoliate"—growing through the joined leaf bases—are perhaps more striking than the large, flat heads of greenish white flowers. The name "thoroughwort," so faithfully applied to eupatoriums in manuals (though seldom elsewhere) is really only applicable (it means literally "growing through") to this species among the plants discussed here. Few have their stems growing through the leaves. *E. perfoliatum* is of historical interest as an old-time remedy for broken bones, hence the common name. It grows anywhere, but is most common in wet meadows.

The most showy of eupatoriums is *E. coelestinum*. So distinct that it is often segregated from others in a separate genus, *Conoclinum*, the species is nonetheless quite similar to other plants mentioned here except in the soft lavender-blue coloration of its flowers. It is an exception to the general rule that native plants are not often cultivated, for it is a frequent inhabitant of old gardens in the East.

I first met the species, called "Blue Mistflower" in manuals, in my mother's garden, where she called it "Hardy Ageratum." Neither she nor I had the faintest notion that it was not only a native plant but close kin to the Joe-pye growing in ditches nearby. For a number of years I grew a stand, descended from my mother's, in my own garden. By this time I knew what it was, but was convinced that it was a southern plant not met naturally in my region. Then one day I found it living on a roadside in lower Delaware, growing in conditions very different from those I had always given it—a brackish marsh overrun by the giant Reed-grass *Phragmites communis* verged right up to the roadside. The reed-grass was mowed along the shoulder, and here grew the eupatorium, its roots in the wet soil, its heads above the truncated stubble of the grasses. It made a wide ribbon of delicate blue against the green wall of grasses, accented here and there by mauve *Lobelia puberula* and bright yellow *Helianthus angustifolius*. The species is really quite beautiful. Witmer Stone reports in *Plants of Southern New Jersey* (p. 738) on the show it makes: "In late summer these grassy . . . stretches [of marsh near Cape May] are covered with the pink *Sabatia stellaris*, the purple *Gerardia purpurea*, and the blue misty heads of the present species, making a fine display of color." From this I would guess that the species would do well in seaside gardens, provided it had some moisture.

I do not know of any variants of the species available, though my wild-collected plants differ somewhat in leaf shape and texture from the garden strain. The plant spreads quickly by means of underground runners and, like many species which propagate similarly, may rely on asexual means rather than sexual to multiply. This would mean reduced variability, of course.

The fact that it spreads by stolons has perhaps more practical applicability to the gardener if he realizes that the plant is a potential invader always. In my garden this potential has never been realized, though, because I have grown the plant in situations which limit its spread—very dry soil in semi-shade or in grassy meadows mowed two or three times a season. My old stand grew in soil so dry that I now marvel at its survival. It grew only a foot or so tall (in wet soils it reaches two) and along with a stand of depauperate *Bidens polylepis*, a yellow "daisy" (see p. 230), made a low groundcover that was beautiful in bloom. Mistflower, with its heads of precisely the shape and color of the annual ageratum but with long, slender stems, makes a very fine cut flower, especially nice when arranged with lemon-yellow marigolds.

Use Blue Mistflowers as a groundcover with BIDENS POLYLEPIS.

The Joe-pye Weeds form a marked group of eupatoriums distinct in their tall growth, striking foliage, and pink to purple flowers. There are about four species in the East, so closely related that they are confusing to all but botanists. All grow with stout, un-branched, upright stalks along which whorls of shapely leaves emerge at regular intervals and at the top of which an enormous compound cluster of flowers is formed in late summer. The pale glaucous or green stem is in many individuals strongly flecked with maroon or purple. The pointed leaves vary from oval to almost linear. Even without flowers the plants of all Joe-pyes are strikingly architectural.

The four species may be distinguished by various (sometimes rather obscure) details: *E. fistulosum* has a hollow stem; *E. purpureum* has a solid stem without spots, and oval leaves; *E. maculatum* has an unspotted stem and very narrow leaves; *E. dubium* has also a spotted stem, but oval leaves like those of purpureum. *"Dubium,"* Latin for "doubtful," indicates the attitude many botanists have toward its intermediate characters.

For garden purposes one needn't concern himself with technical details, of course, especially if he collects his plants. In my area, *E. purpureum* usually grows in woods, while the others occur in open areas—roadside ditches and swales, usually in company with Swamp Milkweed. *Purpureum*, then, might be selected for shady gardens; the others for sun. Unfortunately *purpureum* is somewhat of a misnomer, for its flowers are hardly purple; in fact, they are a pale flesh-mauve, less striking than those of either *maculatum* or *dubium*, which are often a fine red-purple, very showy.

Joe-pye Weeds? E. PURPUREUM *for shady gardens;* FISTULOSUM, MACULATUM, *and* DUBIUM *for sun.*

All Joe-pyes are easy to cultivate either in wild gardens or perennial borders. The plants have such good architecture that they are worth growing as specimens in lawn or among shrubbery also. They cut well and are excellent for wild bouquets (a row has been grown in the cutting garden at Winterthur for many years). They begin blooming in early August.

The odd common name derives from a legend that an Indian medicine man named Joe Pye used the plants in his pharmacology. The name *Eupatorium* also alludes to the plant's medicinal uses: Mithridates Eupator (132–62 B.C.) was a physician, in addition to being king of Pontus.

Ironweed easy to grow.

No discussion of fall flowers would be complete without mention of Ironweeds, *Vernonia*. These close relatives of eupatorium are among the showiest flowers of field and wet meadow in late summer and early autumn, their vibrant, rich red-purple color contrasting strongly with the yellow of goldenrods and the grayed white and rose of Swamp Milkweed, Boneset, and Joe-pye Weed with which they grow. The individual blossoms resemble those of eupatorium except that they are larger and more loosely aggregated in broader clusters. The bold foliage, red stems, and tall, upright habit also recall Joe-pye Weed. Ironweed is very common but merits wider use in gardens. It is extremely easy to grow. In the East the commonest species is *V. noveboracensis*. There are many other species farther south and west, all of them quite similar.

What is for all intents a climbing eupatorium is *Mikania scandens*, an inhabitant of the Coastal Plain in Delmarva, native on a country-wide scale from Ontario to Florida and Texas. 'Climbing Hempweed,' as it is called in manuals, or 'Climbing Boneset' is a rather delicate vine which twines for about ten feet over adjacent vegetation. Its leaves are more or less heart- or halberd-shaped, in pairs, from the axils of which the clusters of frosty pink flowers appear in late summer. It is listed as common, but I have only encountered it growing on the edges of salt marshes and in wet dune hollows, where it usually twines over mallows, making a pretty companion to them. It transplants easily and makes an excellent addition to gardens where the soil is damp, grown on fences or among shrubs in the wild garden. Since its stems die down each year, the plant is no danger (as woody vines like honeysuckle may be) to the shrubs through which it twines. Seashore gardeners should also try it, since it is resistant to salt.

The gentians are to herbaceous plants what witch-hazel is to shrubs—the absolutely final burst of flowering of the year. William Cullen Bryant wrote of the Fringed Gentian:

> Thou waitest late, and comest alone
> When woods are bare and birds have flown,
> And frost and shortening days portend
> The aged year is at his end . . .

He exaggerated a little. The woods are not quite bare when gentians bloom, although shortening days and even early frosts do portend the end of the year. Even so, most of the native gentians are worth cultivating almost as much for their odd blooming period as for their beauty.

And they are indeed beautiful plants. The fabulous Fringed Gentian, *Gentiana crinita,* one of the first casualties of civilization throughout its range, is possibly the most beautiful of them all, with its great fringed cups of pure blue in autumn. It is so very rare everywhere that its transplantation should not be attempted unless total destruction of its habitat is absolutely certain. Since it is a biennial, it is an impermanent plant at best. On top of this it seems impatient of cultivation, apparently requiring a moist meadow in order to exist. The safest way to acquire it is to collect and scatter seeds in a likely wild spot in the garden. I have never grown it and frankly doubt that I ever will be able to.

Fortunately, there are other native gentians which, though they lack some of the beauty of the Fringed, are more accommodating in the garden. These are the "closed" gentians *G. saponaria* and *G. andrewsii.* Both are long-lived perennials, vase-shaped in habit with wandlike stems to two feet, each clothed in whorls of deep green willow-like leaves, in the axils of which grow the clusters of closed flowers in deep, true, soul-satisfying blue.

Closed gentians adaptable to the garden.

I found my first closed gentian (though which species it was I could not then say) when I was a boy of fourteen. Like most bloodthirsty adolescents I was more enthusiastic about hunting animals than wildflowers and had recently acquired my own beagle. On autumn days before the hunting season began, it was my custom to walk with a group of friends and my brothers into the fields to train the new dog. One afternoon in late October we trailed the bellowing beagle through a field of dry broom-sedge which sloped sharply toward the nearby tidal marshes of the Christiana River. The barren field was separated from the water by a belt of scrub willows, stunted maples, and cat-brier. The dog, on the trail of what we thought was a rabbit, turned into the sparse briers with a mob of excited boys on its heels. As we surged into the smilax, stepping high to avoid the ankle-punishing thorns, the ground around us seemed to bubble, boil up, and explode. All of us, including the dog, froze with thumping hearts, numb bodies, and dazed brains as the covey of quail which the dog had been trailing dispersed in every direction, two dozen fat little bodies careening on vibrating wings over the thickets. As the last bird dropped out of sight I stooped to look for evidence of the covey in the broom-sedge and smilax at my feet and gazed with amazement into the face of a gentian, the bluest flower I had ever seen.

Now it may be that the adrenalin coursing through my system at that moment rendered me more receptive to the flower's beauty, but beautiful it certainly was, the more so because of its bleak surroundings. It was above all the quality of the color that impressed me. I seemed to be looking at the mother of blueness itself, the primal, original, very source of blue. At the time poetry was meaningless to me, but years later I understood perfectly what Bryant was attempting to say (not quite successfully perhaps) with:

> Blue, blue, as if that sky let fall
> A flower from its cerulean wall.

Here at the bitter end of the summer bloomed a flower as fresh, cool, and lovely as any of spring. My young mind reeled at the wonder of it.

That place with its broom-sedge, scrub, and gentian is no more.

Even then it was owned by a gravel company which eventually expanded until the whole of that area was dug out. Now it is a gaping, red wound in the earth clearly visible from Interstate Highway 95. The state recently (until members of nearby communities protested) considered using it as a "landfill," that is, what everybody used to call, in the days before politicians became aware of ecology, a dump.

Ten years later I rediscovered gentians in precisely the same sort of habitat: among stunted maples, mountain-laurel, sparse smilax, and broom-sedge in the moist belt between a dry, acid field and a woodland swamp. This time I was able to identify the species as Soapwort Gentian, *G. saponaria*. I dug a couple of plants which lived but did not thrive in my too-dry wild garden. The species and its near relatives are not difficult to grow as long as they have a fairly acid soil, some sun, and a fair supply of moisture. The sort of spots in the garden where cardinalflower, geum, and *Primula japonica* thrive are ideal for them. They grow from crowns with cordlike roots which radiate in all directions, the type of growth which is very amenable to transplanting.

The plants themselves are handsome, often with reddish stems set at intervals with smooth, linear leaves in pairs or whorls of four. The flowers occur in clusters of a half dozen or so at the apex of the stem and in smaller clusters in the upper leaf axils. These are tightly closed ovals in *G. andrewsii* and slightly open at the mouth in *G. saponaria*. Both species are often called Blind or Bottle Gentian, though the flowers are not really bottle-shaped at all. They look more like little eggs or footballs than bottles.

Two perennial species with beautiful open flowers are *G. autumnalis* and *G. puberula*, the first, called usually Pine-barren Gentian, inhabiting pine woods and barrens on the Coastal Plain from New Jersey to South Carolina, and the latter inhabiting barren places west of the mountains from Ontario south to Georgia west to Kansas and the Dakotas. I unfortunately have no information as to the performance of either of these lovely rarities in cultivation. Mr. and Mrs. Julian Hill have told me of finding the Pine-barren Gentian in New Jersey invariably accompanied by holes indicating

CLOSED GENTIAN
Gentiana andrewsii

that plants had recently been dug. The species is too rare for indiscriminate collecting. So long as its habitat is intact (though the Pine Barrens are by no means safe from "progress," as a trip through them will show) the Pine-barren Gentian should be allowed to grow in peace.

AUTUMN FOLIAGE

At perhaps no other season of the year does nature so intrude itself into the consciousness of even the most callous of individuals as in autumn, when remnants of the mixed deciduous forest which at one time covered much of the East turn from green to many hues before leaf-fall. Yet I have found that few gardeners, even those who make pilgrimages to the mountains or to New England to see the best autumn color, plan gardens around its effects. It is paradoxical that in Great Britain, whose "soft" climate produces a fall display much inferior to ours, gardeners are much more conscious of it. I was reminded of this fact not long ago when an English friend, looking at a stand of Sweet Gums on my property, asked, "Have you selected any for outstanding autumn color yet?" The thought had never occurred to me.

First choice specimen tree: Black Gum.

Yet it is another important factor to consider in choice of any tree or shrub for the garden. Black Gum (*Nyssa sylvatica*) is a hardy, deep-rooted tree with good green foliage, all points in its favor. Weighing against it are its difficulty in transplanting and its lack of showy flowers. So extremely colorful is its autumn foliage, however, that in my opinion the scales are tipped very much in its favor. I would consider it as a first choice as a specimen tree for the home.

Autumn coloration is somewhat tricky. Some species naturally have bright color, while others have little. Moreover, some species are limited to certain colors; hickories, for example, are always yellow, while Sweet Gums vary from pinkish to purple, and Black Gums are crimson to scarlet, but never yellow. Variable species like Red Maple may be light yellow, bright scarlet, or anything in between. Situation and season have much to do with color. Plants in more exposed localities color earlier and more vividly than those in shade and shelter. Warm, wet autumns inhibit the formation of bright color in most trees. Finally, color is also a matter of individual variation. Just as some members of a population of plants will invariably produce larger flowers or longer leaves than others, so do some show a brighter autumn coloration than others. It behooves the color-conscious gardener, then, to select the most colorful clones, no matter what the species.

Honors for brightest fall color are divided between three native trees, all worthy of a place in the garden. The first of these is Red Maple, *Acer rubrum*, a fine, multi-purpose tree which has also bright red flowers in spring. This species is offered by most nurseries, but it is very variable in color of both leaf and flower. My experience is that the leaves of clones with bright red flowers turn a correspondingly bright red in autumn, and vice-versa. Some specimens have very pallid flowers, and autumn leaves of a pleasing but unspectacular yellow. These are, of course, less desirable.

Black Gum's foliage is probably the brightest red of any native tree, a pure glistening scarlet under the best conditions. It colors early in the season, and is not particularly variable as to coloration. The species is dioecious—trees are either male or female, not both— but this is not particularly important since the flowers are not showy. The female plant bears rather attractive dark blue fruits in the fall, though. These are edible but very tart. When I was a child we called them (for some reason totally inconsonant with taste) "wild raisins." The memory of their taste puckers my mouth still, though more than twenty years have passed since I indulged in "wild raisins" of an autumn. Both Black Gum and Red Maple will grow in swamps in the wild, so are worth consideration in poorly drained soil.

Third member of the triumvirate of autumn trees is Sweet Gum, whose star-shaped leaves turn shades of red in autumn. It is variable, some clones turning earlier than others, some becoming a mere pinkish and others a wine or purple so deep as to appear almost black. It bears globular, spiky fruits which are attractive in winter (and make good Christmas decorations either natural, or silvered or gilded). Its ridged, corky gray bark is also attractive during the winter. Like sycamores, it may be considered by some a "dirty" tree because of the fallen fruits.

Other large trees which provide good color are: (yellow) Sugar Maple, Hickory, Ash, Sassafras, Tulip-poplar, Beech; (red to purple) Persimmon, Scarlet Oak. Smaller trees and shrubs: Spice Bush (yellow), Chokeberry (red), Blueberries (red), Sumacs (red), Dogwood (wine-red).

Sumacs are interesting natives not grown as often as they should be, perhaps because their common name is linked by the public with thoughts of acute dermatitis. Only a few of the species are poisonous; in my area there are only three—the Poison "Oaks" and "Ivies," *Rhus radicans* and *toxicodendron*, two highly successful weeds, and the much rarer Poison Sumac (*R. vernix*), found only in an occasional swamp. None of these species is similar to the harmless sumacs. The first two are vines or low suckering shrubs with trifoliate leaves. The last is a small tree with compound leaves and axillary clusters of *white* berries. All of the harmless sumacs have enormous, tropical-looking compound leaves and great pyramidal terminal clusters of red or chestnut fruits.

In my area there are three of these, all common, two of which are large shrubs (or small trees) and one a low shrub. These are: *R. glabra*, Dwarf Sumac, *R. typhina*, Staghorn Sumac, and *R. copallina*, Shining Sumac. Of the three, *glabra* is perhaps the least desirable, simply because it looks very much like *typhina* but lacks the latter's stature. It is usually seen as a colonial shrub less than six feet in height. Its very deep blue-green leaves are about two feet in length. The leaf stalk is purple, and its clusters of berries are cinnamon in color.

Staghorn Sumac is so similar that for years I thought that the two species were the same. It lacks the purplish leaf stalk, has leaves of a somewhat lighter green, and can always be distinguished from *glabra* by a look at the young branches: those of *glabra* are smooth ("glabrous," in botanical parlance, hence the scientific name), while those of Staghorn are densely covered by a red-brown felt resembling the "velvet" which covers the new antlers of deer, and no doubt accounting for the common name. The branches of both species are stout and forked, reminding one indeed of deer antlers.

For garden purposes, however, the major difference between the two lies not in pubescence but in size and stature, for while *R. glabra* is a low shrub, *R. typhina* sometimes achieves the dimensions of a tree—thirty or forty feet—with a rounded head and horizontally spreading branches. It is a fine lawn tree, extremely tropical in appearance. Even better—one of the most elegant small trees in existence—is the variety *dissecta*, in which each leaflet is cut or incised so heavily that the leaf looks like a fern frond.

Staghorn Sumac, variety DISSECTA, *an elegant small tree.*

Quite different from either of the preceding is Shining Sumac, *R. copallina*. Its leaves are smaller, of a shining green with leathery texture. It forms a denser shrub or small tree to thirty feet (even though one of its common names is "dwarf sumac," a misnomer), and blooms later in the season, bearing its clusters of green-yellow flowers very late in summer, when those of the others are already ripening into chestnut-red fruits. The foliage is this plant's best ornamental point—a deep rich green with slight olive tint, and always so glossy as to seem sprayed with liquid plastic.

Shining Sumac for a dense shrub.

Sumacs have limited but important uses in the landscape. Very few hardy plants give the sort of lush, tropical effect that is theirs. With their bold growth and large leaves they (particularly *typhina*) are reminiscent of palms or tree ferns, rather than temperate-zone plants. All are good as lawn specimens. *Copallina*, a denser shrub, is excellent for any sort of massed border. It is also good for beach planting.

The individual flowers of sumacs are not showy, but are borne in such tremendous clusters that they make a display. The red-brown fruits of all three (probably brightest, almost cinnabar-orange, is *typhina*) are extremely showy in late summer and autumn, and are also valuable as food for the wild birds. The fruits of *copallina* color later than those of the other two and are duller, being purplish crimson rather than almost red. (Sumacs are dioecious, thus it is advisable to select a female plant for fruits.) The color of sumac fruits derives from their dense covering of, to quote Sargent, "acrid hairs." An acid drink can be made from the berries of *glabra* and *typhina*. I have no information on the other species. Sumacs belong to the *Anacardiaceae*, a largely tropical family which includes, besides many sources of lacquer and varnish, such illustrious members as the

Mango, the Cashew, and the Pistachio-nut. *Anacardiaceae* are characterized by a distinct resinous sap, which gives mangoes their distinct flavor, produces lacquer from the Asiatic Varnish-tree, and, in the "poisonous" species, causes skin irritation.

One important attribute of the three harmless native sumacs is their magnificent autumn coloration—some shade of red, from coral to crimson, enhanced by the large heads of reddish fruits. They color early and, due to the large size of their leaves, make a great splash of red. *R. typhina* is very popular for this reason in Europe. I once saw a naturally growing plant in my area which couldn't have been more happily placed by the sharpest gardener. It grew at the corner of an old barn foundation which now functioned as an enclosed garden. The owners of the property had sense enough to clean out an absolute minimum of vegetation when they renovated the property, removing only brambles and scrubby wild cherries. The finished effect—grass accented only by the corner Staghorn Sumac, with the solid but rubbly wall as contrast—was quite striking.

Hercules' Club a spectacular lawn plant.

One other native deserves mention here, simply because it gives the same sort of tropical effect as the sumacs and is at its best in late summer and fall: *Aralia spinosa*, a tree to about thirty feet high with horribly prickly trunk and branches, huge doubly compound leaves, and enormous terminal panicles of foamy white flowers in August which become black berries in autumn. It is a plant of the Austral Zones, occurring only to southern Pennsylvania in the East and west up the Mississippi to southern Indiana. In Delmarva it is rare in the Piedmont but one of the showiest and most characteristic plants of the forest-edges far south. The plant is interesting even in winter by reason of its persistent fruit (on which birds feed for most of the season) and its large, clublike thorny shoots. I know of few thornier plants—even the petiole of the leaf bears spines. The common names Hercules' Club, Devil's Cane, and Prickly-ash allude to this characteristic. As a lawn plant Hercules' Club is spectacular, though it needs a good bit of space. The leaves may grow to four feet in length and over half that in width! Its autumn coloration is a soft pinkish orange, good in contrast to the red-stemmed, black-berried panicles of fruit. The plant is hardy in Massachusetts.

XII

Planting
Problem Gardens

For those who have problem spots in their gardens (or, for that matter, "problem gardens") where an excess of any element or condition—sand, clay, moisture, acidity, alkalinity, sterility, dryness —prevents or discourages good growth of common garden plants, local wildflowers may provide a solution to problems and a source of color and interest all season long. Most garden plants are adapted to median conditions of soil and moisture—moderate fertility, sufficient but not excessive watering, a pH which is neither strongly acid nor strongly alkaline. In other words, highly specialized plants do not often become garden flowers, no matter how beautiful or interesting they may be, precisely because they *are* specialized— adapted to some extreme condition which cannot easily be met in the average garden.

But a look at the countryside will show that plants grow everywhere, in dry or wet, sun or shade, in the dry dust of roadsides,

Local wildflowers ideal for problem gardens.

271

in sunny fields, in the gloom of dense woodlands, in crevices of sheer rock faces, in swamps and bogs and pond-edges, even on the surface of the water and in the depths of the pond itself—all situations which require a degree of specialization.

GARDENING IN POORLY DRAINED SOILS

Years ago I spent several seasons helping to plant a problem garden. I was a college freshman then, and the garden belonged to a married couple, very close friends, though about ten years older than I. The wife was a painter, with a painter's appreciation of beautiful flowers, and great skill and artistry in flower arranging. She wanted badly to have a border of annuals and perennials to supply cut flowers, the rest of her yard being given over to shrubbery and a play area for the children. But their property, located in a suburb of Wilmington accurately entitled "Claymont," lay at the foot of a large hill and its soil consisted of a narrow layer of humus covering many feet of solidly packed white clay. To complicate matters further, the land on the side opposite the hill also sloped slightly upward, creating a pocket where excess water lay for weeks on end during wet weather. This pocket was the back yard where we planned and planted a perennial border.

The garden was a disaster from the beginning. Besides the soil problems there was also a deficiency of sunlight, an oak wood crowding the site from the north, and neighboring houses and buildings shading it from other directions. For several years we dug tons of oak leaves, peat moss, and compost into the soil every spring and replanted the languishing perennials. We limed and fertilized lavishly, dug in sand, tried deflocculants on the clay. In the end, we had comparatively good results; shasta daisies, gaillardias, perennial cornflowers, zinnias, marigolds, cosmos, and roses survived and even bloomed abundantly enough to provide cutting material, but none ever really flourished.

The irony of this story is that not far away a wet meadow overlay the same sort of soil, producing the same sort of conditions. It was bright all summer long with hardhack and meadowsweet, milkweed, asters, ironweed, boneset, Joe-pye weed, bur-marigolds, vervains, and a dozen others, and my friend's wife often cut bouquets there. Yet none of us ever thought of chucking the bearded irises and Oriental poppies and starting again with wild plants.

If I were doing the same thing today, I would not attempt to thwart nature so. I would plant local wildflowers which flourish in similar situations—pink Hardhack (*Spiraea tomentosa*) and Swamp Milkweed (*Asclepias incarnata*), both of which are excellent as cut flowers and garden plants; Culver's Root, *Veronicastrum virginianum*, for a white accent; Ironweed, Boneset, Joe-pye Weed, and New England Aster; *Heliopsis* for an orange-yellow daisy, and the double garden varieties of the same plant as substitutes for zinnias and marigolds; Cardinalflower; Heleniums, both wild and cultivated, in yellows and mahogany-reds; Star-grass (*Aletris farinosa*); the long-stemmed Blue Bog Violet (*Viola cucullata*) and perhaps also the tiny marsh violets with white flowers; Blue Lobelia; Swamp Rose (*Rosa palustris*); blue and yellow Water Flags (*Iris* spp.); Closed Gentians (*Gentiana andrewsii*, *G. saponaria*); *Phlox maculata*; various *Lythrum*; and moisture-tolerant species of *Bidens, Helianthus, Silphium*, and *Rudbeckia* for yellow daisies.

I would not be above mixing Americans and exotics which flourish in moisture-retentive soil. Golden Globeflowers (*Trollius*) from America, Europe, and Asia, for example, with the native Blue Dogbane, *Amsonia tabernaemontana*, a tall plant of faintly milkweedish appearance with summer flowers of a beautiful turquoise.

One other group of plants I would certainly try—the Meadow-beauties or Deer-grasses, *Rhexia*. Up until recently I thought of these plants as candidates for the bog garden rather than the perennial border. Then I saw how well my friend Jackie Root grows them in her garden. They certainly rival exotic plants, with their large, showy rose or magenta flowers with conspicuous, oddly jointed yellow stamens. There are two species common in the East, *R. virginica*, with inch-wide, four-petaled, out-facing flowers of flamboyant magenta, and *R. mariana*, with similar flowers of pale rose or blush pink. In the South are several other species, at least one of which has yellow flowers. The two northern species range from Florida and Georgia north to Massachusetts and (in the case of *R. virginica*) as far as Nova Scotia.

Aside from the difference in hue of flowers, *R. virginica* may be distinguished from *mariana* by its four-angled stem of bright coppery red and its urn-shaped seed capsules of the same color. Its eight stamens carry long, curved anthers of bright yellow which change to coppery red as the flower ages. The combination of coppery red stem, bright stamens, bronze-green leaves, and magenta petals makes for a showy effect in the fields of summer. The species has tuberous roots. Care must be taken in transplanting that these are not severed from the plant.

R. mariana is more restrained but just as pretty. Its stem is not four-angled, is green and beset with soft bristles, and its leaves are greener and narrower. It does not have tuberous roots. Both will grow in shallow water, the bases of their stems then becoming much enlarged and covered by a corky bark. Neither usually exceeds two feet in height, and both bloom in late summer, when they give very valuable color. They look well together.

There are ways of dealing with poorly drained, boggy or swampy land other than attempting to thwart nature (usually unsuccessfully) by dredging, ditching, draining, or working in tons of sand. The logical way to do this involves first a change in mentality rather than in garden terrain: get away from roses and petunias, hard as it may be to do. (If you must have them, grow them in raised beds or in containers on your patio.) Look carefully through catalogues for plants of any sort which thrive in wet soil—trollius, primulas, beardless irises, forgetmenots—and then look carefully at the wild lands around you. Do you see color there? What plants provide it? Every niche in nature is filled, and even the least promising-looking habitats support interesting and beautiful plants.

Wetlands are really of two sorts, those which are under water part of the time, such as the shores of tidal streams or bottomlands which are flooded during periods of heavy rains, and those which are constantly wet but seldom under water. Add to these areas which are always wet—streams, ponds, and so forth—and you have three potential habitats for plants. Now, the usual "problem spot" in gardens is a flat and uninteresting stretch of soggy ground which supports little save sedges and scrub trees. The first creative step in dealing with such an area is to vary its contours. For a fairly reasonable sum of money, a skilled operator on a piece of large machinery can in a short time do marvelous things. The lowest, wettest part should be gouged out to form a basin which collects water. This basin accomplishes two things: it makes the surrounding land relatively dryer because it is better drained, and it provides a definitely wet environment where true aquatics can be grown. Aesthetically, it provides an expanse of water which, no matter how small, gives focus and interest to an otherwise vague and dull area.

First step: vary contours of area.

The earth from the excavation may be used in several ways—to form, for example, one or more hills or hummocks where plants which require drier conditions than those the area formerly provided can grow. Already you have three habitats where previously you had one. On the knolls you can grow various woodland or meadow flowers (depending on the amount of overhead shade) and shrubs. In the pond, again depending on the amount of shade, you can grow aquatics like waterlilies and irises. In between you can grow a host of bog and marsh plants.

A note: don't worry about mosquitoes breeding in the pond. They breed successfully in water-filled tin cans on trash heaps as well as in major water systems, so that the addition of a small body of water will not contribute materially to their number. Besides, frogs and fish will keep their numbers down. You should stock your pond with fish. Goldfish are pretty, tame, and interesting, but somewhat delicate in the North. They also muddy your water. The Japanese carp called "Koi" are as attractive and interesting and are hardier. Golden Orfe are much more active than either and are quite hardy. All these are available at nurseries which specialize in aquatics. Native shiners and minnows are also pretty and satisfactory. The common Mill Roach, for example, with its gleaming silvery body and orange-red fins is a beautiful fish.

Any body of water increases the wildlife population substantially.

For instance, in the spring of 1972 I had a pond dug on my five acres (the site was a poorly drained section under water during the winter months and baked during the summer, which supported little besides rushes, scrub maples, and Poison-ivy). In this pond six five-and-dime goldfish in a year's time became a veritable school. Enormous frogs appeared from I don't know where—since the nearest natural body of water is miles away. In the spring of 1973 two families of mourning doves nested in my pines for the first time and I seemed to have longer contingents of cardinals, catbirds, robins, mockers, and orioles than usual. By 1974, I had counted a dozen new species, including an upland plover, a little blue heron, and a glossy ibis.

No ducks if you want pond plants.

A logical concomitant of a pond is ducks. They are both interesting and beautiful, especially the brightly patterned ducks like mallards. They add life to a dead landscape. They will not, however, agree with pond plants, which they eat with gusto. So you must decide (unless your pond is very large, of course) between a duckless pond and a plantless one—you can't have both. Six petite mallards resided on my pond for the first year, to the delight of everyone, child and adult alike, who visited the garden. They did, however, destroy my waterlilies, and they rendered the pond-edge a muddy pitted, vegetationless morass before I reluctantly penned them elsewhere and began to replace the plants. European shelducks, though, are beautiful and quite harmless to plants.

A pond with a surrounding edge of damp soil allows you to grow many marvelous plants denied to the average gardener. If the area is sunny, the following natives might be tried. (For the sake of convenience I have divided them into three categories: A. true aquatics, those plants which must have water (sometimes occasionally deep water) in which to grow; B. semi-aquatics, those which grow either in shallow water or very wet soil; and C. ordinary bog or swamp plants.)

A.   TRUE AQUATICS

    1. *Nymphaea*—the true waterlilies. There are three species native in the East. *N. odorata*, with white, fragrant flowers

is by far the commonest. *N. tuberosa* is similar but lacks fragrance. *N. tetragona* is a dwarf species which has a wide range but is not very common. The European *N. alba*, similar to *odorata*, is also naturalized in places; its pink variety *rosea* is abundant on the Eastern Shore of Maryland. All the waterlilies must have plenty of sun in order to bloom.

2. *Nuphar*—Spatterdocks or Cow-lilies. These have leaves like their relatives the true waterlilies, but these usually stand above the water rather than float upon it. The flowers are yellow and not very showy. *N. advena*, a coarse plant of ponds and tidal streams in my area, is common. There are several other species, some much more delicate, native to this country. Culture like that of *Nymphaea*.

3. *Nelumbo lutea* (*Nelumbium pentapetalum*)—Lotus. The one native species is wide-ranging but nowhere common, an aquatic with enormous long-stalked, orbicular leaves and almost equally large yellow flowers in summer. The distinctive leaf is peltate—that is, the petiole joins the blade not at the edge but at the center, like the handle of an umbrella. A spectacular plant. Leaves and flowers stand high above the water. Culture like that of *Nymphaea*. Indians used both seeds and tubers of the plant for food. It spreads very rapidly.

4. *Nymphoides*—Floating-heart. There are two native and one introduced species in this genus of small floating plants which look like miniature waterlilies. *N. cordata* and *N. aquatica* (both called also "Water-snowflake") have white flowers less than an inch wide; those of the introduced *N. peltata*, the commonest of the three in my region, are an inch or more in width and are butter-yellow. These plants spread widely by underwater stems, so should be watched for invasiveness. The umbels of flowers are very pretty during the summer. Culture as for *Nymphaea*.

5. *Peltandra virginica*—Arrow-arum. This widespread plant looks exactly like the common florists' calla-lily in leaf and habit of growth. Its flower is similar also, but green instead

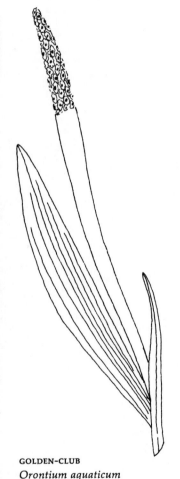

GOLDEN-CLUB
Orontium aquaticum

of white, and borne below the leaves. It is worth growing for its statuesque appearance alone, since its flowers are unshowy. The very deep root requires an inordinate amount of muscle and care to dig intact. Will grow also in wet soil at pond-edge. The Indians, who used its shoots and roots for food, called the plant "Tuckahoe." One of the commonest plants of the estuarine tidal marshes of the East.

6. *Orontium aquaticum*—Golden-club. Like the above, an aroid, but lacking the spathe, its naked yellow and white spadix quite colorful in early spring. The lance-shaped leaves are gray-green and either floating or erect. They are peculiar in that they shed water like the feathers of a duck's back; it simply will not adhere to them. A folk name for the plant is "Never Wet." This is a handsome and interesting plant which belongs in every water garden. It grows well in shade.

7. *Sagittaria*—Arrowhead. Both scientific and common names for these plants refer to the shape of the mature leaves in most species. For some obscure reason, many aquatics have evolved with more or less arrow-shaped (sagittate, in botanical parlance) leaves. Underwater leaves of arrowheads are grass-like (some species are used in fish tanks), only those above water acquiring the characteristic arrow shape. Commonest is *S. latifolia*, which grows in almost every wet spot in the East. There are a dozen or more others, with varying leaf size and shape. All have tall clusters of showy three-petaled white flowers in summer. A double form of *S. latifolia* occurs, a most desirable plant with long-lasting flowers that are balls of white. The edible tubers of *Sagittaria* are much prized by Oriental people (as they were by our Indians). Common names for various species include Swamp-potato, Duck-potato, and the Indian name "Wapato."

B.   SEMI-AQUATICS

1. *Caltha palustris*—Marsh-marigold. This yellow-flowered native is one of the earliest of all plants to bloom, beginning

here in March. Its flowers, like glistening buttercups, are extremely showy. It will grow in mud or in shallow water, and tolerates deep shade. The foliage disappears in summer. A very desirable plant, beautiful in combination with the pale lavender *Primula denticulata* from the Himalayas.

Combine: Marsh-marigolds and PRIMULA DENTICULATA.

2. *Calla palustris*—Wild Calla. Not to be confused with the preceding. This is an aroid, while Marsh-marigold is a relative of buttercups and anemones. Wild Calla is native to cold swamps and bogs of the northern half of our continent and may not be adaptable to hot climates. It is a handsome creeping plant with heart-shaped leaves and white "calla-lilies" in summer.

3. *Symplocarpus foetidus*—Skunk-cabbage. This common aroid is interesting for its purple and green hooded spathes which appear in earliest spring and for its huge, bright green leaves which are handsome all summer. Its smell is only unpleasant when the foliage is bruised or broken.

4. *Lysichitum americanum*—Western Skunk-cabbage. Quite different from its eastern relative, this plant has showy canary-yellow spathes in early spring followed by large foliage which is narrower than that of the eastern species. A native of the Pacific Coast, it has proved hardy and amenable in Delaware.

5. *Acorus calamus*—Sweet-flag. An aroid which superficially resembles an iris. Its linear leaves are bright green, pointed, rising to a height of two feet or so from a creeping, branching rhizome. There is no spathe. The rhizome is pink inside and exudes a sweet and aromatic fragrance when cut or bruised. The plant looks like an iris with bright green leaves and no flowers. The rhizome is the "calamus" of old-time medicine.

6. *Decodon verticillatus*—Water-willow or Swamp-loosestrife. A relative of Purple Loosestrife (*Lythrum*) with similar lavender flowers in summer. It differs in being at least partly shrubby, with long arching branches which root where they

Water-willow unusual and easy to grow.

touch water, so that the plant proliferates this way. It will grow in mud or in water, forming thickets of arching stems. The underwater stems develop a very thick, spongy bark. Leaves narrow, willow-like. This is an unusual plant for the wild bog garden, very easy to grow. Will stand shade.

7. *Iris*—There are several species of water iris valuable for their pretty flowers and statuesque clumps of foliage. The Blue Flag, *I. versicolor*, has soft lavender flowers in late May and June. It will grow in shallow water. The form known as "Keremesina" has pretty flowers of white and red-magenta. Very similar is *I. pseudacorus*, a European immigrant now more common in tidal marshes of the East than its blue counterpart. The European Water Flag has bright yellow blossoms. *I. prismatica* is a slender native species which is lavender-flowered and not very robust. There are several more in the South which come in an astonishing array of colors. "Louisiana" irises of gardens are largely hybrids or selections of these. One hybrid, the rich purple D. K. Williamson' (*fulva* x *brevicaulis*) is fully hardy with me and forms enormous clumps in wet soil or shallow water. Irises need some sun in order to bloom.

8. *Myosotis*—Forgetmenot. The true Forgetmenot is *M. scorpioides*, a European which has been extensively naturalized in this country. Its multitudes of blue flowers are lovely from mid-spring to late summer. *M. laxa*, a native, is very similar. Both will grow readily in wet ground and along pond-edges.

9. *Jussiaea*—Primrose-willow. These are perennials belonging to the Evening-primrose family with showy yellow flowers and stems which creep in the mud or float in shallow water. The glossy leaves are narrow and willow-like. Several species, none common in my area, but a few offered by nurseries specializing in aquatics.

10. *Saururus cernuus*—Lizard's-tail. This is a rather coarse but attractive plant with large, heart-shaped leaves and spikes

of small white flowers in summer. It grows two or three feet in height, with flower spikes sometimes a foot in length. These are elongated and have a distinctly nodding tip, which gives rise to the common name. It is also called Water-dragon and Swamp-lily. The plant is valuable for its tropical appearance and for the fact that it will grow in dense shade. It spreads rapidly.

Lizard's-tail for dense shade.

11. *Typha*—Cat-tail. This plant is probably known to everyone. There are two species common in the East, *T. angustifolia*, the Narrow, and *T. latifolia*, the Broad Cat-tail. The former is much more delicate and possibly more desirable as an ornamental. *T. glauca*, with rather narrow leaves, is native west of the Alleghenies, and *T. domingensis*, a tall species with narrow leaves, is native to the southern half of the country, from coastal Delaware to California. Cat-tails are handsome aquatics but should be planted (in shallow water) in containers to prevent their spreading. Other names by which they are known or sold are the British "Reed-mace" and the erroneous "Bullrush." They must have sun.

12. *Taxodium distichum*—Bald-cypress. One of the few trees which grow in water, the Swamp-cypress is ornamental in its own right, with handsome pale green needles, a thick, red-barked trunk, and an upright, pyramidal habit. It attains a hundred feet or more with age. When growing in water it produces "knees" from its branching roots which rise above the surface and presumably convey oxygen to the submerged roots. A magnificent specimen grows in a pond at Longwood Gardens, near Kennet Square, Pennsylvania. Native from southern New Jersey south on the East Coast and up the Mississippi to southern Illinois and Indiana, the tree is not too hardy, but should be grown where it is. Will grow in fairly dry soil also. Several magnificent specimens may be seen on the mall in Washington, D.C. Though a conifer, it is deciduous. It is one of the last trees to leaf out in spring.

BALD-CYPRESS
Taxodium distichum
Cone

LIZARD'S-TAIL
Saururus cernuus

13. *Cephalanthus occidentalis*—Button Bush. This shrub or small tree may often be found growing in shallow water. In sun *Cephalanthus* makes a rounded bushy shrub, while in shade it becomes an angular, gnarled tree to twenty feet or so (taller in warmer climates). The white flowers, arranged in tight spherical heads, are attractive in summer.

C. ORDINARY BOG OR SWAMP PLANTS

1. *Lobelia cardinalis*—Cardinalflower. One of the most beautiful of all flowering plants, with magnificent spectrum-red flowers in late summer. It will do well in shade or sun, and will even grow in very shallow water.
2. *Chelone*—Turtlehead. Requiring the same conditions as Cardinalflower, though far less handsome, turtleheads bloom in late summer. The common species is *C. glabra*, with white flowers shaped very much like the head of a turtle (or a snapdragon without the frilly lower lip). Several southern species have purplish or pink flowers. Of these, *C. lyoni* is recommended.
3. *Mimulus*—Monkeyflower. Two species native in the East, both tall herbs with flowers of pale lavender, shaped something like the flowers of foxgloves.
4. *Lythrum salicaria*—Purple Loosestrife. This is not native, but an introduction from Europe that is now widespread in the United States. It is a robust plant which bears spikes of bright mauve or purple blossoms in July or August until frost and is very showy. Several named clones are in the trade, varying mainly in color of flowers (all, however, are some shade of purple). The wetlands just south of Philadelphia are covered with this plant and are absolutely spectacular. It is very easy to grow but should be watched, as it is invasive.

In addition to the plants listed above, there are many others which have been discussed in other portions of this book. Some of these are the following: *Viburnum nudum, Itea virginica,* gentians, *Helenium, Hibiscus, Rhododendron viscosum, Clethra alnifolia, Magnolia virginiana, Helonias bullata.*

If, as is often the case, your problem spot is under trees that you do not wish to eliminate, it might be well to forget the cat-tails and waterlilies and create instead a woodland pond, with sphagnum moss around the edges and laurels and wild azaleas on its fringes. Sweetbay, Swamp Azalea, Clethra, and Itea are a few of the shrubs that will do well in such a spot. Bald-cypress and Eastern White-cedar (*Chamaecyparis thyoides*) are fine also, as is Black Gum and Red Maple. Decodon will arch up and over in shallow water like a stand of tropical mangroves, bearing its lythrum-like flowers in summer and looking ornamental in general. Golden-club, the two Skunk-cabbages, Swamp-pink, and Lizard's-tail all will do well here. Such rarities as sundews, pitcher-plants, and certain bog orchids may also thrive once you have sphagnum moss established.

Sphagnum moss for woodland ponds.

Each summer I see in the gardens of southern Delaware and New Jersey or the Eastern Shore of Maryland plants which suffer because they are not adapted to conditions on the Coastal Plain. Garden Phlox, which demands the rich, moist soil of its native river valleys, is chlorotic and distorted by attacks from red spider. Chrysanthemums are stunted and twisted, with blackened leaves on the lower half of each stem. Peonies, like chrysanthemums gross feeders, are discolored and dejected-looking. Yet along nearby roadsides one sees a multitude of wildflowers—asters, golden-asters, Butterflyweed, and Blunt-leaved Milkweed—blooming gaily and growing lustily.

PLANTS FOR DRY, SANDY SOIL

If I were gardening on the Coastal Plain or, indeed, any place else where the soil was too dry or porous to support the ordinary garden plants during the summer, I would turn to nature to see what grew well beyond my fences. There are countless plants adapted to dry, sunny gardens.

Three handsome members of the Pea Family come immediately to mind: Wild Lupine (*Lupinus perennis*), Goat's-rue (*Tephrosia vir-*

THE PEA FAMILY

giniana), and Yellow False-indigo (*Baptisia tinctoria*). All three have a similar range—from New England and southern Ontario west to the Mississippi and south to Florida and Texas—and all are found in dry fields and wood-edges and clearings, especially in sandy pine-woods. Wild Lupine's spikes of lavender-blue flowers are extremely beautiful, as are its bright green, finely divided, wheel-shaped leaves. In nature it grows with Birdsfoot Violet and the following species, blooming between the two chronologically. It is decreasing in abundance. I have seen it only in the New Jersey Pine Barrens and on eastern Long Island. It grows from a long, woody root and is impossible to transplant when mature. Seedlings transplant more easily, and seeds germinate readily.

Tephrosia virginiana, because of its enormously long root, is known as Cat-gut and Devil's Shoestring as well as Goat's-rue. Its compound, locustlike leaves are covered with silvery hairs which give the whole plant a kind of glaucous bloom perfectly complementing the pastel yellow and pink hues of the flowers. I first found this plant growing bloomless in the sandy soil of a southern pine forest near the Delaware/Maryland line, and was much taken then with the handsome foliage. In June of the following year I found it in full bloom in the New Jersey Pine Barrens, fresh and lovely in the blazing sun compounded by the glare of the white sandy roadside banks. Its short spikes of flowers seemed at first to be somewhat compact snapdragons, but their sweetpea-shape became apparent on closer inspection. It is extremely difficult to transplant except in small sizes. My plants have persisted but not thrived in my garden in northern Delaware, probably because my soil, though dry, is not sandy enough to please it. Though a herbaceous perennial, Goat's-rue gives a shrublike effect in the landscape. It seldom exceeds a foot in height.

For dry, sunny gardens: Yellow False-indigo.

A third pea, *Baptisia tinctoria*, blooms later than the two preceding species, in July. It forms a two-foot bushy, much-branched bright green plant with cloverlike leaves and small clusters of bright yellow flowers. The freshness of both leaf and flower color does much to recommend it. It is deep-rooted, but somewhat easier to establish in larger sizes than the other two legumes discussed here. It does well in my garden. A much commoner species of False-indigo in gardens is the blue-flowered *B. australis*. This species is showier but less resistant to drought.

Goat's-rue's constant companion is a low, spreading plant which has no flower to speak of but is well worth growing for foliage alone— the Ipecac Spurge, *Euphorbia ipecacuanhae*. It is one of the most variable plants in nature, the leaves of no two individuals being alike. Plants growing side by side may have leaves of green, blue-gray, or maroon (or combinations of these) which vary from almost round to narrow-linear in shape. The plant seldom exceeds six or eight inches in height and forms a most attractive, sparse groundcover, where it can be grown—its roots go to China and so it is very difficult to transplant. In sandy soil small plants may be established, but even these did not live long in the heavier soils of my garden.

SPURGES

A close relative, though entirely different in appearance, is *E. corollata*, Flowering Spurge. This makes an attractive clumping perennial with unbranched stems which reach three feet or so, beset with narrow, gray-green partially whorled leaves. At the summit of each stem a large, airy umbel of small white flowers appears in midsummer. The plant looks much like a perennial baby's-breath. It cuts well. H. F. du Pont grew it in his cutting garden at Winterthur, and one florist I know grows it as a substitute for baby's-breath. Though a dry-soil species, it is not limited to the sands of the Coastal Plain, and is thus a bit more adaptable away from that region. In the Piedmont it is often found in the cinders of railway embankments. It ranges across nearly the whole eastern half of the United States.

As their names imply, the sandworts or arenarias (Latin for "of the sand") flourish in light, dry soil. *Arenaria peploides*, already discussed, is indeed a plant of sand dunes, and its relative *A. carolina* frequents the dry sands of the plains not far back from the shore. This species blooms in late spring, a mat of woody stems and tiny, dark green, needley leaves from which rise small, starry white flowers on slender stems to a height of only a few inches. I have found this

SANDWORTS AND ST.-PETER'S-WORTS

*Combine: Sandwort,
Birdsfoot Violet, and
Wild Lupine.*

pretty little thing only along the roads which wind through the Pine Barrens of New Jersey, where it grows in really beautiful combination with Birdsfoot Violet and Wild Lupine. The Pine-barren Sandwort, as the species is called in manuals, has a long woody tap-root which makes transplanting touchy. Seedlings transplant well.

Two interesting low shrubs of dry barrens are members of the genus *Ascyrum*, which with their close relatives the St.-John's-worts, *Hypericum*, share the odd distinction of bearing common names derived from those of saints. They are similar, though often lower, to the shrubby St.-John's-worts except that they have four- (not five-) petaled flowers. By some workers they are included in *Hypericum*.

St.-Andrew's-cross, *A. hypericoides*, looks like a gray-leaved boxwood clipped to a foot or so tall. It bears small yellow flowers in its leaf axils in midsummer. Taller, larger, and handsomer in flower, but not so attractive in habit is *A. stans*, St.-Peter's-wort. It is an upright, open shrub, not dense and compact like its relative. Both species occur in dry soil in sun or partial shade. *A. stans* also, curiously enough, grows as well in wet ditches and bogs as on barrens. Both transplant easily.

CACTI AND OTHER SUCCULENTS

*Dry area groundcover:
Eastern Prickly-pear.*

No plants are better adapted to dry conditions than members of the cactus family. One species is native in the East: *Opuntia humifusa*, the Eastern Prickly-pear. A typical member of its genus, it has leaves reduced to minute scales; flat green, jointed stems, each joint shaped like the tail of a beaver; large yellow flowers in late spring or early summer; and edible pink, pear-shaped fruits. The joints are studded with small rosettes of tiny, barbed prickles which cause a great deal of irritation to the skin.

Though of considerable interest as a garden subject and really gorgeous in bloom, this cactus should be used with care in the garden. Plant it in an area so barren that no other plants compete with it, or mulch it heavily with gravel. If you must weed around it, wear heavy gloves so as to avoid its wicked, nearly ineradicable prickles. Its joints root wherever they touch ground. The plant is simple to propagate by severing the joints and plunging them into sand or dry soil. Where it is happy, *Opuntia humifusa* will become a veritable groundcover. It thrives by the sea as well as on barrens on the Coastal Plain and rock outcroppings upland, and is quite hardy, with a range from Massachusetts west to Minnesota, south to Georgia, the Gulf, and west to Oklahoma. Synonyms for the species are *O. compressa*, *O. vulgaris*, and *O. opuntia*. There are equally hardy species west of the Mississippi.

Yuccas (p. 165) are logical plants to grow along with prickly-pears, since both occur together in nature. Technically they are hard-leaved xerophytes rather than succulents, but they withstand drought nearly as well as the water-storing cacti. The genus *Agave*, including the famous century plants of the Southwest, is a third group of drought-resistant plants which lies somewhere between the yuccas and the cacti in succulence. Only one member of the group is found in the East, this an extremely interesting but uncommon plant.

Combine it with Yucca.

Agave virginica, American Aloe, False Aloe, or Rattlesnake Master, is a yucca-like plant which is scattered across the Southeast from Virginia (or, according to some manuals, Maryland) west to Missouri. For years I tried to find a source for it and failed, until a few years ago the American Horticultural Society offered it in its members' seed list (this is one of the obvious advantages of belonging to plant societies, by the way). Today I have half a dozen specimens which appear to be doing well, one of which bloomed for the first time in the autumn of 1974.

Its narrow, fleshy, pointed leaves, the outermost of which lie prostrate and twisted on the ground and reach a length of eighteen inches, are pale green with a glaucous bloom, striped purplish in the form known as *tigrina*. From the center of the rosette rises in autumn a scape to six feet tall surmounted by a spike of greenish flowers which are not showy but are fragrant at night. The species is often separated from *Agave* in a distinct genus, *Manfreda*. One writer says that it is not an agave at all but a tuberose, *Polianthes*. My plants certainly look more like tuberoses than century plants.

Growing with my American Aloes in the impoverished soil at the base of a Scrub Pine are several specimens of one of the most

STIFF-LEAVED ASTER

*For drought conditions:
Stiff-leaved Aster.*

distinct and pretty of the asters, *A. linariifolius*, the Stiff- or Savory-leaved Aster. Its hard, narrow leaves at once proclaim it a plant adapted to drought conditions, as indeed it is. Several foot-tall stems grow in a tuft from its woody crown, each surmounted by a cluster of several inch-wide lavender to white flowers in October, rather late in the season even for an aster. Its scientific name means "leaves of *Linaria* (Toadflax or Butter-and-eggs)." Actually, the plant out of bloom looks more like some Mediterranean herb such as rosemary than linaria. Its dense, tufted habit and deep, glossy leaves are decidedly handsome. "Savory" in one of its common names no doubt refers to the herb by that name. It is one of the best of the genus, and there is nothing in the least weedy about it. Because of certain obscure differences in botanical details, the species was formerly separated in another genus, *Ionactis*, where in some manuals it still may be found.

All the plants discussed in this section have evolved various means of coping with the heat and drought of Coastal Plain summers. Yuccas and *Aster linariifolius* possess thin leaves covered by a waxy, water- and air-proof integument; agave and opuntia have developed organs—leaves or modified stems—which store moisture; *Tephrosia virginiana* and Wild Lupine are distinguished by incredibly deep roots which penetrate deeply into the sand in search of water. One interesting plant has evolved yet another method for survival: its root has become an organ in which moisture and food are stored against hard times, and reaches enormous proportions as a result.

MAN-OF-THE-EARTH

*Groundcover for sandy,
sunny banks:
Man-of-the-Earth.*

Man-of-the-Earth, Man-vine, or Wild-potato Vine is a true morning glory, related closely to those of our gardens and to the sweet potato of commerce, another species with a tuberous root. Botanically *Ipomoea pandurata*, the species is a trailing plant, climbing only when it is shaded and then weakly, with attractive bright green heart-shaped or pandurate (fiddle-shaped) leaves and large flowers of typical morning-glory shape. These are usually white with a crimson throat, quite beautiful.

Because, I suppose, of its deep root, the species is often listed as a weed. In my experience it is a very restrained plant, which should make a stunning groundcover on sandy, sunny banks.

As stated at the beginning of this chapter, excesses of drought or moisture are not the only problems encountered in gardening. On the Coastal Plain especially one may find that soil acidity prevents the growing of all but a limited number of specialized (but fortunately beautiful) plants like kalmias, rhododendrons, wintergreens, shortias, and the like. One may counteract the acidity of his soil by constant liming or by specializing in acid-soil plants or, preferably, by both. In the Midwest the opposite conditions often prevail. Here gardeners may attempt, as many do, to grow rhododendrons and their relatives in artificial peat beds. They may also investigate the possibilities of some of the marvelous prairie plants which abound in the alkaline regions west of the Mississippi. No matter the excess or lack—wind, sun, rain, shade, heat, cold, sand, clay, organic matter—regional plants are adapted to the condition and will thrive in regional gardens. One need only go into the adjacent wilds to find them.

I find as I end this book that I still have much to say. One of my notes states, "mention Christmas colors of Cardinalflower—*pure* red flowers and *clear* green leaves, never marked, flawed, distorted." Another inquires querulously, "Other lobelias??" Another sketches plans for a whole chapter on plants of the Heath Family, while another lays the groundwork for an essay on wild orchids. All have been put aside for lack of space.

Cardinalflower's virtues may become obvious to him who grows it. I wish, however, that space permitted discussion of its beautiful blue analogue *Lobelia siphilitica*, or that I might take room to extol the virtues of Box Huckleberry among shrubs or Virginia Bluebells and Rue-anemone among spring flowers. I wish also that I had room to discuss the virtues of winter gardening with evergreen shrubs and berried plants, or to warn that ferns (subject for another chapter at least!) should, like all delicate woodlanders, be planted on slopes or knolls in the wild garden, not in depressions where they will be smothered by fallen leaves.

But to do all this would make the book excessively long. I therefore draw the line at this page. To those whose favorite wildflower is overlooked or inadequately discussed, my apologies. That I can write so many pages on native plants and still find more to say seems to me living proof of the complexity and fascination of our wildflowers, shrubs, and trees.

Appendix

Sources for Wildflowers

The most obvious source, and the one on which I have relied most heavily, is of course their native habitat. It goes without saying that rules of good conservation should be observed when collecting plants from the wild. While there is no doubt in my mind that far more plants are destroyed each year by one bulldozer than by a whole army of plant collectors, this is still no excuse for wanton or careless collecting. A grave responsibility rests on the wildflower collector. To collect one specimen of a rare species and subsequently fail with it is, however disheartening, a justifiable experiment. To collect most or the whole of a population and lose it is absolutely criminal. Never collect rare plants or those which are sparsely represented in the environment unless you are sure that their habitat is going to be destroyed. Then, of course, almost anything goes. If the habitat is fairly secure and the species well represented therein, you are justified in taking a specimen or two or, better yet, divisions of a plant or two. In the case of rarities, it is good conservation to rely on divisions or, if the plants are not easily divisible, on seeds or cuttings.

There are several wildflower nurseries in this country, which should be relied on especially for plants which are rare or extinct in your area. The quality of these nurseries varies: most declare that their stock is nursery-grown, when the truth of the matter is that they collect at least part of it from the wild. Reprehensible as this is, one may console himself with the knowledge that the plants have been collected by experts (albeit unscrupulous experts!) and properly dug and handled before they reach one's garden. Not all wildflower growers rely on collected plants, however; some people who offer them are among the most ardent of conservationists. (Would that we knew which were which, so that we could patronize the latter exclusively.) There follows as comprehensive a list as I have been able to compile of nurseries which specialize in native plants of one sort or another:

ALPINES WEST, R. 2, Box 259, Spokane, WA. 99207. Western wildflowers.

Claude A. Barr. PRAIRIE GEM RANCH, Smithwick, S.D. 57782. Plains and prairie flowers.

CHARLES H. BICKFORD, Box 510, Exeter, N.H. 03833. Native wildflowers.

S. D. COLEMAN NURSERIES, Fort Gaines, GA. 31751. Native azaleas.

CONLEY'S GARDEN CENTER, Boothbay Harbor, ME. 04538. Wildflowers, native trees, and shrubs.

DEITRICK GARDENS, R. 2, Dexter, MI. 48130. Specialists in unusual forms of bloodroot and rue-anemone.

DUTCH MOUNTAIN NURSERY, R. 1, 7984 N. 48th St., Augusta, MI. 49012. Wildflowers and plants which attract wildlife.

ERICKSON, 20516 S. Sprague Rd., Oregon City, OR. 97045. Seeds of Pacific Coast irises and other wildflowers.

FERNDALE NURSERY, Askov, MI. 55704. Wildflowers, in business since 1906.

GARDENS OF THE BLUE RIDGE, Ashford, N.C. 28603. Appalachian wildflowers and shrubs.

GRIFFEY'S NURSERY, Rt. 3, Box 17A., Marshall, N.C. 28753. Wildflowers, shrubs, etc.

RUTH HARDY'S WILDFLOWER NURSERY, Falls Village, CONN. 06031. Wildflowers and ferns, grown by a true conservationist.

JAMIESON VALLEY GARDENS, Jamieson Rd., R. 3, Spokane, WA. 99203. Western wildflowers, rare plants.

LAMB NURSERIES, E. 101 Sharp Ave., Spokane, WA. 99202. Native rock plants and others.

LAURA'S COLLECTORS' GARDEN, 5136 S. Raymond St., Seattle, WA. 98118. Rare alpine plants.

LESLIE'S WILDFLOWER NURSERY, 30 Summer St., Methuen, MASS. 01844. Large and fine selection of wildflowers.

LOUNSBERRY GARDENS, Box 135, Oakford, ILL. 62673. Good selection of natives as well as other plants.

MIDWEST WILDFLOWERS, Box 644, Rockton, ILL. 61072. Seeds only.

MILES W. FRY & SONS NURSERY, R. 3, Ephrata, PA. 17522. Specialists in conservation plantings.

MINCEMOYER NURSERY, County Line Rd., Jackson, N.J. 08527. Wildflowers, also aids to organic gardening.

ORCHID GARDENS, R. 3, Box 224, Grand Rapids, MI. 55744. Good selection, plus much information as to culture.

PUTNEY NURSERY, Putney, VT. 05346. Wildflowers and ferns.

RAKESTRAW'S PERENNIAL GARDENS, 3094 S. Term St., Flint, MI. 48507. Mainly rock garden specialties.

CLYDE ROBIN, P.O. Box 2855, Castro Valley, CA. 94546. Western natives and many others, plants and seeds. Wide selection.

THE ROCK GARDEN, R. 2, Litchfield, ME. 04350. Mainly rockery plants.

SKY-CLEFT GARDENS, Camp St. Ext., Barre, VT. 05641. Mainly wildflowers and alpines, but many others. Fantastic selection.

THE SHOP IN THE SIERRA, Box 1, Midpines, CA. 95345. Western natives.

FRANCIS M. SINCLAIR, R. 1, Rt. 85, Exeter, N.H. 03833. Mainly wildflowers.

THE THREE LAURELS, R. 3, Box 15, Marshall, N.C. 28753. Wildflowers, aquatics, etc.

VICK'S WILDGARDENS, Box 115, Conshohocken State Rd., Gladwyne, PA. 19035. Wildflowers and ferns.

THE WILD GARDEN, Box 487, Bothell, WA. 98011. Several sorts of native plants.

WILDLIFE NURSERIES, P.O. Box 399, Oshkosh, WIS. 54901. Plants which provide food for wildlife, both upland and aquatic.

WOODLAND ACRES NURSERY, Crivitz, WIS. 54114. Wildflowers, etc.

This by no means exhausts the list. Many ordinary nurseries offer wildflowers and native woody plants as a matter of course, even the rarer species. For example, this year I obtained a specimen of the beautiful *Magnolia cordata* from Carroll Gardens, Westminster, Maryland, a nursery which I had hitherto associated with more usual plants.

Another source for rare plants lies among the many botanical gardens and arboreta scattered across the country. Most institutions are extremely courteous and anxious to help members of the public gain access to rare plants.

Several years ago, after seeing a tree of *Kalopanax pictus* (not a native, but a rare and beautiful plant) at the Arnold Arboretum, I wrote that institution asking for a source. To my surprise they sent me a letter apologizing for not knowing a source, and a full bag of seeds. Americans probably do not take full advantage of the horticultural facilities available to them (how many visitors to Washington, for example, take advantage of the National Arboretum and its magnificent collection of plants, all totally free of charge?); many in fact hardly know that they are available. Besides botanical gardens and similar institutions, state universities often have services available to the public, usually in the form of State Cooperative Extension Services. The U.S. government also offers services to the public through the U.S. Department of Agriculture in Washington, D.C. Finally, specialist societies are often excellent sources of desired plant material. Following is a list of some of those which might apply to wildflowers:

American Fern Society, Dept. of Botany, U. of Rhode Island, Kingston, R.I. 02881.
American Magnolia Society, 2150 Woodward Ave., Bloomfield Hills, MI. 48013.
American Orchid Society, Bot. Mus., Harvard U., Cambridge, MASS. 02138.
American Pentstemon Society, R. 2, Box 61, Cozad, NB. 69130.
American Rhododendron Society, 2232 N.E. 78th Ave., Portland, OR. 79213.
American Rock Garden Society, 99 Pierpont Road, Waterbury, CONN., 06705.
Holly Society of America, 407 Fountain Green Rd., Bel Air, MD. 21014.
North American Lily Society, c/o Fred Abbey, North Ferrisburg, VT. 05473.
American Horticultural Society, 910 Washington St., Alexandria, VA. 22314.
The Pennsylvania Horticultural Society, 325 Walnut St., Philadelphia, PA. 19106.
The Massachusetts Horticultural Society, 300 Massachusetts Ave., Boston, MASS. 02115.

Index

A Note About the Author

Harold Bruce was born in Wilmington, Delaware, in 1934. Following service in the U.S. Navy, he studied both English and horticulture at the University of Delaware, receiving his B.A. in 1964 and M.A. in 1967. From 1959 to 1965 he was Taxonomist at the Winterthur Gardens, Winterthur, Delaware. Since 1967 he has taught at the University of Delaware, where he became an Assistant Professor of English in 1975. He is the author of *Winterthur in Bloom*, published in 1968, and has also written articles for various horticultural magazines.

A Note on the Type

The text of this book was set on the Linotype in Palatino, a type face designed by the noted German typographer Hermann Zapf. Named after Giovanbattista Palatino, a writing master of Renaissance Italy, Palatino was the first of Zapf's type faces to be introduced to America. The first designs for the face were made in 1948, and the fonts for the complete face were issued between 1950 and 1952. Like all Zapf-designed type faces, Palatino is beautifully balanced and exceedingly readable.

The book was composed, printed and bound by American Book–Stratford Press, Inc., Saddlebrook, New Jersey.

The line drawings are by Maida Silverman.

The book was designed by Earl Tidwell.